Salvation as Praxis

Salvation as Praxis

A Practical Theology of Salvation for a Multi-Faith World

Wayne Morris

B L O O M S B U R Y

LONDON • NEW DELHI • NEW YORK • SYDNEY

Bloomsbury T&T Clark

An imprint of Bloomsbury Publishing Plc

50 Bedford Square	1385 Broadway
London	New York
WC1B 3DP	NY 10018
UK	USA

www.bloomsbury.com

Bloomsbury is a registered trade mark of Bloomsbury Publishing Plc

First published 2014

British Library Cataloguing-in-Publication Data
A catalogue record for this book is available from the British Library.

ISBN: HB: 978-0-567-47401-8
PB: 978-0-567-53209-1
ePDF: 978-0-567-34517-2
epub: 978-0-567-44336-6

Library of Congress Cataloging-in-Publication Data
Morris, Wayne
Salvation as Praxis/Wayne Morris
p.cm
Includes bibliographic references and index.
ISBN 978-0-567-47401-8 (hardcover)
ISBN 978-0-567-53209-1 (pbk.)

Typeset by Newgen Knowledge Works (P) Ltd., Chennai, India
Printed and bound in Great Britain

For
Linda Joy Morris
(1949–1986)

CONTENTS

ACKNOWLEDGEMENTS

This book has been nearly five years in writing, and I would like to express my deep gratitude to all who have supported me throughout. First, my gratitude is extended to colleagues and friends of the Department of Theology and Religious Studies at the University of Chester, United Kingdom. Thank you especially to colleagues who made my research leave in 2009 possible, but to the whole academic and administrative team, past and present, who have made and continue to make this such a stimulating and collegial place to work.

I would also like to express my thanks to our students at Chester. I have variously shared pieces of this research with our undergraduates and with students on our Professional Doctorate in Practical Theology. Not only do our students readily engage with the new ideas that I have been formulating and exploring, but they have also been invaluable critical friends offering robust engagement and criticism with what I have laid before them. Without them, this work would have been a much lesser product.

During a visit to University of Birmingham, United Kingdom, to deliver the Cadbury Lectures, Professor Amos Yong kindly agreed to meet with me and discuss my research in both disability theology and what was, at the time, a new area of research for me (this book). His wise counsel and guidance were instrumental in my early thinking about the direction of this book and I am most grateful to him for giving me his time.

The editorial team at T&T Clark, Tom Kraft initially and later Anna Turton, have been a great support in the writing in this book, in particular in being willing to extend deadlines for submission as my role at the University of Chester changed considerably midway through this project. Thank you to both of them for their generosity and patience.

I would like to express my gratitude to Kevin Jones. He remains a great support to me in so many ways and without him I am not sure this book would ever have been finished. His generous and kind presence enriches my life greatly and I am profoundly grateful for all that he does to make my work possible.

Finally, my colleague, Hannah Bacon, merits special mention. I have sat in her office many times expounding my ideas for this book and she has listened patiently and graciously every time. She has further read through drafts of this work and offered invaluable insights and critique, often with little time to turn them around. Her questions are always insightful and she has challenged me many times to go back and start thinking about things again. I too often take her friendship for granted and I depend on her support greatly. I am deeply honoured to know her and wish to express my thanks to her for being such a wonderful and reliable friend.

Introduction

I believe that there are two fundamental challenges facing western nations today. One is how we live with our planet. The other is how we live with each other. The second – in Sir Isaiah Berlin's phrase – 'living together graciously' – is in my view the more urgent.[1]

This book seeks to make a particularly Christian theological contribution to thinking about how Christian persons might practice more gracious ways of living alongside and with people of other faiths and spiritual pathways. Historically, as will be argued, people of other faiths have mostly been viewed with suspicion, as a threat to Christianity and as an offence to its God with the result that, far from seeking to live graciously together, Christian engagements with people of other faiths have often been characterized by mistrust, hatred, conflict, war and even genocide. Underpinning such approaches towards people of other faiths has been soteriological theories and practices that have led to a Christian 'presumption of superiority'[2] that they, and they alone, possess all that is necessary for entry into a future eschatological existence in full communion with God. Without first becoming Christian themselves, it has been assumed, no human person could possibly be saved. This soteriological focus on the hope of future eschatological possibilities for the Christian was used to justify the political and economic agendas of many Western nations that used theology to conquer and colonize contexts where other faith traditions and perspectives were dominant in the name of 'saving souls' in the life beyond death.

In a post-Holocaust era, many churches in Europe found themselves subject to a critique from both outside and inside their own structures, regarding their lack of resistance to Nazism that had led to the massacre

---

[1]T. Phillips, 'Not a River of Blood, but a Tide of Hope: Managed Immigration, Active Integration', *Equality and Human Rights Commission*, www.equalityhumanrights.com/key-projects/race-in-britain/modern-multiculturism/not-a-river-of-blood-but-a-tide-of-hope/, accessed on 1 February 2013.

[2]M. H. Suchocki, 'In Search of Justice: Religious Pluralism from a Feminist Perspective', in *The Myth of Christian Uniqueness: Toward a Pluralistic Theology of Religions* (eds J. Hick and P. Knitter; Eugene, OR: Wipf & Stock, 2005), pp. 149–61 (154).

of millions of Jews during the Second World War.[3] Subsequently church institutions and the academy alike began to engage in the inevitable theological struggle this created as they sought to make sense of a God who would allow such an atrocity to occur.[4] Together with a long legacy of Christian anti-Semitic beliefs and practices it was argued that the Church was, at least in part, culpable. Theologians and church institutions thus began to reflect on these historic practices, and the beliefs and theologies that had shaped them, most notably those related to Christology and the focus of this work, soteriology. This new post-Holocaust context demanded new ways of thinking and acting towards people of other faiths and this would mean careful examination and in many instances, deconstruction and reconstruction of the associated doctrines.

Key voices that shaped early theologies of religions in the post-war era, especially with reference to soteriology and people of other faiths, were Karl Rahner and John Hick. For both figures it did not seem to make logical sense that, in a faith tradition which claimed that its God was a God of love, such a God would condemn the majority of the world to oblivion, especially those who had never heard of Christianity or who happened to be born in a part of the world where Christianity was at best, a marginal minority expression of faith.[5] With a shift in Catholic teaching regarding people of other faiths articulated in the documents of the Second Vatican Council,[6] together with Rahner's and Hick's explorations in soteriology, a new way

---

[3]Exceptions include the writings of, for example, those recorded in, H. de Lubac, *Christian Resistence to Anti-Semitism: Memories from 1940–1944* (San Francisco: Ignatius Press, 1990).

[4]Jürgen Moltmann in particular acknowledged this theological struggle, and his book, *The Crucified God*, was written as a way of seeking to respond to that struggle. See. J. Moltmann, *The Crucified God: The Cross of Christ as the Foundation and Criticism of Christian Theology* (Minneapolis: Fortress Press, 1993) and also J. Moltmann, *A Broad Place: An Autobiography* (Minneapolis: Fortress Press, 2009), p. 189.

[5]These views are expounded by both Hick and Rahner in, for example, J. Hick, 'A Pluralist View', in *Four Views on Salvation in a Pluralistic World* (eds S. N. Gundry, D. L. Okholm and T. R. Phillips; Grand Rapids, MI: Zondervan, 1996), pp. 29–59 (45), and K. Rahner, *Theological Investigations: Volume Six* (London: DLT, 1969), p. 391.

[6]*Unitatis Redintegratio*, the Council's document on Ecumenism, sought to set out some 'considerations' that would provide a foundation and also facilitate dialogue with churches not in Communion with Rome which signified an increased openness to the possibility that salvation could be realized outside the visible Roman Catholic Church. The document, *Lumen Gentium*, suggested that both 'truth' and 'sanctification' could be found outside of the 'visible Church' and that 'those who have not yet received the Gospel are related in various ways to the people of God'. Particular mention is made of people who are Jewish and Muslim. See Second Vatican Council, *Unitatis Redintegratio*, www.vatican.va/archive/hist_councils/iI_vatican_council/documents/vat-iI_decree_19641121_unitatis-redintegratio_En.html, last accessed on 1 February 2013, and Second Vatican Council, *Lumen Gentium*, www.vatican.va/archive/hist_councils/iI_vatican_council/documents/vat-iI_const_19641121_lumen-gentium_En.html, last accessed on 1 February 2013. Other key documents include, Second Vatican Council, *Nostra Aetate*, www.vatican.va/archive/hist_councils/iI_vatican_council/documents/vat-iI_decl_19651028_nostra-aetate_En.html, last accessed on 1 February 2013.

forward opened up for Christian thinking and acting towards people of other faiths, one that would hopefully mean that the horrors of the past might never be justifiable with reference to Christian theology again.

Since the Second Vatican Council, and Hick and Rahner's groundbreaking works, much of the subsequent literature that emerged with regard to Christian understandings of salvation and people of other faiths has attended to questions of whether a person of another faith can experience salvation, either through their own faith, or because of the universal significance of Christ or the activity of the Holy Spirit. The many and varied perspectives on soteriology that have emerged are discussed in much greater detail in Chapter 4 though, as we shall see, with the exception of a minority of scholars, the question of the salvation of a person of another faith has continued to be almost entirely concerned with saved souls in the life beyond death. In many ways this is an important question to address, because it is precisely beliefs in future eschatological soteriology that have largely underpinned and been expressed in the practices of the churches towards people of other faiths historically. However, salvation in the Christian tradition has always been concerned with more than questions about future, eschatological, post-mortem possibilities. Salvation has been understood to speak to present, temporal, earthly realities in which human persons, perhaps in communion with the rest of creation, can experience the kind of reality now that is promised for the future. Present and future soteriologies are inextricably linked. While present soteriologies may be preparations for future salvation, 'foretastes' of eschatological possibilities, or a full realization of a transformed state of being here on earth, what is important in Christian soteriology is that the present matters and it always has. These dimensions to Christian soteriological discourses have, it is argued, largely been absent from debates in the theologies of religions attending to questions of salvation.

Recent developments in contextual theological voices, especially those from historically marginalized and oppressed groups, have initiated a shift in their focus on soteriological discourses towards an understanding of salvation as principally relating to the transformation of *this world* for the better. This book draws on that corpus of literature. The majority of the world's Christians no longer live in prosperous Western nations but are among the poorest of the poor, exposing the colonial notion that belief in Christ brings prosperity as erroneous. Further, the hope of a better life in some future heavenly world provides a deeply inadequate response and an empty hope to the suffering that many of those Christians experience in this world on a daily basis. Indeed, such an other-worldly understanding of salvation has been used to justify, it is argued, passive acceptance of suffering in this world.[7] Instead, present salvation, the transformation into a

---

[7] R. R. Ruether, *Introducing Redemption in Christian Feminism* (Sheffield: Sheffield Academic Press, 1998), p. 102.

new and improved existence has been reconstructed and is constituted by an end to oppressive and destructive systems and practices such as patriarchy, capitalism, racism, Euro-centrism and so forth in favour of more just and egalitarian systems and practices. However, as we shall see, experiencing salvation as a transformation of the present is no new theological innovation of twentieth and twenty-first century-contextual theologies, but a part of the Christian understanding of salvation that goes back to this faith community's inception.

In seeking to recover traditions of salvation that are concerned with more than a hope for a post-mortem existence, but rather provide a way of speaking about transformative Christian praxis in this world, this book seeks to explore what such an alternative understanding of salvation might mean for Christian engagement with people of other faiths. In so doing, it aims to contribute to develop conversations in theologies of religions that can instigate a further departure from Christianity's legacy of engaging with people of other faiths that have historically been so destructive. Theologies of religions need to give much greater attention to Christian praxis in interfaith engagements if living more graciously together is to be a real possibility for the future. If what has been described thus far is the general focus and argument of this book, prior to outlining the structure that develops this argument, it is important to define some terminology, much of which has already been used.

Explaining key terms

'Salvation'

The whole of this book is directed towards articulating a Christian understanding of 'salvation' that might help to shape and be expressed in new Christian praxes, and so any attempt to explain what is meant by this term here can only be provisional. At this stage, and for the purposes of this work, to speak of salvation is, broadly, to speak about transformation from one present reality into a new and better reality. While this may seem rather vague and not in any sense explicitly Christian, it is important to note that unlike pluralists such as Hick and Knitter, I am not attempting to find a definition of salvation that can be applied to any faith community's self understanding of the present possibilities or the ultimate ends of their adherents. Salvation narratives in Christianity and the ancient Jewish traditions that they draw on, I argue, all speak about a human state in need of change and of the promise of a new and improved existence, whether it be the hope of entering into the 'promised land', the possibility of realizing the 'kingdom of God' on earth or entering into it in heaven, or participation in some other-worldly existence in communion with God in the life beyond death. This transformation into something new is understood to be into the kind of improved reality that Christian traditions suggest that its God intends for all creation, a state in which human persons in particular and the whole of creation in general is not, at present, residing. While, as has already been suggested, many contextual theologies have shifted to an emphasis on a state of salvation as something that can be realized in this world, it is the contention of this book that the gaze of most theologies of religions continues to be fixed on future eschatological possibilities for people of other faiths.

'Practice' and 'Praxis'

Elaine Graham has usefully defined 'practice' with reference to its use in the discipline of practical theology and this informs the use of the notion of 'practice' in this work. She argues, 'practice' is 'purposeful activity performed by embodied persons in time and space as both the subjects of agency and the objects of history'.[8] She explains that religion is 'one form of purposeful practice',[9] that is intentionally engaging in particular activities as expressions of religious identity. However, practices are not, for Graham, simply 'expressions of the Christian presence in the world' and nor should they be understood as the 'application of theological understanding'.[10] So that, while it is the case that 'tradition, classic texts and contemporary social analysis' provide the 'sources and norms' for performed activities, those activities themselves are also 'bearers of living principles'.[11] Practical theology, therefore, is concerned not only with an examination of the written texts and traditions that inform how Christian persons live and act in the world; it attends to 'living human documents'[12] too. It is concerned to examine lived practices of human persons so as to understand what they reveal about the social and cultural 'norms and values' that, indeed, interpret or may not even be found within written texts and traditions.

This book aims to examine the historic purposeful soteriological beliefs and practices of Christian individuals, communities and institutions towards people of other faiths, so as to be able to deconstruct those that have been historically destructive, and attend to alternative understandings of salvation that might lead to more gracious practices of living together. In reconstructing alternative practices, practical theology has a responsibility to do so in such a way that historic and present injustices are addressed. Thus, what is constructed or proposed is more than simply new ways of doing things, but what I here refer to as 'praxis'. Praxis simply means

---

[8] E. Graham, *Transforming Practice: Pastoral Theology in an Age of Uncertainty* (Eugene: Wipf and Stock, 2002), p. 110.
[9] Ibid.
[10] Ibid., p. 111.
[11] Ibid.
[12] Anton Boisen's term documented in E. Graham, H. Walton and F. Ward, *Theological Reflection: Methods* (London: SCM Press, 2005), p. 35.

'committed action'. 'Praxis' is a Greek word transliterated into English and originally means 'a doing, deed, act'[13] and provides the etymological root for the English, 'practice', so the two concepts are related. The concept of 'praxis' has, however, taken on a new theological significance, in particular in its use in Liberation Theology, and more widely since.

Jon Sobrino argues that praxis refers to the response to what takes place in the social realm as Christians engage in the 'construction of the kingdom' and 'construction of communities'.[14] While Graham's understanding of 'practice' as 'purposeful activity' and Sobrino's notion of 'praxis' as 'committed action' are in many ways very similar, I have opted to use 'practice' to speak here of the descriptions and interrogation of historic and present purposeful acts of Christians towards people of other faiths that, I argue, need to be addressed. I propose that the term 'praxis' better described the acts of radical commitment to social transformation informed and shaped by a particular understanding of the Christian Gospel that I aim to construct here. This is intended not to set up a Christian paradigm to which it is suggested that all people should conform, but rather it is to make a distinctively Christian contribution to thinking and practice regarding relationships with people of other faiths by seeking to develop alternative Christian soteriological understandings and praxes. Such alternative praxes are ultimately realized in communities and contexts in which theologians, in solidarity with oppressed and marginalized people, exercise a 'commitment to create a just society, a community of sisters and brothers'.[15] This commitment to working towards the realization of such a society and world, however inadequate this particular offering may be, underpins the whole of this book.

'Salvation as Praxis'

James Cone argues that '. . . when Christians really believe in the resurrection of Christ and take seriously the promise revealed through him, they cannot be satisfied with the present world as it is'.[16] With Cone, I am located within the Christian tradition as one who believes that Christianity is as much a movement concerned with the transformation of the present as it is about future eschatological possibilities. In Stephanie Mitchem's review of womanist theology, she draws on the work of Patricia Hill Collins who suggests that there are three questions that should always be used to reflect on social theory. Mitchem argues that these can equally be used for reflecting

[13]G. Abbott-Smith, *Manual Greek Lexicon of the New Testament* (Edinburgh: T&T Clark, 1994), p. 376.
[14]J. Sobrino, *No Salvation Outside the Poor: Prophetic-Utopian Essays* (New York, NY: Orbis Books, 2008), p. 91.
[15]G. Gutierrez, *The Power of the Poor in History* (London: SCM Press, 1983), p. 60.
[16]J. H. Cone, *A Black Theology of Liberation: Twentieth Anniversary Edition* (New York, NY: Orbis Books, 1990), p. 14.

on theology and these questions are first, does theology 'speak the truth to people about the reality of their lives?' second, does theology 'equip people to resist oppression?' and third, does theology 'move people to struggle?'[17]

Soteriologies, perhaps more than other aspects of theological discourse, in the spirit of Mitchem's proposal, ought to be concerned with naming the sins of injustice, inequality and suffering that humans experience, and seeking ways to resist and transform it. Such soteriologies are soteriologies of praxis; salvations that speak out of and into contexts where new and improved ways of living are envisaged and shaped by struggles against and resistance to oppression. Soteriology is, therefore, here about praxis, about transformed belief and committed action that leads to new and better relationships with and perspectives on people of other faiths; that is, conscious praxes that result in improved relationships and realities constitute nothing less than the state of salvation itself.

'People of other Faiths'

Identifying an appropriate term with which to speak about the persons, communities and institutions of the many religious, spiritual and faith traditions with whom this book seeks to improve Christian engagement, is complex. No single term adequately includes the many religious, spiritual and faith traditions practiced in contrasting ways around the world. However, the terms 'people of other faiths' or 'people of other faith communities' have been chosen for the following reasons. Influenced by my work with people with disabilities,[18] I am profoundly conscious of the need to avoid terminology that labels individuals and groups as though they are entirely 'other' to another individual or group, and thus, it is implied, form a supposed homogenous whole. Such terminology has a tendency to depersonalize and dehumanize people who are different to one's self. For this reason terms like 'religious other', popular in many recent theologies of religions, for example, are deeply uncomfortable because while the notion of otherness usefully implies difference to one's self, the term suggests that all others can be spoken about as though they are all effectively the same. In contrast, the language of 'people of other faiths', as with 'people with disabilities', serves as a reminder that first and foremost this book is concerned with *people*, with human beings in all their uniqueness and difference.

Further, Emmanuel Lartey rightly explains that all human persons are, in some ways, like all others, some others and no other.[19] This provides an

---

[17]S. Y. Mitchem, *Introducing Womanist Theology* (Maryknoll, NY: Orbis Books, 2004), p. 74.
[18]W. Morris, *Theology without Words: Theology in the Deaf Community* (Aldershot: Ashgate, 2008) and R. McCloughry and W. Morris, *Making a World of Difference: Christian Reflections on Disability* (London: SPCK, 2002).
[19]E. Y. Lartey, *In Living Colour: An Intercultural Approach to Pastoral Care and Counselling* (London: Cassell, 1997), p. 12.

important marker for talking about people of other faiths by beginning with a recognition of the common humanity of all people; the so-called 'religious other' is never entirely different – 'other' – to the Christian as they are all born, will all die, and all have blood in their bodies, for example. At the same time, there are certain qualities, characteristics, beliefs and practices that individuals share in common with others that they do not share with all human beings. Participation in a faith community with others provides one example. However, this does not mean that a person of one faith is entirely different to a person of another faith. Indeed, in previous work with Deaf people in the city of Birmingham in the United Kingdom,[20] the most important location of common ground between Deaf people was their Deaf identity which nearly always had priority over religious affiliation. Thus, Christians, Jews and Muslims could often be found in the 'Deaf Church' and 'Deaf club', meeting and socializing together. Adherence to one faith tradition may be something that a person shares in common with others, but the Muslim and Christian Deaf person also found common ground with one another that they did not find with most other Christian and Muslim people. Finally, however, every person is also unique so any discussion about homogenous groups in their entirety, and that includes members of Christian communities too, must tread very carefully so as to avoid simplistic generalizations or assumptions about any group or community and the individuals that form them. Thus we cannot talk about Christians, Jews, Muslims, Hindus, Buddhists or any other religious, faith or spiritual group as though they are all precisely the same as everyone else under the same label and entirely different to every other person labelled differently. Thus, while this book talks about 'people of other faiths' as distinct from Christianity, it should be noted that there is often much that is already shared in common across faith communities as well as there being internal conflict and difference within faith communities.

The term 'faith', like religion, may seem problematic and an imposition of a particularly Western Christian notion of an intellectualized form of religious or spiritual affiliation and expression. The language of 'religion' has been critiqued for such tendencies[21] and any such term has the possibility of including some and not others. In using 'faiths' or 'faith communities' (plural), however, I define this as an inclusive term referring to the many and varied ways in which human persons might engage in what can be broadly termed religious or spiritual practices. Finally, the language of 'other' faiths potentially homogenizes the person who does not identify with Christianity into one homogenous whole, thus creating the very problem I have sought

---

[20]See Morris, *Theology without Words.*
[21]M. Engelke, *A Problem of Presence: Beyond Scripture in an African church* (Los Angeles, CA: University of California Press, 2007), p. 38.

to avoid, though I hope the use of the plural in 'people of other faiths' or '. . . faith communities' aims to mitigate against such homogeneity.

No term is adequate and Christian engagement with different faith communities does vary depending on which communities are the focus of Christian interaction. With this in mind, however, this book is concerned with a particularly Christian theological perspective on the persons and communities that are generally identified, often most strongly by themselves, with a label other than that of 'Christian'. Conscious that classifying individuals and groups together with terms such as 'faith communities' may indeed represent useful but flawed constructions for academic discourses, it is important to start somewhere or else be unable to speak about engagement with people of other faiths at all. Having thus attempted to define and explain some of the most important terminology used in what follows in this work, let us now turn to the structure of the book.

The Structure of this Book

Chapter 1 outlines the methodological framework that shapes this book, examining in particular the importance for engaging with questions of practice and praxis in a multi-faith world. 'Critical conversation' as descriptive of the method used in this book will be outlined, and further detail of the nature of this approach to practical theology will be discussed. In Chapter 2, a brief overview of the ways that Christian soteriology has been variously understood within the many received traditions identifiable with Christianity will be provided, noting that there are generally three aspects or dimensions to most soteriological discourse:

1   a description of the state from which it is understood salvation is necessary;
2   the process by which salvation is realized and the extent of human participation alongside the role of Christ in making salvation possible;
3   an articulation of what the final end state of salvation will be like.

Chapter 3 will argue that particular aspects of Christian soteriological traditions and practices have been emphasized historically over others in order to reinforce a Christian 'presumption of superiority' over people of other faiths. The practices of Christian faith communities and institutions towards people of other faiths demonstrate that underpinning such practices has been more than a desire to 'save souls' as acts of altruism, but rather such theologies have justified all kinds of atrocities to the personal and material advantage of those who enact them. Examples will be explored that include the way soteriological traditions paved the way for the Holocaust, how they were used to justify the Crusades, how they justified colonialism and the suppression of indigenous faith traditions, and how they continue to inform and shape neo-colonial practices in the West.

Chapter 4 will then provide an overview of contemporary theologies of religions and their contributions in particular to soteriological discourses. It will be argued that in theologies of religions since the Second World War, the soteriological gaze of such theologies has been directed towards future and other-worldly possibilities. It will be argued that because of this particular focus within theologies of religions, despite a reorientation of focus within other contextual theologies more broadly, that the notion of soteriological praxis is necessary to begin thinking about Christian practices differently, and to begin shaping alternative praxes towards people of other faiths. Throughout these first four chapters, the aim is to articulate why an alternative practical theology of salvation that understands salvation as a form of human earthly praxis is needed, and the framework for developing such an alternative theology is outlined.

In the second part of this book, three ways of speaking soteriologically will be developed and brought into conversation with the historic and destructive practices of the past with a view to proposing alternative Christian praxes towards people of other faiths for the present and future. Chapter 5 begins by examining the soteriological tradition of *deification* and seeks to develop an understanding of what it might mean to become God, or to become like God, through an engagement with the doctrine of the Trinity and, in particular, social understandings of the Trinity. With particular reference to the Trinitarian theology of John Zizioulas, this chapter seeks to reflect on the praxis of salvation in multi-faith contexts for the purposes of community building and for creating spaces for dialogue.

Chapter 6 develops an understanding of salvation as a praxis of *healing*. This will draw in particular on New Testament healing narratives in which 'to be made well' can be understood as a soteriological act. These narratives, it is argued, demonstrate that God cares about human bodies and what happens to them. While such narratives may suggest that to be fully a member of society, a person must first be 'normalized', this chapter seeks to resist such interpretations of the healing narratives. Instead, it argues that one form of Christian soteriological praxis is to exercise a concern for the earthly well-being of people of other faiths – real embodied human persons – and that this matters soteriologically speaking as much, if not more than, what happens to a person's soul in the life beyond death. Salvation as 'embodied well-being' is thus brought into the conversation regarding Christian engagement with people of other faiths.

Chapter 7 turns to the notion of salvation as *liberation*. It will argue that when sin is interpreted as concrete acts that affect human lives detrimentally, such sins should be challenged and transformed. Drawing on the particular notion within liberation theology that suggests God has a 'preferential option for the poor', it will argue that praxes of salvation themselves may well be found in communities outside of Christian traditions. This chapter will also reflect on the dangers of articulations of a state of liberation that reflect a Western, liberal ideal of a good and flourishing life which can subsequently be imposed upon people of other faiths.

These three approaches to salvation as a form of praxis are offered in the hope that they might contribute to new ways of Christian thinking and action towards people of other faiths that fosters more gracious ways of living together in a multi-faith world.

PART ONE

Why a practical theology of salvation?

1

A practical theological perspective

Introduction

Soteriological beliefs have historically served to justify many kinds of oppressive Christian practices towards people of other faiths, also including sometimes one Christian tradition towards other forms of Christian expression. These beliefs have been based on an understanding that salvation, possessed by an elite few and understood as a future post-mortem possibility, is only achievable through subscription to a particular set of beliefs and practices to the exclusion of all others, reinforcing a particularly Western and Christian 'presumption of superiority'. More recent discourses in the so-called theologies of religions have sought to articulate some alternative theologies whereby it has been argued that it may be possible for people of other faiths to participate in a future post-mortem existence without conformation and subscription to particularly Christian beliefs and practices. However, it is contended here that insufficient attention has been paid to both deconstructing these historic and present practices towards people of other faiths and reconstructing alternative approaches to practice – praxis – in the formulation of these revised soteriological perspectives.

This chapter argues, to use Elaine Graham's term, that theologies of religions need to more fully engage in a 'turn to practice'[1] as they seek to respond to the horrors of historic Christian approaches to people of other faiths, conscious that in a post-Holocaust context, alternative practices and beliefs are necessary. In light of this, it is argued here that while attention to questions of practice are essential for all theological discourse, it is

---

[1] See E. Graham, H. Walton and F. Ward, *Theological Reflections: Methods* (London: SCM Press, 2005), p. 194.

particularly so for theologies regarding people of other faiths. The practical
theological method used to try to do this will be that of 'critical conversation'
and this will be explored and presented as the key methodology in this
chapter that best describes the approach taken in this book. This chapter
will then turn to consider why this work is necessarily a 'particular' form
of theology as well as theology that may have 'public' significance. It is
'particular' because it first and foremost aims to be a theology that seeks
to transform 'particularly' Christian belief and practice rather than impose
anything on to people of other faiths and none. It aims to speak to both
members of Christian communities in particular, but also to contribute
to wider public debates about the role of Christian faith communities in
a twenty-first century multi-faith world. Finally, Campbell's notion that
practical theology must aim to tread cautiously a path between 'practical
relevance' and 'theological integrity' will be explored as a guiding principle
for this work.

Theology and practice: Inseparable bedfellows

The practical and contextual nature of *all* theology

It is a widely held view, especially among those whose perspectives have
historically been marginalized and excluded in the churches and academy,
that all theology is essentially contextual.[2] That is, all theology emerges
out of and is shaped by the concrete realities of life and uses the language,
assumptions and philosophical frameworks of the individuals and groups
who are engaged in the process of doing theology to speak theologically.
Elaine Graham, however, also proposes that all theology is essentially
practical as well as contextual in nature.[3] By this, she expresses agreement
that all theology emerges out of a context and is articulated in and for a
context, but that theological principles themselves are also expressed and
discovered in the 'purposeful practices' of faith communities too.[4] Theology
is, therefore, not simply found in magisterial texts, ancient scriptures
or significant theological tomes of the past and present that may emerge
out of any contextual position, but is also found in the lived expression

---

[2] S. B. Bevans, *Models of Contextual Theology* (New York, NY: Orbis Books; rev. edn, 2002), p. 3.

[3] E. Graham, *Words Made Flesh: Writings in Pastoral and Practical Theology* (London: SCM Press, 2009), p. 138.

[4] E. Graham, *Transforming Practice: Pastoral Theology in an Age of Uncertainty* (Eugene: Wipf and Stock, 2002), p. 110.

of communities of faith in worship, devotion, relationships, social action, community engagement and so forth. As a result, practical theology should 'refuse a distinction between words and deeds, faith and action'.[5] Moreover, Graham rightly argues that theology has always been developed and expressed in these ways explaining that, 'indeed, to establish itself, it [Christianity] had to embrace the cultural patterns and philosophies of its day' and that this 'integral aspect of its self-understanding has always been a part of theological formulation and Christian practice'.[6] Both theory and practice are, and always have been, inseparable bedfellows, each influencing and impacting upon one another. Thus theology is always practiced and practice itself is a theological resource worthy of interrogation.

This is true in theologies of religions just as in any other aspect of theology, but a survey of publications in this area, as we shall see in Chapter 4, would largely suggest that, in broad terms contextual and practical questions and concerns have driven the search for alternative soteriological discourses. However, too much attention has been paid to questions of how salvation might be understood differently with too little explicit exploration of what the implications of such alternative soteriologies might mean for Christian praxis. As we shall see in Chapter 3, however, practice and theology regarding people of other faiths have always been inextricably linked, and attention to questions of practice is ignored at our peril. If all theology is practical and contextual, and I contend that it is, let us consider in more detail why, in general, explicit attention to practice is so important.

Paying attention to practice

Emilie Townes argues that all study of theology and religion should seek to be engaged with questions of practice. She acknowledges that it is 'imperative' for scholarship in theology and religious studies to 'be rigorous, relentless, and responsible to the issues of the day while pushing our understanding of what is before us in our modern/postmodern worlds'[7] and many theologians and religious studies scholars would agree with her. However, she goes on to argue that all scholarship' should also help map out strategies for creating a more just and free society and world'.[8] As a critique of the contemporary methods of much theological scholarship, Pattison argues that 'too much contemporary theology seems to be a kind of whispered conversation on matters esoteric conducted in a foreign language behind closed doors in a distant attic'.[9] Pattison goes on to suggest that 'its supreme achievement has

---

[5]Graham, *Words Made Flesh*, p. 138.
[6]Graham, *Transforming Practice*, p. 118.
[7]E. Townes, 'Walking on the Rim Bones of Nothingness: Scholarship and Activism', *Journal of the American Academy of Religion* 77(1), (2009), pp. 1–15 (4).
[8]Ibid., p. 4.
[9]S. Pattison, *The Challenge of Practical Theology: Selected Essays* (London: JKP, 2007), p. 212.

been to make even the idea of God boring'.[10] Likewise, Terry Veling purports that if theology remains a purely 'speculative enterprise'[11] as it is understood, in his view, by some systematic theologians, there is a danger that

> our serene theories with their grand visions of life too often deny to knowledge any origin in the practical difficulties of life, but rather seek to transcend these difficulties into a vision of Being that is pristine and unaffected by human affairs.[12]

Without addressing itself to matters that affect people's lives, to practice, theology becomes little more than an irrelevance, boring and detached from the reality of lived experience. For theology to continue in such a vein would be potentially dangerous because religion and theology shapes practice. This is because, as Townes argues, the study of theology and religion that takes seriously the world beyond the academy is crucial in order to 'help make sense out of the chaos and spinning top of wars we now live in as part of the mundane and everyday in far too many people's lives'.[13]

Townes argues that the reason that all theological and religious scholarship should be attentive to questions of practice is past experience and that no published work is discrete and without the capacity to affect people's lives outside the academy. She thus calls for scholars of theology and religious studies to be conscious and aware of how their ideas might be received and how they might impact on people's lives. She further argues, 'I believe that what should drive our research in large measure is that we are exploring traditions that have driven people to incredible heights of valour and despicable degrees of cravenness. In other words, the research we do is not a free-floating solitary intellectual quest. It is profoundly tethered to people's lives – the fullness and the incompleteness of them'.[14] Scholarship that does not consider the way that it may be used by others and the impact it may have on others is, for Townes, irresponsible.

With Amos Yong, I argue that, 'all too often the relationship between Christian theologies and religion and Christian practices vis-à-vis the religions has not been spelled out'[15] and that, therefore, 'Christians need to give much more sustained reflection to the implications of their theologies of religion for Christian attitudes and actions regarding other faiths'.[16] It is

---

[10]Ibid., p. 213.
[11]T. Veling, *Practical Theology: "On Earth as It Is in Heaven"* (Maryknoll, NY: Orbis Books, 2005), p. 5.
[12]Ibid., p. 6.
[13]Townes, 'Walking on the Rim bones', p. 12.
[14]Ibid., p. 9.
[15]A. Yong, *Hospitality & The Other: Pentecost, Christian Practices, and the Neighbour* (New York, NY: Orbis Books, 2008), p. 38.
[16]Ibid.

important also, however, not to look only at the implications of theology for practice, but to acknowledge that practices themselves have shaped and express theological beliefs in ways that are sometimes distinct from the written 'sources and norms' of much Christian theology, such as the Bible and traditions of the churches. As Isherwood rightly notes, it is difficult to determine whether theology shapes practice and culture or visa versa,[17] but the likelihood is both, through complex processes of mutual interaction, shape one another. All theology is practical and contextual and so all theology should be concerned to pay as much attention to the implications it may have for practice as it is for the internal and intellectual coherence and rigour of the argument itself. Let us consider, therefore, how this necessary attention to practice is approached in this work.

Towards a practical theological method

Practical theology as applied theology

Much of the literature that explicitly identifies itself as practical theology is concerned to articulate what practical theology is and what, in particular, is distinctive about this approach to theology compared to others. This is due to a combination of scholars such as Elaine Graham, Emmanuel Lartey, Stephen Pattison, James Woodward, Heather Walton, John Swinton and Zoe Bennett, to name a few who have written on this subject from a British context, variously seeking to both define the discipline and push it in new directions. This has been further accompanied by the construction of an apologetics for the discipline, conscious that it has often historically been understood as marginal to the 'real' work of systematic and dogmatic theologies.

Graham, Walton and Ward, and Richard Osmer have each suggested that what is distinctive about contemporary practical theological methods can be traced back to the contributions of Friedrich Schleiermacher.[18] Schleiermacher's threefold theological model of philosophical theology, historical theology and practical theology has historically shaped the place that practical theology has held in thinking about what theology is and how it relates to the world beyond the academy. This threefold model understood practical theology as essentially an application of philosophical and historical ideas to questions and issues that confront (usually an ordained minister) in the church and world. Osmer describes this as a relay race: philosophical

---

[17]L. Isherwood, 'Will you Slim for Him or Bake Cakes for the Queen of Heaven?', in *Controversies in Body Theology* (eds M. Althaus-Reid and L. Isherwood; London: SCM Press, 2008), pp. 174–206 (178).

[18]See Graham, Walton and Ward, *Theological Reflections: Methods*, p. 3 and R. R. Osmer, *Practical Theology: An Introduction* (Grand Rapids, MI/Cambridge: Eerdmans, 2008), pp. 232–33.

theology begins the race, historical theology takes the middle leg and 'practical theology is located in the final position, running the anchor leg. It has the task of bringing the baton across the finish line to the church'.[19] This understanding of practical theology locates an engagement with practice as a final step in a longer process that can only take place as an act of application, subsequent to the theologian being literate in established historical and philosophical theological traditions. As has already been argued, however, that theology is not only expressed in historical and philosophical documents and then applied to concrete live situations, but rather belief and theology can also be found in lived human practices themselves that may shape the interpretation of historical and philosophical traditions, while also leading to the creation of new written 'sources and norms' for Christian practice. Thus, such an approach to theology fails to recognize that practice itself is 'generative of theological insight'.[20]

For example, the Council of Nicaea did not formulate the doctrine of the Trinity as a merely interesting intellectual exercise, and so-called heretics were not killed as a mere application of doctrine. The doctrine itself emerged in response to the political agenda of the emperor Constantine to secure political unity in the empire and his own position as emperor. Religious conflict over central theological questions regarding how the Church should understand who Jesus was posed a threat to such unity. Practice and context drove the theological formulations of Nicaea, and Christian practices towards those it branded heretical expressed the significance that this articulation of belief would mean for the Church. That is not to suggest that the Holy Spirit may or may not have been working through this council of the Church, we cannot quantify that either way, but what this does suggest is that theology is not simply formulated in the mind or learned in the classroom and practical theology is no mere application of such thinking and learning to practice. Schleiermacher's major contribution, however, is the identification of 'practical theology' as a term to describe a distinctive approach to theology that is concerned with questions of practice.

Practical theology and pastoral studies

A second important contributing factor to shaping contemporary practical theology has been the influence of pastoral studies and pastoral theology dominant in the twentieth century. Graham, Walton and Ward note, for example, that pastoral studies was largely understood as 'helps and hints' for ministers as it was taught in seminaries and, therefore, remained as still a form of applied theology.[21] Pastoral studies in many seminaries meant

---

[19]Osmer, *Practical Theology*, p. 238.
[20]Graham, Walton and Ward, *Theological Reflections: Methods*, p. 3.
[21]Ibid.

providing trainee clergy with skills and insights that would enable them to perform their pastoral duties, such as leading liturgy and worship, caring for the sick, and so forth. Pastoral studies was thus located in the concrete activities of clerics but, in the second half of the twentieth century new voices began to emerge that both questioned the premise that the work of the pastor was mere application of doctrine, but also questioned who engaged in pastoral activities and to what end. Two key voices illustrate how pastoral studies were developed in this period.

First, Graham is critical of the essentially clerical paradigm underpinning the discipline that was identified as pastoral studies.[22] The language of 'pastoral' draws on the shepherding metaphor whereby the human (usually male) shepherd cares for the docile sheep. Not only does this locate pastoral thinking and practice historically in the hands solely of ordained men, but everyone else is perceived as being a quite separate species to the cleric. To think about theology in this way preserves the authority of those whose voices have been most dominant historically in the churches and academy while also reinforcing the passivity of all others as the recipients of pastoral care. Taking seriously the experience of pastoral care as it has been practiced reveals that pastoral activity has never been the sole preserve of ordained persons anyway. Rather, it is descriptive of the work of the whole people of God, a more democratic practice. With the rise of many different approaches to contextual and practical theology more broadly that critique dominant theological discourses for marginalizing and suppressing the voices of the majority in favour of an educated elite, such a critique of pastoral studies was inevitable. That is, not least as Graham brought feminist discourses into conversation with the pastoral studies model of practical theology.[23] Practical theology thus became concerned not just with the practices of the ordained, but with those of the whole people of God.

Second, Emmanuel Lartey was also critical of established pastoral paradigms that too often, in his view, saw the work of the 'pastor' as concerned with responding to problems facing the minister or other Christian persons. The pastor was perceived to be a 'trouble-shooter', or 'super-hero' who rides in on (usually his) horse to sort out the various dilemmas, problems and difficulties in which the 'sheep' found themselves. Lartey, however, argued that pastoral theology should be attentive to and respond not only to human crises at the point of need, but that a truly responsible pastoral theology should be engaged in social analysis, reflection and subsequent transformation to seek to prevent such problems arising in the first place.[24] Pastoral theology that leads to the real care of human beings

---

[22]Graham, *Transforming Practice*, p. 48.

[23]E. Graham, *Making the Difference: Gender, Personhood and Theology* (London: Mowbray, 1995).

[24]E. Lartey, *In Living Colour: An Intercultural Approach to Pastoral Care and Counselling* (London: Cassell, 1997), p. 9.

should, therefore, do more than 'clean up' the mess created by pastoral crises, but also be proactive in addressing social and political injustices. Politics, economics and doctrine, among other things, impact on individuals and one cannot care for an individual without also addressing these wider concerns. Pastoral theology, thus goes beyond being the activity of local ministers, and becomes something practiced in local contexts and is characterized by a proactive engagement in the transformation of ideas and structures that contribute to pastoral crises occurring.

Graham and Lartey both advocate that practical theology is neither a form of applied historical or philosophical theology and nor is it solely about ministerial practice and seeking to make that better. Explicitly practical theology should also consciously be more actively engaged in thinking about wider social, political, economic as well as local pastoral questions, conscious that the local and wider concerns are usually inter-related. This book, therefore, is not a piece of practical theology that is concerned only with how Christians might live graciously together with people of other faiths at a local level, though this is important, it also recognizes that gracious living together at a local level is only possible with the transformation of wider social, political, economic and theological attitudes and practices too. It acknowledges that if such new forms of praxis are to be realized, it will involve not just Christian leaders and pastors, but the whole people of God.

Practical theology: Towards liberation

Practical theology as a discipline and this particular piece of practical theology on salvation and people of other faiths, are further, however, indebted to the influences of liberation theologies. Graham, Walton and Ward recognize that liberation theology has helped to shape practical theology in the approach to theological reflection that they describe as 'Theology in Action: Praxis'.[25] Liberation theologians, they argue, insist 'that proper theological understanding cannot be formed independently of practical engagement'.[26] Going beyond Emilie Townes' proposals described above, such theology should not only be attentive to questions of practice but theologians and theology itself must be orientated towards 'value-committed action'[27] (praxis). The principal value that informs this approach to theology is a view that the Christian Gospel is concerned primarily with ending human suffering, fostering well-being, and seeking human liberation, freedom and equality, and that God is always on the side of the poor as they struggle for freedom. If that is so, therefore, theology and the church should also be on the side of the poor and on the side of any human persons

---

[25]Graham, Walton and Ward, *Theological Reflections: Methods*, pp. 170–99.
[26]Ibid., p. 170.
[27]Ibid.

who 'struggle for human emancipation'.[28] This work is shaped by such a commitment to transformation of contexts of oppression and injustice based on an understanding that, with liberation theologians, the Christian Gospel is orientated towards the transformation of human suffering in this world. The soteriological significance of liberation theology for people of other faiths will be discussed in further detail in Chapter 7. Suffice to say here that, with James Cone, the task of this theology is to 'put into ordered speech the meaning of God's activity in the world' and to recognize that the task of working towards the creation of more just and fair societies and world 'is not only *consistent with* the gospel, but *is* the gospel of Jesus Christ'.[29]

Practical theology as theological reflection

If this practical theology represents a method of theology that attends to questions of both belief and practice, conscious that the local, regional, national and global are inter-related, with a view to developing principles that attend to and inform praxis with regard to people of other faiths, then how does it do this? Various methods have been proposed that intend to both describe the method and provide tools to help students of theology to engage in practical theology better. Such methods are usually referred to as 'theological reflection'. In Laurie Green's important publication in 1990, *Let's Do Theology*, he developed a theological method of reflection that started with practice. He developed a fourfold cycle of reflection that has been adapted and re-presented in many different formats.[30] Of significance, he too suggested that theological reflection as a method of doing theology need not be restricted to clerical or academic individuals, but could be practiced in community by local members of church congregations. His method of theological reflection was designed to facilitate that. Such methods of theological reflection drew on secular cycles of reflection but were also influenced by liberation theology to provide tools to aid the liberation process.[31] Graham, Walton and Ward have, however, identified a total of seven distinct methods or approaches to theological reflection that, they argue, represent the principal ways in which theological reflection has been practiced in many different theological genres, from Augustine to Paul Tillich to Gustavo Gutierrez to Rosemary Radford Ruether to Green's

---

[28]Ibid.
[29]J. Cone, *A Black Theology of Liberation: Twentieth Anniversary Edition* (New York, NY: Orbis Books, 1990), p. 1.
[30]L. Green, *Let's Do Theology: A Pastoral Cycle Resource Book* (London: Continuum, 1990). Examples of adaptations of this model can be found in P. Ballard and J. Pritchard, *Practical Theology in Action: Christian thinking in the Service of Church and Society* (London: SPCK, 1996), pp. 74–79 and E. Y. Lartey, 'Practical Theology as Theological Form', in *The Blackwell Reader in Pastoral and Practical Theology* (eds J. Woodward and S. Pattison; Oxford: Blackwell, 2000), pp. 128–34.
[31]Graham, Walton and Ward, *Theological Reflections: Methods*, p. 5.

cycle of reflection.[32] Shaped by the insights of practical theology and the commitment to a particular understanding of the Gospel described above, it is, however, Pattison's notion of 'critical conversation' as a method of theological reflection that I would like to propose best describes the theological approach of this book. It is not so much that 'critical conversation' provided a way of thinking about salvation as praxis here, but that, retrospectively, this most closely describes the methods used that have been employed. Below, therefore, the method is outlined as some further guiding principles that have informed this practical theology of salvation.

Practical theology as critical conversation

Stephen Pattison argues that his preferred metaphor used to describe theological reflection is that of 'critical conversation'.[33] Pattison and Woodward argue that 'practical theology is a place where religious belief, tradition and practice meets contemporary experiences, questions and actions and conducts a dialogue that is mutually enriching, intellectually critical, and practically transforming'.[34] Graham offers an important corrective to this view of practical theology when, as we have seen, she argues that belief, tradition and practice should not be separated and understood to be unrelated to one another. However, producing descriptive methods of theological reflection, as with the articulation of any method or model, necessitates seeking to artificially distinguish various contributing factors that make up the process, conscious that each factor may indeed be related to or overlap with others. This is so in understanding theological reflection as a process of 'critical conversation' as each identified dialogue partner should not be understood as completely separate and distinctive to the others.

Developing the metaphor of critical conversation as a model of theological reflection, Pattison identifies a number of characteristics that constitute a process of dialogue including that:

- 'A real conversation is a living thing which evolves and changes'
- 'The participants in a conversation are changed' as a result of the dialogue
- 'Participation in a conversation implies a willingness to listen and be attentive to other participants'
- 'Participants do not always end up agreeing'.[35]

---

[32]See ibid.

[33]S. Pattison, 'Some Straw for the Bricks: A Basic Introduction to Theological Reflection', in *The Blackwell Reader in Pastoral and Practical Theology* (eds J. Woodward, and S. Pattison; Oxford: Blackwell, 2000), pp. 135–45.

[34]S. Pattison and J. Woodward, 'Introduction to Pastoral and Practical Theology', in *The Blackwell Reader in Pastoral and Practical Theology* (eds J. Woodward and S. Pattison; Oxford: Blackwell, 2000a), p. 7.

[35]Pattison, 'Some Straw for the Bricks', pp. 139–40.

In addition and of note, Lartey argues that,

- 'each participant is committed to stating and clarifying their own views. They are also committed to exploring the views of others'.[36]

Let us consider each of these five characteristics in turn, but in a slightly different order that makes more sense for the purposes of this particular work.

Conversation as a live event

Conversations take place in real time and involve real living people. They are, to use Pattison's term, 'concrete events'.[37] As such, the nature of the conversation is largely dependent on who is involved and the wider context in which the conversation is taking place. It is important, therefore, as Osmer argues, that the practical theologian should be 'reflexive about the choices and assumptions guiding their work',[38] or perhaps more precisely to acknowledge who is at the table of dialogue and why they have been invited. Further discussion on some of the guiding principles that inform this work from liberation theology has already been discussed, but in addition, it is important to note that the nature of the conversation that takes place is dependent on the author, what matters to me, why the question of salvation and people of other faiths matters, and so forth. To acknowledge that this approach to theological reflection is a 'live event' is also to note that any outcomes from the conversation are temporary. They are from the moment and of the moment in which the conversation takes place and, as such, are not intended to be universal timeless principles, but perspectives on soteriological praxis that emerge out of some of the immediate questions that face Christian theology and its reflection on the lived relationships of Christian persons to people of other faiths today.

Conversation involves listening and attention to others

Practical theology is largely characterized by its willingness to engage with a range of disciplines. Osmer, for example, emphasizes the importance of social scientific empirical research methodologies through which the practical theologian can engage in a process of really 'attending' to others.[39] The purpose of this book is to explore alternative 'sources and norms' for guiding Christian practice and to consider what the implications of these

---

[36]E. Y. Lartey, *Pastoral Theology in an Intercultural World* (Peterborough: Epworth, 2006), p. 82.
[37]Pattison, 'Some Straw for the Bricks', p. 139.
[38]Osmer, *Practical Theology*, p. 57.
[39]Ibid., p. 34.

'sources and norms' might be. Empirical research to test out these 'sources and norms' or to identify how they may already be worked out in concrete praxes is beyond the remit of this book but would be an obvious next step beyond this work. Graham listens to the voices of others in her practical theology when she uses feminist philosophy and theology to critique historical perspectives on practical theology and pastoral praxis,[40] while in my own work on theologies of disabilities, it has been important to engage in both scholarship in disability studies, as well as empirical research among people with disabilities to develop meaningful theologies.[41] Thus, practical theology is attentive to and listens to perspectives from a range of disciplines, and not only intra-theological discourses.

Other disciplines become partners in the dialogue that can question and speak to the practical theologian. But practical theology attends to and listens to lived experience and practice too. Those voices may be heard through empirical research or communicated in other ways, such as through literature. The important point here is that however other perspectives are communicated, the practical theologian seeks to listen to voices that are not from their own tradition or worldview and take them seriously and they should do so not from a presumption of their own superiority but in a spirit of openness to learn from others. Practical theology does not necessarily adapt theological positions to those of other disciplines (though it might) but nor does it pretend to have all of the answers to society's questions either.[42]

Conversation involves speaking

It is important that all partners in any conversation can find a space in which to articulate their particular contributions to the subject of discussion. It has been a very real danger historically, that Christian theology has been so assured of its own rightness and superiority over other faith perspectives that its voice in any dialogue has been so loud as to ensure that other perspectives are not heard. In contrast, because of this legacy, alongside the once predominant notion that moral and political 'neutrality' could only be realized by expelling 'religious arguments from the political agenda',[43] Christian theologians and practitioners have often been silenced in the public square. However, this book emerges from a perspective of someone who is located within the Christian tradition and believes that Christian

---

[40]See Graham, *Transforming Practice*.

[41]See Morris, *Theology without Words*.

[42]See Hiltner's critique of Tillich discussed in Graham, Walton and Ward, *Theological Reflections: Methods*, p. 158.

[43]K. J. Klop, 'Equal Respect and the Holy Spirit: The Liberal Demand for Moral Neutrality in the Political Sphere and Christian Respect for Creation', in *Public Theology for the 21st Century* (eds W. F. Storrar and A. R. Morton; London: T&T Clark, 2004), pp. 95–106 (103).

theology has something useful and valuable to contribute to theological and social thinking and praxis in a multi-faith world. As a result, Christian theology therefore has a responsibility to speak to the questions that face the multi-faith and globalized world of the twenty-first century, but to do so in respectful and open dialogue in its speech to others so that as it speaks, it also listens.

Participants are changed through dialogue

Critical conversation is not a method of theological reflection that proposes dialogue for its own sake, but is, in this work, orientated towards transforming human injustice and suffering. Genuinely listening to others, as well as speaking out from one's own perspective, should invariably lead to some level of transformation in all the dialogue partners. Dialogue with people of other faiths is, in many ways, a relatively new phenomenon, necessary to address a history of conflict and mistrust between faith communities. Thus even the process of conversation itself signifies a transformed and renewed relationship, a new soteriological praxis between people of contrasting faith perspectives. But not only is the process of conversation transformative, but there is potential for the content of the dialogue to be transformative too. Through listening to and speaking with survivors of the Holocaust, for example, Jürgen Moltmann's theology and understanding of Christian notions of hope were transformed through attentive engagement with experiences that questioned the very foundations of Christian theology. Moltmann's theology necessitated change and he too was changed as a result of his encounters.[44]

In discussing David Tracy, Graham et al. note that he argues that 'in the process of hearing the claims of modern culture in all its urgency and complexity, Christian theology itself must be prepared to undergo *revision*'.[45] Further, drawing on the work of Ruether, they suggest that Ruether argues that 'the Christian tradition stands in need of a radical corrective through the inclusion of extra-theological voices'.[46] So this theology of salvation as praxis seeks to be open to such possibilities of change to theological discourse as well as practice. This change, I suggest, should be sought only in the spirit of speaking and listening described above. Imposing change on one or another for its own sake may become a new form of oppressive practice, the very thing from which this book seeks to escape. Ultimately, the dialogue is driven towards transformation of Christian praxis in a multi-faith world, so that while dialogue constitutes transformation, this dialogue is orientated towards a particular goal.

---

[44]Moltmann, *A Broad Place: An Autobiography* (Minneapolis: Fortress Press, 2009), p. 189.
[45]Graham, Walton and Ward, *Theological Reflections: Methods*, p. 159.
[46]Ibid., p. 163.

Conversation partners may not end up agreeing

Theology does not always conclude with neat solutions or responses to practical or theoretical questions. To some extent, this book exemplifies the reality of this statement. Different conversation partners will come to the dialogue with different starting points, worldviews, philosophical frameworks, beliefs and ideologies (including me as facilitator of this particular conversation in this book) and it is not always possible to reconcile such contrasting perspectives and, indeed, nor is it necessarily desirable. To do so would involve repeating the weaknesses of many pluralist theologies that have homogenized contrasting religious beliefs into homogenous wholes, often imposing and mapping Western Christian notions and discourses onto other world religions. Practical theology is necessarily unsystematic in its approach. That is to say, because theory and practice are always in dialogue with one another, what may seem to make logical sense, is not meaningful until it is tested in practice. Practical theology must, therefore, live with and seek to address itself to the messiness and confusion of the world and the possible contradictions that may develop within newly constructed theories. In the second part of this book, in seeking to develop alternative soteriologies that may shape new praxes in the Christian community, there is a constant danger that perhaps these alternatives will again be used to impose Christian notions of liberative praxis onto people of other faiths who may not wish to be on the receiving end of such praxes. Thus any theology must continue, beyond the pages of this book, to engage in on-going critical conversation in dialogue and mutual respect, and to be open to the critique of engagement with practice to seek to avoid such dangerous pitfalls.

Critical conversation: An important limitation

There are, however, some important limitations to note with regard to the 'critical conversation' approach. Perhaps most importantly is that such methods of doing theology arguably serve a Western liberal agenda,[47] whereby the Bible, tradition, experience and reason and so forth become equal partners in dialogue with each other. Such equality will not be appropriate or acceptable in many Christian traditions[48] and look strange to many outside of Christianity too. In a context of teaching theological reflection to students from a range of contrasting ecumenical traditions, Bennett recalls that an Orthodox student in her class was not sympathetic to the idea of doing theological reflection using the methods presented to him:

> This was in part because it asked him to reflect theologically and sociologically on a pastoral situation in a way which seemed to the

---

[47]Ibid., p. 168.
[48]Z. Bennett, *Incorrigible Plurality: Teaching Pastoral Theology in an Ecumenical Context* [Contact Pastoral Monograph 14] (Edinburgh: Contact Pastoral Trust, 2004), p. 24.

Orthodox to presuppose that modern insights, for example from psychology, hold an equal place with the writings of the Fathers of the Church.[49]

Likewise, she notes that some evangelical students raised similar questions with regard to how they were being asked to reflect on the Bible. She notes that theological reflection 'presupposes a liberal tradition of reflection'[50] and even more than that, as a result, it has the potential to be 'totalising and imperialistic'[51] by assuming that its approach to theology is normative.

Who is invited to a piece of critical conversation in the first instance, and then who has the most influential voice, is largely dependent on how culture, context, belief and theology are shaped by the one who facilitates the conversations. For some, it is important to note that the methods employed in this book are inappropriate because I do not privilege the received interpretation of certain texts and traditions over the need to be relevant to the questions that confront the multi-faith world today. However, I hope to avoid a method that is totalizing and imperialistic. I do so by reiterating again that this book is intended as a 'contribution to thinking' that will be variously useful to the audiences for whom it is intended, but not at all the definitive or final word on this subject. We will come back to unpack further the 'particularised' nature of this work and the contribution it may make to ecclesial and public thinking towards the end of this chapter, but first, it is important to consider who the main dialogue partners will be in this practical theology of salvation for a multi-faith world, again conscious that each partner may not easily be distinguishable from others.

Critical conversation: Identifying key dialogue partners

Dialogue partner one: Historic and contemporary contexts

The first dialogue partner in this conversation is found through seeking to understand something of the historical ways in which Christians have engaged with people of other faiths, the legacy of that, and the concrete situation of the multi-faith and globalized world in which we live today. There are particular issues and concerns that face the world today that history has shaped and in which the role of faith communities remains significant. This is true internationally as well as at national and local

---

[49]Ibid.
[50]Ibid.
[51]Ibid.

levels. In my own context in the United Kingdom, there are many positive
examples of inter-faith engagement and attempts by faith and spiritual
leaders and people more widely to improve relationships among people
of faiths; in such instances, improved relations between faith communities
are often prospered.[52] At the same time there can be suspicion, mistrust,
even fear of people of faith, in particular people of minority faiths both
within Christianity and outside it, and that is often shaped by uninformed
suspicion and mistrust that can, in turn, lead to community tensions and
even violence as we shall see in Chapter 3. It is this second dimension of
inter-faith engagement that has for much of history been the principle way
in which people of faiths have engaged with each other. This conversation
partner is crucial in this dialogue of practical theology as it is in seeking
to understand and learning from the past and the present, in particular
the ways in which Christian beliefs and practices regarding people of
other faiths have operated, that provides the backdrop against which this
practical theology of salvation is written and the contexts to which it seeks
to formulate a response.

Dialogue partner two: Soteriological traditions

The second dialogue partner is Christian theologies of salvation and their
role in Christian approaches to people of other faiths. First, in Chapter 2,
the many and varied ways in which soteriology has historically been
understood in the Christian tradition will be explored. Second, the narrow
definitions of soteriology that have historically been used to inform and
shape Christian practices towards people of other faiths, despite the
diversity of perspectives present in the Christian tradition, will be discussed
in Chapter 3. In particular, there is a focus on how such soteriologies have
been used to reinforce Christian notions of their own superiority. Third, in
Chapter 4, contemporary theological discourses on salvation and people of
other faiths will be discussed and, it will be argued, that these approaches
to soteriology are largely inadequate for shaping new forms of praxis.
Transforming Christian engagement with people of other faiths to take
Christian practices in alternative directions to the past necessitates bringing
alternative theologies of salvation to the table of dialogue because, as has
already been argued, soteriologies have been central to Christian attitudes
and practices towards people of other faiths for centuries. Thus, if more
gracious living together is to be realized, soteriology must either be taken out
of the discourses regarding people of other faiths or else be deconstructed
and reconstructed.

---

[52]See, for example, accounts of inter-faith engagement in M. Torry and S. Thorley (eds),
Together & Different: Christians Engaging with People of Other Faiths (London: Canterbury
Press, 2008).

Dialogue partner three: Other disciplines and perspectives

The third dialogue partner in the conversation will be disciplines and perspectives from outside of Christian theology that might contribute to understanding the past and present and help to shape new ways of thinking about salvation for present and future engagements with people of other faiths. Townes notes that in 'allowing our minds, our scholarship to dance, we can welcome new conversation partners – not to control or dominate – but to allow the richness of insights and experiences beyond what we know and don't know to fill our scholarship with deeper meaning'.[53] This practical theology will take a multi-disciplinary approach to theology conscious that it can learn from traditions outside of theology and perhaps be open to the possibility that God is active and revelation may take place outside of the academy and churches. Perspectives from other disciplines are engaged with throughout this work but perhaps, most notably, in Chapter 3 where history and contemporary social analysis on Christian engagements with people of other faiths is articulated to explain why a practical theology of salvation such as this is needed.

Dialogue partner four: The author

The fourth dialogue partner in this conversation on salvation is the author himself. As with any piece of theology, I bring my own 'ideas, beliefs, feelings, perceptions and assumptions'[54] to the table. I write from a particular geographical, theological and ecclesiastical location and these inform the way I contribute to the conversation and the way I facilitate the conversation of the others. As has already been discussed, the fact that I am willing to engage in this kind of conversation at all is reflective of my own Western liberal theological position. I write from a white, British, Christian, Anglican perspective having worked in academic theology for over ten years. I am a theologian committed to the principle that the Gospel is at its heart concerned with human liberation and the transformation of injustices, inequalities and human suffering. All of this contributes to, and shapes the conversation as it proceeds. There will be dangers that I read into dialogue partners what I want to read and ignore what I do not want to hear. I come with an agenda to both engage with and use theology in such a way that it facilitates a particular end (as all theology does), and I have a concern to address the injustices and suffering that human beings might experience, a concern shaped by my faith tradition and theological leanings outlined above. This is not intended as a 'get-out' clause that gives me permission

---

[53]Townes, 'Walking on the Rimbones', pp. 14–15.
[54]Lartey, *Pastoral Theology*, p. 82.

to argue whatever I want without defending it, but rather it is an attempt to be honest about where this theology comes from, where it is going and what it is intending to achieve. Others may not share the same motivations, methods and goals as I do, but at least the reader may understand how and why I am arguing this particular case in this book.

Dialogue partner five: The reader

Arguably, there is a fifth dialogue partner in this practical theology of salvation for a multi-faith world; that is the reader. As Pattison rightly notes, conversation involves living beings who change and evolve as a result of the conversation. The reader is invited in this book to observe the conversation, but hopefully the reader will also be inspired to go beyond the pages of the book and become a participant in the conversation. The reader will at times agree, disagree, challenge and be challenged by what is contained herein. Frances Young notes that as a theologian she has at times 'spoken of a kind of arrival, a return to faith, a sense of salvation and healing, as if the journey was a linear process with a goal attained'. She now recognizes that 'the important thing is the journeying, not the arriving'.[55] This book is not meant to be the final word on this subject, but a theology in flux aiming to respond to a question, and seeking to take theologies and praxes forward. Because of this, it is hoped the reader through engaging with this book may in some way think about and practice soteriology differently or refine what is contained here with a view to transforming soteriological praxes further.

Summary: This practical theology

This practical theology of salvation, consistent with the discipline more widely, is no mere application of doctrine to questions facing the Christian community and its contribution to the complex multi-faith world at the beginning of the twenty-first century. Rather, it is a theology that takes practice seriously, conscious that theology itself is revealed and expressed in the intentional acts of Christian communities. Further, such practices must be interrogated because they often reveal a soteriological viewpoint that has reinforced Christian notions of its own superiority over people of other faiths that have led to acts of profound hostility and violence. This practical theology thus seeks to bring a range of dialogue partners into conversation with one another with a view to constructing an understanding of salvation as praxis that might lead to new Christian expressions towards people of

---

[55]F. Young, *Welcoming Difference* (Friends Day Lecture, 2002). (Birmingham: Queens Foundation, 2002), p. 12.

other faiths in words and deeds. That may involve, in turn, constructing new or renewed forms of belief and practice. That being so, it is important to consider some further final parameters for shaping the kind of dialogue and subsequent practical theology of salvation that will be constructed in the remainder of this book.

A very particular and public theology

The need for particular and public theology

Many theologies of religions have been accused of failing to recognize the particularity from which they speak. Summing up the principle objections to Rahner's notion of 'anonymous Christianity', for example, Karen Kilby explains that Rahner is often,

> accused of condescension and arrogance. The Christian who follows Rahner supposes he [sic.] knows better than everyone else what they really believe and experience. He [sic.] pays no attention to the differences between religions, but immediately claims them all as 'anonymous' versions of his [sic.] own.[56]

Kilby notes that Rahner's inclusivism assumes that Christianity is the only religion to really have grasped the truth about God, but condescends to suggest that most religions are essentially, albeit anonymously, Christian. The notion of the 'anonymous Christian' itself has not been widely used beyond Rahner. However, other inclusivists, such as Pinnock and Yong, for example, have both suggested that the Holy Spirit may be at work in other religions and that Christians may discern that activity in other religions.[57] Indeed, John Paul II has also suggested that the Spirit 'is mysteriously present in the heart of every person'.[58] However, with D'Costa, I would argue that 'it is not clear why an "anonymous Christ" is imperialistic' or carries the marks of Christian 'condescension and arrogance' and an '"anonymous Spirit" is not'.[59] Similar accusations can be made towards many other perspectives on theology and salvation with regard to people of other faiths, as we shall see

---

[56]K. Kilby, *The SPCK Introduction to Karl Rahner* (London: SPCK, 2007), p. 34.
[57]See A. Yong, *Beyond the Impasse: Toward a Pneumatological Theology of Religions* (Carlisle: Paternoster, 2003) and C. H. Pinnock, 'An Inclusivist View', in *Four Views on Salvation in a Pluralistic World* (eds S. N. Gundry, D. L. Okholm and T. R. Phillips; Grand Rapids, MI: Zondervan, 1996), pp. 95–123 (105).
[58]John Paul II, 'General Audience, Wednesday, 9 September 1998', www.vatican.va/holy_father/john_paul_ii/audiences/1998/documents/hf_jp-iI_aud_09091998_En.html, last accessed on 1 February 2013.
[59]G. D'Costa, *Christianity and World Religions: Disputed Questions in the Theology of Religions* (Oxford: Wiley-Blackwell, 2009), p. 18.

in Chapter 4, that seek to construct discourses of universal significance from
a Christian perspective.

Greggs argues for the need for Christian theology, therefore, to speak from
a position of particularity, that is, to be able to speak out of the distinctiveness
of its own position and traditions. He explains, 'put concretely, a Christian
should engage with a Muslim on the basis of Christianity. A Muslim should
engage with a Christian on the basis of Islam'.[60] It is important to note,
however, that Christianity is not a single homogenous whole and nor, for
that matter is Islam. The question of particularity is not simply of the
broadly 'religious' tradition from which one speaks, but also the theological
and ecclesiological position and socio-economic-political location of the one
speaking. That the theologian should speak from their particular position
and location and that people of other faiths should do the same does
potentially open up a space, however, for a more open and fruitful dialogue
between people of different faith traditions.

This represents an important development in more recent theologies of
religions. Where practiced, it means that Christian voices are not silenced
at the table of conversation in public contexts or in places of inter-faith
engagement, but likewise should avoid the dangers of the past whereby the
Christian theological voice insists on its own dominance. To avoid such
imperialism, Christian theologians can only speak from their own traditions
and should resist any attempts to colonize any other religious or spiritual
tradition or practice by interpreting them through Christian theological
ideas and frameworks. Christian voices must speak for themselves out of
their own particularity and allow other faith and spiritual traditions to do
the same. What is created is a space in which universalizing claims that
would have significance for people of other faiths cannot be made. While
Greggs himself advocates a form of universal soteriology, for example, he
does so without wishing to say anything about how another faith perspective
might realize that salvation. He speaks as a Christian theologian from the
particularities of his own Christian perspective.

However, if this practical theology of religions speaks out of its own
particularity, it speaks not only to a Christian audience but also into the
public square, not least as it seeks to address the use of Christian language,
ideas and motifs in contemporary social and political discourses. In that sense
it is also a form of public theology: it speaks for itself, but it speaks to others.
Storrar argues good public theology engages 'in the politics of democratic
transformation and not simply in the politics of protest and prophetic
resistance'.[61] This involves 'participating in the public sphere with civility to

---

[60]T. Greggs, 'Legitimizing and Necessitating Inter-Faith Dialogue: The Dynamics of Inter-Faith
for Individual Faith Communities', *International Journal of Public Theology* 4(2), (2010),
pp. 194–211 (196).
[61]W. Storrar, '2007: A Kairos Moment for Public Theology', *International Journal of Public
Theology* 1(1), (2007), pp. 5–25 (16–17).

strangers and attentiveness to their opinions'[62] thus reinforcing the importance of listening and speaking at the table of critical conversation. Further, however, de Gruchy rightly suggests that 'good public theological praxis gives priority to the perspectives of victims and survivors, and to the restoration of justice'.[63] Notwithstanding the reality that many Christians are and continue to be among the victims and survivors of oppressive persons, institutions and regimes, that does not mean it is appropriate or acceptable to overlook or ignore the way Christian persons, nations and institutions have also often been the forces of oppression that have led people of other faiths to suffer and not always survive. This means that the voice and experience of people of other faiths, particularly those who have been suppressed at the hands of Christian persons, often need to be privileged in order to develop alternative soteriological discourses to those that have served the churches for so long. This will not always sit comfortably with those in the Christian tradition who subscribe to the notion of Christian superiority over people of other faiths but, nevertheless, such a shift in position is indeed necessary for Christian beliefs and praxes to exercise and enact a commitment to creating a more just and egalitarian society. Thus, as well as being a practical theology of religions for the Christian community, this also aims to be a public theology from a Christian theological perspective aiming at offering a particularly Christian theological contribution to thinking and praxis in a multi-faith world.

In Alastair Campbell's words, this particular practical and public theology of salvation, in seeking to speak to the Christian community and into the public square in a non-imperialistic way does so by aiming to tread 'a difficult path between practical relevance and theological integrity'.[64] If this theology is to speak at all to the audiences to whom it seeks to make any difference, it does so from the particularity of the traditions that they and I value as part of Christianity. To do so, it must be in some way recognizably 'Christian' to members of Christian communities, but it needs also to seek to meaningful and relevant to Christian praxes inside and outside of churches. Thus with Campbell, this book does indeed aim to tread a difficult path between practical relevance and theological integrity. But how are such things measured? The answer to the question of what constitutes practical relevance and theological integrity is not singular and cannot be used universally. For a Protestant Christian, for example, theological integrity may mean among other things, an appeal to a defence of existing future eschatological understandings of soteriology with reference to Scripture. In Roman Catholicism, it may involve an appeal to the Magisterium and in Orthodoxy to the Church Fathers. Further, what is practically useful and

---

[62]Ibid., p. 17.

[63]J. W. de Gruchy, 'Public Theology as Christian Witness: Exploring the Genre', *International Journal of Public Theology* 1(1), (2007), pp. 26–41 (39–40).

[64]A. Campbell, 'The Nature of Practical Theology', in *The Blackwell Reader in Pastoral and Practical Theology* (eds J. Woodward and S. Pattison; Oxford: Blackwell, 2000) pp. 77–88 (86).

expedient in one context may be precisely the opposite in another. As we have seen, Zoe Bennett found this to be the case in aiming to teach theological reflection in an ecumenical context where different texts, traditions, priorities and philosophical frameworks influenced her students' approaches to and levels of engagement with theological reflection.

I have developed three approaches to soteriology as praxis in this book, drawing on the notion of *deification*, an important theme in the writings of the Church Fathers and in Eastern Orthodoxy though developed and adapted here; *healing*, which draws on a particularly biblical understanding of salvation, though by no means the only one; and finally, *liberation*, which has been an important theme in Roman Catholic soteriologies, not least in South America, but in many contextual theologies around the world too. Each of these three soteriologies will, in turn, I hope, contribute to thinking about how different praxes across multiple theological and ecclesiological traditions might be formed, conscious that the legitimacy and usefulness of each can only be determined after they have been tested in a variety of contexts. These three approaches to salvation are already recognizable across a range of Christian traditions, therefore, so that while they push the boundaries of soteriological thinking and praxis regarding people of other faiths, they do so by drawing on and reinterpreting traditions already present in and identifiable with Christianity.

Conclusion

Christian theologies of religions need to engage in a turn to practice. It has been argued that it is imperative that scholars seriously think through the consequences and potential impact of new theological ideas and that to fail to do so fails to recognize and learn from the past and the power that ideas can have to shape what human beings do for good and bad. Such a turn to practice for theologians is necessary in a world where wars, political agendas and divisions of human persons justified by religious discourses have and continue to be rife. It is also necessary that such discourses are, where appropriate, challenged. That being so, a practical theological method has here been developed that seeks to openly engage in a process of critical conversation of listening to and speaking to a range of dialogue partners in the hope of constructing new, alternative and more liberative beliefs and praxes for the multi-faith world of the twenty-first century. It is hoped that this will be achieved by speaking from within the Christian tradition to Christian communities and to do so meaningfully by treading Campbell's path between practical relevance and theological integrity. In Chapter 2, the notion of theological integrity in particular whereby I hope to demonstrate that the very idea of salvation as praxis is no new innovation, but a concept that has always formed a part of Christian soteriological discourses from the beginning, will be explored.

2

Salvations in the Christian tradition

Introduction

Jon Sobrino writes, 'There is *personal* salvation and *social* salvation, there is *historical* salvation and *transcendent* salvation'.[1] While multiple perspectives on salvation can be found in various Christian traditions, a dominant perspective has emerged in the West that has historically shaped Christian practices towards people of other faiths. Further, as will be proposed in Chapter 4, it is this dominant perspective that has also underpinned most contemporary soteriological thinking regarding people of other faiths too. Most theological discourses on salvation, it was proposed in the Introduction to this book, have three main aspects or dimensions to them:

1 a description of the state from which it is understood salvation is necessary;

2 the process by which salvation is realized and the extent of human participation alongside the role of Christ in making salvation possible;

3 an articulation of what the final end state of salvation will be like.

In what follows, the dominant Western perspective on salvation will be discussed according to these three dimensions of soteriological discourse. It will then be argued that alternative salvations that focus on the social and historical dimensions of salvation can be found in Christian traditions too. With reference to a number of contextual theologies of salvation that have

---

[1] J. Sobrino, *No Salvation Outside the Poor: Prophetic-Utopian Essays* (New York, NY: Orbis Books, 2008), p. 57.

uncovered these alternative soteriological positions, the notion of salvation as a lived transformative praxis will begin to be developed.

Christian soteriology: Multiple salvations

In contrast to many pluralist theologies of salvation, Mark Heim proposes that 'it does make sense to speak of salvation in the plural'[2] because it is only possible to speak about 'multiple religious aims, salvations'.[3] Seeking to homogenize contrasting religious truth claims into a single definition does not, he claims, take religious diversity seriously enough, despite the claims of many pluralists that this is the foundation of their work. It is not possible to speak about salvation across religious traditions and to articulate a single definition that is inclusive of all religious claims about the final aims and ends of human persons. Those who have attempted such inter-religious soteriological definitions have invariably imposed the truth claims of their faith tradition onto others or else provided a definition that bears no relation to the truth claims of any tradition.[4] While Heim's term, 'salvations' is not employed here, given the multiple ways in which salvation is spoken about in the Christian tradition, it could arguably be equally appropriate to only speak about *salvations* in the plural when speaking about Christian soteriologies.

Giving consideration to the many different ways in which salvation as a whole, or aspects of salvation, have been articulated and practiced gives a sense of the breadth of soteriological understandings that can be found in the Christian tradition. Language provides one indicator of the diversity of perspectives and O'Collins identifies just five key theological terms that are used: 'redemption, salvation, atonement, reconciliation, and expiation'.[5] However, there are many other terms that any scholar of soteriological discourses might use, including, substitution, satisfaction, pre-destination, justification, deification or theosis, healing, liberation and sanctification. While some of these terms are associated with particular denominations or traditions more than with others, nevertheless, they point to aspects of different Christian perspectives on why salvation is necessary, what it means to be saved and the process by which salvation is realized. Further, each term does not represent one set of views or perspectives on salvation either. The Lutheran notion of justification, for example, has been debated and contested since Luther first emphasized this understanding of salvation,

---

[2] S. M. Heim, *Salvations: Truth and Difference in Religion* (New York, NY: Orbis Books, 1995), p. 6.

[3] Ibid., p. 7.

[4] See the discussion of this in Chapter 4.

[5] G. O'Collins, *Jesus Our Redeemer: A Christian Approach to Salvation* (Oxford: Oxford University Press, 2007), p. 2.

with multiple perspectives on what it means to be justified resulting from the conversations.[6]

There are multiple ways in which individuals, communities and institutions that identify as 'Christian' speak about salvation. Chapter 4 demonstrates this in relation to perspectives on the 'scope' or 'reach' of salvation as discussed in contemporary theologies of religions, but equivocity can be found in all aspects of what might be summed up as soteriological discourses. Gerald O'Collins suggests that the reason for this is that 'conciliar clarification has never take place in soteriology'[7] as it has in relation to Christology and pneumatology, for example. While not every individual who identifies themselves as Christian would necessarily subscribe wholeheartedly to the Trinitarian definitions of Nicaea (325 CE) or Constantinople (381 CE), they have nevertheless proved useful in articulating the particularities of Christian identity and defining orthodoxy and heresy regarding Christian understandings of God at ecclesial, organizational and institutional levels. Niceno-Constantinopolitan definitions, for example, are used today by ecumenical organizations to determine eligibility of church institutions for membership.[8] No such statements exist on soteriology, hence the plethora of different ways of thinking and speaking soteriologically that can be discovered in the Christian tradition. Though, as we shall see shortly, a dominant view on soteriology has emerged in Western traditions regarding salvation and it is this dominant soteriology, focused on personal and transcendent salvation, that has largely informed Christian practices towards people of other faiths across the centuries of Christian history.

Dominant western soteriology: An overview

Reasons why salvation is necessary

Ivor Davidson provides a classic account of the dominant understanding of the human and the divine conditions that have been used to explain why, in the first instance, human salvation by a divine agent was necessary:

> ... the God who gave the world its being acts to redeem it from its current conditions of disorder, thus restoring otherwise lost creatures to fellowship

---

[6]See, for example, the discussions in V. M. Kärkkäinen, *One with God: Salvation as Deification and Justification* (Collegeville: Liturgical Press, 2004).

[7]O'Collins, *Jesus Our Redeemer*, p. 1.

[8]The World Council of Churches, for example, uses belief in the Trinity as one of the hallmarks of its identity and therefore for eligibility for membership. See World Council of Churches, *Constitution*, www.oikoumene.org/en/resources/documents/assembly/porto-alegre-2006/1-statements-documents-adopted/institutional-issues/constitution-and-rules-as-adopted.html?print=1_print%20african%20churches%20address%20p, last accessed on 1 February 2013.

with their creator. . . . There is nothing about creation that God needs, nor
is there anything within creation that, either in anticipation or actuality,
summons an obligation on God's part. Creatures have inexplicably
chosen death rather than life, and brought disaster upon themselves. . . .
Their folly deserves judgement, the tragedy of estrangement from their
intended relationship with God. In the unfathomable love that God is,
God does not give up on his [sic.] world, but moves in mercy to bring it
back to himself [sic.].[9]

Delores Williams identifies four historic so-called theories of the atonement
that have been predominant in Western understandings of soteriology that
provide further insights into a Christian perspective on the nature of God
and human beings. The first is Origen's understanding of the atonement
as 'ransom'. In this approach, 'the cross represented a ransom paid to the
devil for the sins of humankind'.[10] The second is Anselm's understanding
of the atonement as 'satisfaction'. Here, God is 'dishonoured' by the sins of
humanity which demands that God either punishes those who cause such
offence, or that God's honour must be satisfied in some other way. Given
how great the sin of humanity was, nothing can satisfy God's anger but the
death of the Son on the cross.[11] Abelard represents for Williams the third
approach to the atonement which she describes as the 'moral theory of
the atonement'. This understanding of atonement 'emphasized God's love'
so that 'when humans look upon the death of Jesus they see the love of
God manifested'.[12] The cross thus causes humans to repent, allowing their
forgiveness. The fourth understanding of the atonement Williams identifies
is Calvin's theory of 'substitution'. Because human beings were so sinful,
they deserved punishment, she argues, but because 'God is both just and
merciful' Calvin argued a substitute, Jesus, was provided 'who would bear the
punishment of human sin'.[13] Anthony Reddie rightly notes that 'Salvation, the
act of being saved, implies that one is being saved from something, while also
being saved into or for some other purpose or place'[14] so what is it, according
to Davidson's theology and Williams' analysis of history, that necessitates
salvation as a consequence of the way humans and God have been thought to
exist in the dominant model in the West; from what is salvation needed?
    According to Davidson, human beings and God express different and
contrasting conditions, so much so that the two are irreconcilable in their

---

[9] I. J. Davidson, 'Introduction: God of Salvation', in *God of Salvation: Soteriology in Theological Perspective* (eds I. J. Davidson and M. A. Rae; Farnham: Ashgate, 2011), pp. 1–14 (1).
[10] D. S. Williams, *Sisters in the Wilderness: The Challenge of Womanist God-Talk* (Maryknoll, NY: Orbis Books, 2004), p. 162.
[11] Ibid., p. 163.
[12] Ibid.
[13] Ibid., pp. 163–64.
[14] A. G. Reddie, *Is God Colour-Blind? Insights from Black Theology for Christian Ministry* (London: SPCK, 2009), p. 96.

current states. Human beings are essentially corrupt and sinful and in a state of total disorder while God is perfect, good and above reproach. Human activity alone only leads to the ultimate destruction of human beings who will attract divine judgement and subsequent punishment for the way they act. Understood in light of Augustine's concept of original sin, while human beings inherit sin and can do nothing about their sinful condition, in this dominant approach humans are, nevertheless responsible for their sin and, without an intervention from God, will be judged for their sinfulness. God, in Davidson's account, is distant and removed from creation. Human beings are, in theory at least, of no consequence to God, as God does not need creation and is not obliged to care for it. Nevertheless, God is merciful and determines to care for creation and so does intervene in order to ensure that human beings are not eternally punished and lost in the way they would be if they were left to their own devices. Thus the dominant Western understanding of the divine and human conditions in salvation discourses is that humans are in an unworthy, wretched and inherited sinful state that deserves eternal punishment for which they are responsible, and God is one who is offended by this but who chooses to restore the human condition out of generous mercy for creation.

Williams provides further insight into the nature of God and human beings in this dominant perspective as historic notions of the atonement in Western forms of Christianity have been dependent on particular understandings of the condition of both God and of human beings. Human beings are so sinful that they deserve some form of punishment, as Davidson suggests, but what Williams makes clear is that this sin is not necessarily about particular acts of evil, but the original and inherited sin that characterizes the human condition from 'cradle to grave'. Humans are so sinful and so deserving of punishment, in the very core of their beings, that they can do nothing to make right the offence caused to God. While it has been argued that the capacity of humans to sin was a necessary part of creation as the only way through which human freedom would be possible, the sin of the first humans is inherited through original sin, in these understandings, irrespective of the choices and actions of subsequent generations. In the dominant perspectives on salvation, if humanity is so utterly wretched, totally marred by original sin, then what of God?

Having chosen to create the world in such a way, that sin is possible and then can be inherited, God is nevertheless so offended by the sin of humanity that God must punish, either humanity itself or else find a substitute. God is thus imaged as a rather dubious character who is, for example, bound by a 'pact' with the devil and the only way of securing the salvation of humanity is by paying the devil a ransom for humanity. Alternatively, God behaves as a medieval overlord so that, even though God created the world in this way, the divine honour is offended by it and so demands satisfaction. In many of these ways of understanding the divine condition, logical inconsistencies begin to emerge with such views of God and those that speak of God as one who is love, good and above reproach. Attempts have been made that seek to resolve such inconsistencies, but addressing those is not the concern here. Rather, it is important to note that these understandings of the human and divine conditions have shaped the dominant soteriological perspectives on salvation in Western traditions, and have been used to explain why, as a result, salvation into something new is necessary.

The saved state: The goal of salvation

As we have seen in this dominant understanding of salvation God is not in need of any kind of change but, in contrast, the human condition is in need of complete transformation. Rosemary Radford Ruether suggests that the alternative desired saved state of the human is as follows: 'Platonizing Christianity made redemption as being reconciled with God, from whom our human nature is seen as having become totally severed due to sin, rejecting our bodies and finitude and ascending to communion with a heavenly world that is to be our true home after death'.[15] The state of salvation is thus envisaged as principally 'other-worldly' and the aspirations of human beings for an alternative transformed reality are focused almost entirely on future, eschatological, post-mortem possibilities. This focus on another world in the future, in which the human person might hope for an eternal place, implies that any effort to transform this world can only ever be secondary if not largely superfluous to one's salvation.

However, as Ruether suggests, the hope for a place in such another reality that so contrasts this world has led to a rejection of the assumed distinctive characteristics of this world, that is, the embodied state and humanity's inevitable finitude. Thus this dominant soteriological perspective further suggests that humans should view this world as something from which to escape rather than seeking to transform it, orientating the eye of the Christian towards heavenly other-worldly possibilities alone. Ruether further argues that the saved state, while being entirely other-worldly, is described as one in which the human is 'reconciled with God'. As with Davidson, Ruether's presentation of the dominant understanding of salvation in the Western tradition has been that humans have been separated and distanced from God by their sin. Thus to be saved is to have that state transformed by being reconciled to God. Because salvation takes places in another realm that is different from the earth that human beings inhabit, and that salvation involves a renewed relationship with God, such an understanding suggests that God is almost completely removed from life in this world. Reconciliation with God, a transformed alternative reality to the one in which humans live now, is not fully possible in this world, only in heaven. Human beings

---

[15]R. R. Ruether, *Introducing Redemption in Christian Feminism* (Sheffield: Sheffield Academic Press, 1998), p. 63.

cannot enjoy a saved state of being, a state of full reconciliation with God, until they at least depart from this world and the sinful constraints that currently separate them from God. Despite, however, this strong emphasis on a future, eschatological, other-worldly, post-mortem state of improved existence in which the human finds communion with God in the dominant model, as we shall see in Chapter 3, understandings of salvation as a present, earthly possibility have occasionally been invoked when they have served the agendas of, for example, those who historically used Christianity to justify colonialism.

How salvation is realized

Brock and Parker explain that what they learned in 'church and graduate school' was that it was 'the crucifixion of Jesus that saved the world'.[16] If Jesus saves through his death on the cross, it has widely been understood in Western traditions that this is because humans are so sinful, as has just been outlined above, that nothing they can do is sufficient for them to save themselves. Human beings are thus totally dependent on God's 'grace' and initiative to save them and, in the dominant soteriological narrative, this requires an intervention from God. This intervention begins with the incarnation and culminates on the cross, where Christ 'died for our sins'. It is the cross, therefore, that leads to an atonement or reconciliation with God. Dominant soteriological perspectives in the West have, as was argued above, interpreted the death of Christ as an act of appeasement for God's anger with humanity that can only be achieved with a form of payment made or punishment meted out on behalf of humanity. Only God can save and the act of salvation is achieved by God's anger and desire for justice with humanity being 'satisfied' (Anselm) or by Christ taking on the sins of humanity and dying as a 'substitute' (Calvin). What is noteworthy, however, is that despite salvation only being fully experienced by humanity in another world, it is made possible through divine intervention and action in this world.

While humans are incapable of saving themselves, given their irrevocably sinful nature, individual persons are no mere passive recipients of salvation in this dominant perspective. God's intervention in history demands a response from human persons in order for their salvation to finally be possible. That response has included, for example, participation in rites of baptism, public affirmations of a personal faith such as in early baptismal practices, or simply a personal confessional faith in God and the dominant soteriological narrative described thus far. It is further noteworthy that one of the key questions of the Reformation was the extent to which human actions such

---

[16]R. N. Brock and R. A. Parker, *Saving Paradise: How Christianity Traded Love of This World for Crucifixion and Empire* (Boston: Beacon Press, 2008), p. xi.

as the payment of indulgences could quicken the speed at which one entered the heavenly, post-mortem saved state or whether faith alone was the only way of achieving individual salvation. For the most part, therefore, salvation has been understood to be dependent on God's grace, initiative and will to save human beings but that does not completely remove responsibility from individuals for their own salvation. Salvation is fully realized in a future other world, but is only possible as a result of a confession of beliefs or participation in an ecclesial ritual in this world with the result being that humans are, to some extent and only in a small way, participants in realizing their own personal salvation.

Summary: Dominant western soteriological perspectives

Approaches to salvation in Western traditions are multifarious and complex and the above outline of a dominant perspective does not take full account of the many ways that salvation has been understood, expressed and practiced. Nevertheless, the above description of a model of soteriology represents an overview of a set of discourses that have been most prevalent in Western Christian history and have been at the forefront of Western Christian engagements with people of other faiths, shaping Christian practices. This dominant model of salvation views the human condition as one that is utterly wretched and in need of salvation – transformation into a new and improved reality. God mercifully, though without necessity, responds to that need for salvation and intervenes to make salvation possible. The new reality to which the human can aspire in this model is entirely focused on a future, other-worldly, post-mortem existence with the result that the human's principle task is not to transform this world, other than by converting others to this view of reality, but to seek escape from it. God, in Christ, through Christ's death, makes that possible and human persons finally realize their salvation through faith or participation in a ritual to seal their salvation. Before turning to some alternative understandings of salvation, it is important to begin to consider briefly why this approach to salvation became dominant and why it has become the subject of the critique of many contextual theologies from the voices of historically marginalized persons.

Salvation as normalization

A range of contextual theologies, only a few of which there is room to discuss here, have sought to deconstruct this dominant understanding of salvation. The dominant discourse described above has, it is here argued, been emphasized over and above other soteriological understandings because it has justified agendas of normalization by reinforcing the Christian 'presumption of superiority'. That is, the saved state, the ideal existence for the human person, is constructed on the basis of positions in which individuals and communities consider themselves, their beliefs, practices and general way of life to be normative for everyone. In soteriological discourses, they accept that while all fall short of the ideal saved state, they more than anyone else are closer to that ideal. Subsequently they have a responsibility to ensure that those who deviate most from that established normative ideal are, wherever possible, 'normalized'. When that is not possible, or the supposed 'deviant' will not conform to their ideals, such people are assumed to be unable to be saved and, therefore, of less value and worth to God, the church and society more widely. Let us consider just two examples to illustrate this point.

Particular feminist critiques of established discourses of salvation have argued that historically it has been understood that women's salvation is dependent on men or that salvation involves in some way 'becoming male'. Given that human beings are understood to reflect the *imago dei*, and that the *imago dei* in human beings has historically thought to be rational thought free from the confines of a temporal, embodied existence; and given that rational thought has been a quality more closely associated with the male, it has historically been assumed that salvation is less easily attainable for women. The male is set up as normative, because he is like God, while the female is in some way less like God because she is more inclined towards her embodiment. However, she can attain salvation when she conforms to male normativity.

Kari Vogt argues that ancient Koine notions of 'becoming male' referred 'without exception to development from a lower state of moral and spiritual perfection' and that such understandings of the male in contrast to the female (representing spiritual degeneration) found their way in to theological discourses.[17] Therefore, if the quality in human beings that is most like God is the capacity to reason and this is a quality attributed to maleness, and if femaleness represents embodiment as the tradition has assumed (the condition from which humans should seek escape), then women are expected to conform to an understanding of maleness in this life. They do so in anticipation that they will become like men in the next world. Women who subvert this understanding are, it was assumed, less likely (if not totally unlikely) to be saved at all.

People with disabilities have also been assumed to deviate from the supposed normal human that was thought to resemble God and are also further removed than able-bodied people from the ideal state that the human ought to seek to attain if they are to be saved. In particular, soteriological discourses have been constructed that have assumed that they are less likely to be saved than able-bodied people because they are not like God and also because they cannot participate in the practices on earth that

---

[17]See K. Vogt, 'Becoming Male', in *Feminism & Theology* (eds J. M. Soskice and D. Lipton; Oxford: Oxford University Press, 2003), pp. 49–61.

enable salvation in the heaven. If rational thought is the human quality that makes human beings most like God, then the person with a mental illness, dementia, or learning disability is less like God than the non-disabled person. Thus because God is rational, it can also be assumed that the saved state will involve the transformation of all human persons into rational beings. Without this transformation, disabled people will not be saved. Further, if faith is necessary for salvation, and that faith is 'tested' through some form of public confession and affirmation of a set of established beliefs, then people with particular intellectual and mental impairments are also unable to participate in the process that leads to salvation. Thus not only is the able-bodied person representative of the normative state for humanity, to which all humans should subsequently expect to aspire, non-disabled people are the only ones who can be assured of salvation as they are the only ones who can engage in the practices that lead to salvation; the very practices that able-bodied people have created.

The concept of normativity itself need not always have negative implications for how human beings understand the world or how they engage with others. For societies, institutions and communities to operate, there needs to be some shared understanding of what is 'normal' behaviour in order for legal systems to be able to operate, for example. Further a notion of a normal, healthy body can provide science and medicine with criteria against which to determine what might be considered to be an illness and so appropriately invest in research to address such illnesses. Human beings also conform to the norms of a particular language and culture on a daily basis simply to be able to communicate with one another. Norms can enable communities and societies to operate in positive ways. What we observe, however, in agendas of normativity that result in the marginalization and exclusion of women and disabled people among many other groups, are concepts of normativity being used by those in positions of power in order to reinforce their own position of superiority and exercise control over others. In soteriological discourses, they do so by suggesting that God and the saved state constitute a reality that reflects their lives more than others and that others can only be saved if they conform to the norms and participate in practices set up by those with power. Normalization can, therefore, become a mechanism for the abuse of power that reinforces the positions of those who have power while justifying keeping the powerless in their place.

Given that it has been argued that, with Cone, this work is rooted in the principle that the Gospel is essentially a Gospel of liberation, the use of theology for such abuses of power in the name of normalization must be challenged and transformed; they are sinful (a state from which salvation is needed) and those who suffer as a result of them, in their struggle for liberation, rightly seek concrete, earthly salvation from such sins. Soteriological discourses have likewise been used to justify the normalization of people of other faiths too. By assuming that the Christian is normative, that only the Christian tradition possesses the truth to make salvation possible, and that only through subscription and conformation to a belief in that truth will a person be saved, people of other faiths are viewed as both 'abnormal' and in need of normalization. Those who do not conform are problematized, demonized and dehumanized. As we shall see in Chapter 3, Christianity has understood itself as normative and practiced soteriologies that have justified some of the most terrible acts of history in their quest to secure their own superiority and the normalization of people of other faiths to Western Christian norms.

Thus the normalization of difference on the basis of gender, disability and sexuality as means of reinforcing the power and position of able-bodied, heterosexual men should be understood as sinful because it is oppressive. Likewise, the assumption that the Christian pathway is normative for salvation and that any means necessary should be used to ensure people of other faiths conform to such norms ought to also be understood as sinful, because it is oppressive and contrary to the Gospel of liberation. Given that the dominant understanding of salvation in Western Christianity and its use to reinforce male normativity and ensure the exercise of control of those who are considered to deviate from such norms, it is important to explore how this understanding of salvation has begun to be deconstructed by voices that have historically been marginalized and to begin to uncover some alternative perspectives on salvation.

Rediscovering alternative salvations: Salvation as praxis

Humanity and divinity: Alternative perspectives

Freedom, sin and the imago dei

In Western soteriological traditions, as we have seen, the concept of original sin is central. This presupposes that the human condition was originally in a state where sin was absent so that human beings did not offend God. It was only as a result of 'the fall' that the human condition was changed so radically that it was in need of salvation. The precise notion of *original* sin is, however, absent in Eastern Orthodox theology. According to Kärkkäinen, Eastern fathers did not consider human beings to be 'perfect' even before the fall, but rather were created from the beginning with a view to growing into the likeness of God.[18] Kallistos Ware provides some explanation as to how and why this is so: 'Without freedom, there would be no sin. But without freedom man [sic.] would not be in God's image'.[19] Bartos further explains

---

[18]Kärkkäinen, *One with God*, p. 21.
[19]K. Ware, *The Orthodox Way* (New York, NY: St Vladimir's Seminary Press, rev. edn, 1995), p. 61.

that a distinction between being created in the image of God and the task of growing into the likeness of God is 'essential in order to preserve the Orthodox teaching on man's [sic.] continued kinship with God after the fall'.[20] Rooted in the principle that the proto-humans were created in the image of God, a God who is 'free', even before the fall, in order to fully reflect that image, humans were created with a capacity to sin. The fall was an expression of that capacity. Thus, it is the capacity to sin that leads to the eating of the fruit in the Garden of Eden, rather than the eating of the fruit that leads to the development of sin that is irreversible without an intervention from God. The effects of the 'sin of Adam' were not original sin, but rather 'physical death and the obscuring or distortion of the image of God'[21] in human beings.

To grow into the likeness of God was the original intention of God for humanity, in this view, as Kärkäinen explains: 'God's aim [for humanity] is to participate in God's life. The earthly life is for growth and development for this eternal communion'[22] – a process of 'becoming divine' and this is not made impossible, simply disrupted by the fall: sin 'deflected humanity' from the path God intended for them.[23] God's intention for humanity at creation is not destroyed by the fall and a new condition is not created, but rather the unavoidable free condition of humanity, when expressed through sin, disrupts the ultimate intention of God for human beings: to become God. Thus, an intervention from God remains necessary in order to 'save' humanity.

This view of salvation differs from the dominant Western understanding in that the human capacity to sin is seen as a part of the way God intentionally created human beings as 'free' creatures. To speak of sin in this way, and this reading of the creation narratives in Genesis, arguably makes more logical sense than a view that suggests humans were created with the capacity to sin, but that God did not want them to use it, and that when the first humans did sin, despite creating them with this capacity, God is offended beyond the possibility of reconciliation and punishes not only Adam and Even, but the whole of human existence on earth forever. Further, however, and perhaps most significantly, this suggests that the human condition need not be viewed as utterly wretched and lost but, at the very least, that every human person might still in some way reflect the *imago dei*, despite their sinfulness, and that each human person continues to hold the potential to reach the goal that God designed for humanity: to become like God's self. This presents a much more positive notion of the human condition though the *imago dei* in Eastern theology, just as in the West, has been understood to reflect

---

[20]E. Bartos, *Deification in Eastern Orthodox Theology* (Eugene, OR: Wipf & Stock, 2006), p. 136.
[21]Ibid., p. 22.
[22]Ibid., p. 21.
[23]Kärkkäinen, *One with God*, p. 21.

a particular form of normativity: disembodied rational thought. While the notion of theosis or deification is not unique to the Eastern traditions, the Eastern view that the human condition is not to its very core corrupt, but a condition that maintains the potential to grow into the likeness of God even by itself, in preparation for eternal participation in the divine life, provides an important alternative to the notion of original sin. Thus the notion of original sin is not universal to Christianity as a description of the human condition from which humans need salvation.

Inherited systemic sin

In contrast to the view of deification outlined above, Rosemary Radford Ruether rejects the notion of 'original sin' as a tool that can be used for blaming our ancestors, Adam, but more especially, Eve, for the presence of sin in the world.[24] Not only does the concept that sin is original suggest that the presence of sin in the world is not the fault of human beings today, she argues, but it also assumes that contemporary humans have no responsibility, nor the capacity, to do anything about it. Further, to suggest that only divine intervention can finally remove sin in a future eschatological existence encourages human passivity in the face of evil in the world and, in so doing, such a doctrine becomes dangerous. Perhaps this is why a Marxist critique of religion that understood religion as a tool for ensuring the poor and oppressed did not seek their own liberation in this world in the hope of treasures in heaven became so appealing to liberation theologians such as Gustavo Gutierrez.[25] Ruether redefines the notion of original sin as 'inherited' sin.[26] Here she recognizes that sinful practices, such as the historical sin of patriarchy, have been passed on from one generation to the next for centuries. If such inherited practices are understood as being biologically transmitted as 'original' sin, then the implication would be that patriarchy cannot be changed – at least in this world. Instead, however, 'inherited' sins should be understood as systemic sins that can and should be transformed and that they are sins that contemporary humans enact and for which they are responsible.

Anthony Reddie likewise critiques the notion of original sin, but for different reasons. Instead, he critiques the assumption of proponents of original sin that all are guilty and therefore deserving of punishment.[27] Drawing on the work of Anthony Pinn, he asks, 'what sin the tortured and disfigured Black body swinging from a rope in the Deep South, having first been flailed and lynched, committed to deserve being labelled a sinner?'[28]

---

[24]Ruether, *Introducing Redemption*, p. 97.
[25]G. Gutierrez, *A Theology of Liberation: History, Politics and Salvation* (London: SCM Press, rev. edn, 1988), pp. 123, 126.
[26]Ruether, *Introducing Redemption*, p. 74.
[27]Reddie, *Is God Colour-Blind?* p. 98.
[28]Ibid., p. 99.

Original sin thus prevents an appropriate laying of responsibility at the feet of the perpetrators of evil, he argues. If Ruether is right that original sin blames Adam and Eve, and therefore nobody else for the presence of sin in the world, Reddie argues that original sin holds everyone responsible for the presence of sin, including the innocent Black body swinging from the rope just as much as those who perpetrated such hateful and racist acts. Like Ruether, sin needs to be redefined for Reddie, but as something that is 'concrete and specific', a sin that is revealed in 'economic exploitation, racism, sexism and homophobia'.[29] Like Ruether, the sin that needs to be addressed and from which human persons need salvation is the systemic and real sin that leads to the denigration of human existence.

While proponents of the notion of original sin do not arguably explicitly lay the blame for the sin of the world at the feet of others who cannot account for themselves (Adam and Eve), Ruether and Reddie are both right to warn of the dangerous implications of a doctrine of original sin for contemporary Christian practices. Both reject sin as a description of a condition that is biologically inherited from which individuals cannot escape in this life but only hope for in the next. Rather, sin is learned and practiced oppressive behaviour that leads to human suffering and oppression. Sin is thus a systemic problem that leads to the denigration of human life now and salvation is concerned with saving human person from such forms of systemic sin. Such an understanding of sin provides important insights for deconstructing historic and present soteriological practices towards people of other faiths that shall be examined in Chapter 3, while also providing a basis on which to construct new soteriological praxes.

God is on the side of the oppressed

In the dominant understanding of salvation in Western traditions, God is portrayed as one with whom full reconciliation, and therefore, salvation can only be fully enjoyed in another future world. God stands outside of the world, removed from it, and the chief human enterprise is to seek individual escape from this world in order to be in communion with God. If, however, sin, as descriptive of the human condition, is redefined as a systemic inherited sin that should be named and transformed, then a way is opened up for alternative ways for speaking about God too. James Cone, for example, argues that in the Exodus narrative, God revealed himself as one concerned with liberation, redeeming Israel from slavery in Egypt.[30] For James Cone, a God who is indifferent to human suffering, who need not address the human condition but does so out of a sense of mercy, does little to help Cone in his struggle against racism. Instead, Cone finds in the

---

[29]Ibid., p. 104.
[30]J. H. Cone, *A Black Theology of Liberation: Twentieth Anniversary Edition* (New York: Orbis Books, 1990), p. 47.

Exodus narrative a God who is moved by the suffering of the oppressed and acts to save Israel from slavery in Egypt. God engages and intervenes in human experience not only through the incarnation, but in solidarity with the oppressed in their struggle for liberation on a daily basis throughout history. This particular revelation of the character of God as a liberator who sides with the poor and oppressed was, he argues, intentionally 'granted to an oppressed people'.[31]

God's decision to reveal God's self to an oppressed and enslaved people leads Cone to argue for the 'blackness of God'; a God who is on the side of and identifies with black people in the United States in their struggle for liberation from slavery and racism, just as God was on the side of Israel in Egypt. He explains that 'the blackness of God' means that the essence of the nature God is to be found in the concept of liberation, and that God as Trinity participates in this process of liberation: 'as Creator, God identified with oppressed Israel; as Redeemer, God became the Oppressed One in order that all may be free from oppression; as Holy Spirit, God continues the work of liberation'.[32] Thus God is understood by Cone to be one who is concerned with the liberation of human persons from slavery and discrimination into new existences of freedom and equality. God is not distant from and offended by every human being but rather stands alongside those who struggle against the inherited and systemic sins that lead to their oppression and suffering.

Salvation as praxis: Human and divine conditions

Ruether and Reddie, together with traditions of deification, thus provide some examples of alternative approaches to Christian understandings of the human and divine conditions. First, Ware and Kärkkäinen offer a reminder that the notion of original sin is a particularly Western Christian perspective on the human condition and not one that is universal to Christianity. Without this doctrine, Ware has argued that the human condition was intentionally created to be free, that sin is an expression of that freedom, but when expressed, distracted humanity from the path that God intended for it. Ruether and Reddie have both called for new understandings of sin that locate both the nature of sin and the responsibility to resolve it firmly in human hands. As we shall see shortly, by redefining sin in this way, God's participation in salvation is no longer understood as being necessary to appease God's own anger, to satisfy God's honour, to pay off the devil, so as to avoid the punishment that the human offence to God necessitates. Rather, God participates in salvation by joining in the struggles of humanity to transform sin.

---

[31]Ibid., p. 47.
[32]Ibid., p. 64.

Such understandings of the human and divine conditions, therefore, provide the beginnings of the notion of salvation as praxis developed here. The starting point for talking about human beings is not that they are utterly wretched and lost, but that that they were created in God's image, to grow into God's likeness and that, despite their capacity to sin, still reflect the beauty and goodness of their divine creator. The sin from which human beings need salvation is the sin that leads to the suffering and oppression of any human person at the hands of others. It is real and concrete, it is not biologically inherited, and must be named wherever it is found so that it can be transformed in this world. Salvation involves liberation from that sin which can only be realized through praxis, committed action that seeks to address, challenge and transform sin. God also engages in committed action – praxis – in solidarity with those who struggle against sin, so that human persons are saved from sin and participate in a new and transformed existence in this world. Therefore, if these provide alternative ways of thinking about the condition of God and human beings, then what of the state of salvation itself?

The state of salvation: Saved into what?

Redemption: Freedom from slavery

Ruether notes that 'In Hebrew Scripture redemption originally had a very concrete social meaning. It referred to the ransoming of a slave from bondage'.[33] A slave, she explains, was able to buy their own freedom or their freedom could be paid for by others. O'Collins also acknowledges this origin of the notion of redemption and that similar transactions were made for 'ransoming prisoners of war' too.[34] He also explains that in the 'Graeco-Roman world', there was a practice whereby slave-owners would sell slaves to a god and be paid from money that slaves themselves had deposited in the temple. 'Freed from their previous masters', O'Collins notes, 'the slaves became the property of the god' and the god had thus 'purchased the slave for freedom'.[35] Redemption in the ancient Hebrew, Greek and Roman worlds, therefore, can be understood as involving some form of financial transaction that led from a state of slavery and imprisonment to one of freedom. This ancient understanding and language of redemption that led to the transformation from one state of being into another improved reality, found its way into Christian soteriological discourses.

This early origin of the use of financial exchange discourses to speak of salvation helps to make some sense of the economic metaphors that were

---

[33]Ruether, *Introducing Redemption*, p. 15.
[34]O'Collins, *Jesus Our Redeemer*, p. 3.
[35]Ibid., pp. 3–4.

later used in certain theories of the atonement that speak of 'ransom' or 'satisfaction', for example. However, departing from this fiscal aspect of redemptive thinking, more recent reconstructions of redemption have focused on the soteriological significance of moving from slavery and tyranny into a state of freedom. Redeeming human beings from slavery and tyranny does not involve God or oppressed persons offering or making financial transactions to tyrants, oppressors and slave-owners. Slavery and oppression, racism and discrimination are acts of evil, systemic and inherited sin, and should be identified as being so. Such sins should be transformed and those who commit them should not be financially rewarded. Redemption, however, involves a move from a place of slavery and oppression into a state of freedom. The terminology of redemption, therefore, points towards an understanding of salvation that locates the transformation into a new and improved reality firmly located in this world.

Salvation as liberation

Commenting on redemptive themes in Deuteronomy 15 and 16 and Leviticus 19, Jon Sobrino argues that 'God's way of acting – having compassion, doing justice, liberating – should also be Israel's way of acting'.[36] Humans need not, therefore, be understood as utterly wretched and without any capacity to actively contribute to their own salvation. Instead, God's solidarity with Israel in their struggle for redemption provides an impetus and example for human beings to model and so struggle and work towards their own salvation. For Sobrino and others working to re-interpret soteriological discourses in this kind of way (e.g. Cone's interpretation of the Exodus narrative above), such an understanding of redemption is no mere new invention, but a recovery of ancient and biblical notions of what it means to be saved: salvation involves struggle for transformation in this world, with God and humanity being joint active participants in that struggle.

Anthony Reddie argues that 'Black theology does not begin with hypothetical speculations on the nature of God or on salvation conceived purely in terms of "who will go to heaven"'. Rather, its focus is on the 'material and spiritual empowerment of poor, Black oppressed persons in the world, and it seeks to ask in what way the God revealed in the life, death and resurrection of Jesus Christ is in solidarity with the poor and marginalized'.[37] Salvation, then for Reddie, is understood in liberatory terms and is located in the transformation of the present, and that is focused especially on the transformation of the lives of those who experience injustice and oppression into new situations of liberation. Liberation from slavery and oppression is thus understood by Reddie, together with many other theologians of

---

[36]Sobrino, *No Salvation*, p. 78.
[37]Reddie, *Is God Colour-Blind?* p. 77.

liberation, soteriologically. The state of liberation is firmly located in the material and real lives of people in this world. To be saved is thus to be saved in the present. In a number of contemporary contextual theologies, therefore, as Reddie indicates, salvation as a present hope and possibility is central, and the New testament provides a witness, just as the Hebrew Bible does, in uncovering alternative ways of speaking of redemptions; to a God who struggles with the oppressed for liberation. The saved state is a state of complete freedom from tyranny, enslavement and oppression; it is a 'liberated' state.

Constructing the kingdom: The praxis of Jesus

Jon Sobrino argues that the concept of the 'kingdom of God' is central to the Bible[38] and that this was part of the Jewish tradition of 'expressing God's salvific plan and the people's hope' of a vision of a place in which God would rule the earth with justice and truth (Psalm 96.13).[39] This vision of a renewed earth that characterized God's and humanity's hope for the world is, Sobrino argues, the tradition from which Jesus came[40] and that his teaching reflected that tradition of hope and transformation for the world of the present, expressed through discourses regarding the 'kingdom of God'. It is the preaching of this kingdom that Sobrino argues needs to be rediscovered as it represents a form of 'utopia' which contrasts that promised by contemporary ideals like capitalism and globalization that so often lead to poverty. It is among the poor that, for Sobrino, the 'construction' of this kingdom can be found.

While not explicitly using the patriarchal notion of a 'kingdom', in seeking to respond to the problem of the maleness of Jesus and the question of whether a male saviour can save women, Ruether concludes that Jesus' 'lived message and practice' should be emphasized over his biology. Quero further argues that, the maleness of Jesus is insignificant, but rather, that what matters is that God became incarnate so that, she argues, 'we should not use that sublime act [of incarnation] to punish those who do not fit into a binary narrow reading' of Jesus as 'the straight, white, middle-class, able, fit body'.[41] Ruether argues, 'Jesus became paradigmatic by embodying a certain message. That message is good news to the poor, the confrontation with systems of religion and society that incarnate oppressive privilege, and affirmation of the despised as loved and liberated by God.'[42] Sobrino and

---

[38]Sobrino, No Salvation, p. 77.
[39]Ibid., p. 78.
[40]Ibid., p. 79.
[41]M. H. C. Quero, 'This Body Trans/Forming Me: Indecencies in Transgender/Intersex Bodies, Body Fascism and the Doctrine of the Incarnation', in Controversies in Body Theology (eds M. Althaus-Reid and L. Isherwood; London: SCM Press, 2008), pp. 80–128 (112).
[42]Ruether, Introducing Redemption, p. 93.

Ruether together, therefore, while framed differently, provide two readings of New Testament texts that locate transformation into a new and improved reality in earthly terms. Jesus' embodied life and ministry in particular, rather than his death, is where salvation can be discovered and so embodied existence is potentially affirmed. It is also in his teaching and ministry, his praxis, and in his willingness to confront structural and systemic evil by risking his life, that he reveals an alternative understanding of salvation. That is, the establishment of the 'kingdom' or new reality on earth that, just like the liberated state, involves active engagement in the transformation of human lives where they experience oppressive practices that lead to poverty or the marginalization of women, for example, into a state of freedom from such tyrannies. The praxis of Jesus will be discussed further shortly as a part of the discussion on how salvation is realized. What we note here is that his life revealed a particular vision of utopia, the 'kingdom' established here on earth through human praxis.

Salvation as healing

Gerald O'Collins notes the etymology of the English term 'salvation' explaining that '"Salus" with its associated adjectives "salubris" and "salvus", denoted (good) health, wholeness, welfare, well-being, being healed, being "hale and hearty" or being "safe and sound"', and notes that this Latin term is preserved in contemporary Italian as an alternative to buon giorno: 'salve': 'good day'.[43] It is not, however, only in Latin that this dimension of health and wholeness to salvation, which is largely absent in most English usage, can be discovered in the Greek term that is often translated as salvation: *swterion* (salvation) and *swzw* (to save). It is this precise notion of salvation as healing, however, that is present in some of the healing narratives in the Gospels, such as in Luke 8.16, at the conclusion of the story of the healing of the unnamed woman with a haemorrhage when Jesus informs her that it is her 'faith' that has 'made you well'. What is here translated as 'made you well' in most English translations, is in fact a translation of *swzw*, to save. The transformation in this story, this woman's salvation is realized through Jesus and the woman both engaging in acts that 'save' her, and her state of salvation is embodied, earthly and concrete. This understanding of salvation as 'restoration to wholeness' and 'good health' contrasts the dominant Western perspective that Ruether argued encourages human persons to escape their bodies. Instead, the body is valued and its well-being is of great importance. Chapter 6 is dedicated to an exploration of this understanding of salvation for Christian praxis towards people of other faiths.

---

[43] O'Collins, *Jesus Our Redeemer*, p. 10.

'Saving Paradise': Salvation and early Christian art

Thus far, it has been argued that it is possible to speak of salvation as a praxis; that is that a new and improved reality can be realized in the present as a result of human and divine co-operation, for both God and humanity can be understood as active agents and practitioners of salvation. Further, Jesus' life and ministry can be understood as a soteriological praxis that sought a new improved reality for those he encountered while providing a model for subsequent Christian praxis. Brock and Parker also argue that in the Gospels, Jesus is concerned with salvific praxes in his earthly ministry. They discuss the example of the Gospel narrative of the loaves and the fishes and interpret this as an 'act of feeding the hungry',[44] transforming the lives of those without food. Such soteriological understandings could also be found in the early Church, they argue. They explain that 'In the Christian catacombs in Rome, images of the loaves and the fish are frequent motifs' and that this, together with images of the ritual meal of the last supper not only emphasized the importance of ensuring that the hungry were fed, but were also expressions of 'political criticism and economic challenge'.[45] In a context of political oppression and economic struggle at the hands of imperial Rome, where the rich were fed well, paid for by the taxes of the poor, the satisfying of the hunger of the poor took on a particularly subversive nature: the vision of an earthly utopia in which all were fed. Such images, understood in their political-economic context, further indicate that the possibility of a new and alternative improved reality for human beings is not only possible in this world, but its realization is central to understanding the Christian Gospel.

This discussion regarding images of the loaves and fishes is a part of a much wider and seminal study in which Brock and Parker engaged in a search for images of the crucifixion in early Christian art. To their surprise, however, they did not find the cross represented very much at all, but rather discovered that 'paradise . . . was the dominant image of early Christian art'.[46] The death of Jesus, they argue, was not really given much attention in most artistic representations of Christian beliefs and narratives for the first thousand years of Christian history, at least in those images that have survived to this day.[47] It can be assumed that, given the vast majority of the Christian world during that period were not literate, and education about the Christian story would have primarily been delivered orally or presented through images, that the death of Jesus was not in the popular consciousness as an important Christian theme more broadly, or of soteriological significance in particular.

---

[44]Brock and Parker, *Saving Paradise*, p. 30.
[45]Ibid., pp. 30–31.
[46]Ibid., p. xiv.
[47]Ibid., p. xii.

If the cross was missing from Christian art then the most important theme found was, they argue, that of paradise: a hoped for utopian existence. But paradise, they argue, was 'something other than "heaven"'. They explain:

> ... paradise – first and foremost – was this world, permeated and blessed by the Spirit of God. It was on the earth. Images of it in Rome and Ravenna captured the craggy, scruffy pastoral landscape, the orchards, the clear night skies, and teeming waters of the Mediterranean world, as if they were lit by a power from within. . . . The images filled the walls and spaces in which liturgies fostered aesthetic, emotional, spiritual, and intellectual experiences of life in the present, in a world created as good and delightful.[48]

The hope of salvation was arguably, therefore, not a hope for a future existence in heaven that could never be realized on earth. To experience salvation was to transform life in the present for the better to the point that heaven and earth become one reality. Further, creation in all its beauty was celebrated and affirmed. Such possibilities represented a vision of a different, better world from the one in which people currently found themselves, rather than their gaze being fixed almost entirely on the hope of a future 'postmortem life'.[49] This salvation could be expressed in practice; in the intentional activities of communities and individuals in the importance of feeding the hungry, and encouraged soteriological praxis, a committed action that could lead to the establishment of paradise on earth.

The state of salvation is, therefore, a state that is realized through human and divine praxis. It can be argued that Jesus models the forms of praxis that lead to salvation just as the God of the Hebrew Bible did in the liberation of Israel from slavery in Egypt. Earlier, it was argued that sin should be understood as a concrete reality that human beings experience in suffering and oppression at the hands of others. That being so, the state of salvation can thus be understood as a transformation from this state of sin, into an alternative state of liberation and freedom. The possibility of entering into a saved state is lived and practiced in this world. The vision of paradise was perhaps a dream or vision of what this world could be like, a utopia that did not reflect reality in the present, but that these ancient images located paradise in this world suggests that such a utopia remained a concrete hope of what is possible. Inspired by these ancient traditions, it is possible to suggest, therefore, that the state of salvation is a state of transformation from the sins of oppression and suffering, to a state of freedom, communion between human persons in society, a place where the hungry are fed and where bodies are restored to health without perhaps being made to conform to able-bodied normativity. This state of salvation is the state to which

---

[48]Ibid., p. xv.
[49]Ibid., p. 30.

soteriological praxis aims and works towards. If then, such a transformed reality constitutes the state of salvation from the human condition of inherited and systemic sin described above, what processes and action can make this possible?

How salvation is realized: Human and divine collaboration

In the discussion above, the processes and means by which salvation might be attained has already begun to be outlined. First, in the Exodus narratives, God's intervention in history to redeem Israel from slavery provides an example not only of what salvation is for, liberation, but also how God acts to achieve it. For Sobrino, human participation was an important part of ensuring that a saved state of liberation, described as the 'kingdom of God', could be realized. Secondly, Jesus life and ministry itself can be understood as a praxis of salvation through his solidarity with and transformation of the lives of marginalized and excluded people and his challenges to systemic and institutional abuses of power. Thirdly, that a state of salvation as a form of freedom or liberation from oppressive practices of slavery, racism, patriarchy, and so forth, that is attained through God's solidarity with those struggling for freedom, provides another understanding of how salvation is realized through God's co-operation with human beings in acts of soteriological praxis. In what follows, a further discussion of how the state of salvation might be achieved with reference to two possibilities is outlined: Delores Williams' understanding of soteriology as something realized through human soteriological praxis developing further the idea of Jesus as an example of such praxis, and the notion in traditions of deification that, to become God, while finally realized in a future eschatological state is, nevertheless, a process begun in this world that involves human praxis.

Delores Williams: Modelling Jesus' soteriological praxis

Drawing on the narrative of Hagar in Genesis 16, Delores Williams describes as 'surrogacy' Sarai's proposal that Abram should seek to have children with their slave Hagar, because of Sarai's inability to have children. Williams defines 'surrogacy' in this case as being for Hagar a 'coerced experience involving the violation of her body over which she, as a slave, has no control'.[50] Hagar, the slave, contrasts Sarai the slave-owner as someone who's body can be violated for the benefit of slave-owners, men and women. She explains,

---

[50]Williams, *Sisters in the Wilderness*, p. 16.

'While Hagar had no choices in matters of forced motherhood, the law provided options for wealthy free women like Sarai who were barren'.[51] Similarly, African-American women were used by white slave-owners in the same kinds of ways: 'to provide sexual pleasure for white men during the slavocracy'.[52] Dominant Western soteriological understandings that speak of the death of Jesus on the cross as the way by which humans are saved becomes, Williams purports, problematic in light of the African-American experience of surrogacy. Wiliams argues, 'Jesus represents the ultimate surrogate figure; he stands in the place of someone else: sinful humankind'.[53] For African-American women, she argues, if salvation is achieved through the experience of surrogacy (forced or voluntary), then 'African-American women are still left with the question: Can there be salvific power for black women in Christian images of oppression'.[54] Her answer to this question is essentially, 'no'. African-American women need to find alternative ways of understanding salvation that do not involve the violation of Jesus or their bodies so that others can receive benefit from it, she argues.

Others have sought to deconstruct notions that the state of salvation is achieved through the death of Jesus. Brock and Parker, for example, argue that the view that 'the crucifixion of Jesus saved the world . . . contributed to sanctioning intimate violence and war'. They continue by arguing that if Jesus was innocent and indeed, on the cross, experienced violence, and if Jesus is a model for Christian living, then this understanding of salvation 'places victims of violence in harm's way and absolves perpetrators of their responsibility for unethical behaviour'.[55] Because the cross symbolizes the violence and murder of one who is innocent so that the guilty can be redeemed, and if this provides a model for human life, then alternative processes by which salvation can be realized become necessary if soteriology is not to sanction violence (a possibility inconsistent with the Christian Gospel of liberation outlined earlier). Salvations that seek ways of moving from oppression to freedom that do not suggest that the way to put things right is to let the guilty get away with their crimes and the innocent to be punished in their place needs reworking. Williams provides one example of an alternative approach.

Williams proposes an alternative understanding of how salvation might be realized with reference to the methods through which historic traditions of salvation have been developed and constructed. Anselm's understanding of how salvation is realized through the notion of satisfaction, she argues, draws on contextual metaphors from his socio-political context. She explains, 'people owed honour to God just as medieval peasants and

---

[51]Ibid.
[52]Ibid., p. 166.
[53]Ibid., p. 162.
[54]Ibid.
[55]Brock and Parker, *Saving Paradise*, p. xi.

squires owed honour and loyalty to their overlords'[56] and if an overlord
was dishonoured, he must be satisfied either by punishing those who
offended him or by receiving some form of compensation. That Jesus
satisfies God's honour through the cross, she argues, an honour that has
been offended by human sin, is how Anselm interpreted the process by
which salvation is realized.[57] While critical of the notion of satisfaction
for the reasons described above that suggest that salvation can only be
achieved through the forced or voluntary death of Jesus (surrogacy), she
suggests that Anselm's methods provide a framework for the development
of her womanist theology: 'The practice [such as that of Anselm] . . . is to
use the language and socio-political thought of the time to render Christian
ideas and principles understandable. So the womanist theologian uses the
socio-political thought and action of the African-American woman's world'
to construct her theology.[58]

Williams alternative understanding of salvation thus interprets the cross
as 'an image of defilement, a gross manifestation of collective human sin'.[59]
She argues instead that the process and state of salvation is revealed in the
'ministerial vision' of Jesus, in particular his understanding of the 'kingdom of
God' together with Jesus' resurrection. This resonates with the soteriologies
of Sobrino and Ruether discussed above in which the life, rather than the
death of Jesus is where soteriological possibilities for creation are realized.
In Jesus' vision of the kingdom, Williams argues, in which Jesus resists and
challenges evil, he models a soteriological praxis for human persons to
emulate. It is through challenging evil and providing an example of how to
live in relation with others, that Jesus saves. He provides a way of moving
from lives of surrogacy to lives of freedom not through death, but through
life. It is, therefore, in looking to the life of Jesus and his resistance of evil
that Christian persons might also realize soteriological possibilities in the
present. Grace Jantzen has argued for the value of not focusing on mortality
but on natality, not on death but on life,[60] and this seems to be the shift that
Williams is calling for in her understanding of how salvation is conceived.
To be saved should not include the glorification of suffering or 'to render
. . . exploitation sacred'[61] as it only serves to justify such practice in the
present. Soteriological praxis is thus modelled for Williams in the life and
resurrection of Jesus that Christian persons might follow as they seek to
realize a new saved existence.

---

[56]Williams, *Sisters in the Wilderness*, p. 163.
[57]Ibid.
[58]Ibid., p. 164.
[59]Ibid., p. 166.
[60]G. Jantzen, *Becoming Divine: Towards a Feminist Philosophy of Religion* (Manchester:
Manchester University Press, 1998) pp. 128–55.
[61]Williams, *Sisters in the Wilderness*, p. 167.

Becoming God: Begun on earth

Williams, Sobrino, Ruether and others have made significant contributions to re-orientating perspectives on the process through which salvation is realized away from the death to the life of Jesus. It is noteworthy, however, that the notion to incarnation itself as having soteriological significance has an ancient theological heritage. Drawing on the proposition that Jesus became human so that humans might become divine, puts the incarnation at the heart of the process by which God intervenes in history to save. John Paul II acknowledges the significance of the incarnation in realizing salvation: 'God's salvific giving of himself and his life, in some way to all creation but directly to man [sic.], reaches one of its high points in the mystery of the Incarnation'.[62] While still affirming the cross as the high point of the mystery, nevertheless, the incarnation, in becoming human, God, in Christ, begins his work of salvation. However, deification soteriology in Eastern Orthodox theology emphasizes the significance of the incarnation as well as the cross in contrast to the dominant Western perspective that focuses mostly on the death of Christ as the means by which God realizes human salvation. Williams (above) suggests that the life and ministry of Jesus models soteriological praxis rather than the cross. In Eastern traditions of deification, according to Bartos,[63] that God becomes a human being at all is itself an act of divine soteriological intervention. Thus the incarnation can be understood as the means by which salvation is achieved of which the death of Christ is a part.

Further, however, as has already been noted by Bartos earlier, in Orthodox theology a distinction is made between the image of God, in which all humans are created, and the likeness of God, the description of the state into which human beings can be saved.[64] The fall disrupted humanity's relationship with God, but it did not prevent the possibility of relationship altogether. Commenting on the work of Orthodox theologian Dumitru Stăniloae, Bartos explains that instead of viewing this world as totally lost as a result of the fall, the fallen state should be understood as a state that provides an opportunity for human development.[65] As a result, while becoming fully like God is only ever a future eschatological possibility (except perhaps for the saints), this world is a place in which human persons can grow more into the likeness of God.[66] He explains, it is possible for human beings to 'already

---

[62]John Paul II, *Redemptoris Mater: On the Blessed Virgin Mary in the Life of the Pilgrim Church*, www.vatican.va/holy_father/john_paul_ii/encyclicals/documents/hf_jp-iI_enc_25031987_redemptoris-mater_En.html, last accessed on 1 February 2013.
[63]Bartos, *Deification*, p. 136.
[64]Ibid.
[65]Ibid., p. 139.
[66]Ibid., pp. 139–40.

experience this genuine life with God on earth, even if he *[sic.]* is still in the condition of fallen man *[sic.]*'.[67] Thus salvation, in this view, while only ever fully realized in the future for most human beings, can be worked towards in the present and God works with humanity to engage in soteriological praxis to that end: 'In the effort to raise human nature, new ways, new stages adequate to our age, by which God works in co-operation with man *[sic.]* are made accessible'.[68]

Developing and articulating an alternative salvation to the dominant Western paradigm, that understands soteriology as a present praxis need not involve a rejection of the role and significance of the second person of the Trinity in making salvation possible. Through an engagement with contextual theologians such Delores Williams and with notions of deification in Eastern Orthodoxy, the role of Jesus in modelling and realizing salvation is central. Of significance here and in contrast to the dominant Western tradition, however, it has been argued that human participation in realizing soteriological possibilities need not be restricted to participation in rituals such as baptism or in confessions of personal belief. Instead, humans collaborate with God, inspired perhaps by the example of Jesus, to engage in soteriological praxes that can make an alternative state of salvation possible; a state of salvation that can be realized in the present in this world. Salvation as deification will be further discussed in more detail in Chapter 5.

Conclusion: Salvation as praxis

In this chapter, it has been argued that while a dominant understanding of soteriology has developed within Western Christianity, that understanding of salvation has never been affirmed through a council of the church and never fully defined as orthodoxy. This approach to salvation can be understood as having three key aspects: the condition from which salvation is necessary; what the saved state might be like; and how salvation might be realized. There are, however, alternative ways of understanding all three of these aspects of salvation from those represented in the dominant Western perspective. These alternative soteriologies suggest that human beings may not be so utterly wretched, that the saved state might be achievable in this world and that, with an alternative vision of what salvation might be about, Christian persons can engage in soteriological praxis in collaboration with God to make that saved state possible in the present. Such an understanding of soteriology, increasingly prevalent in many contemporary contextual theologies, is rooted in and finds some common ground with ancient biblical and theological traditions that have become marginalized in many Western churches.

---

[67]Ibid., p. 140.
[68]Ibid., p. 139.

Thus it is argued that the notion of salvation as a praxis that works towards the transformation of injustices and the tyrannies of oppression in this world is an approach to Christian thinking and acting that seeks to recover and reinterpret these ancient soteriological ideas. In other words, this is no new innovation as such, but a set of soteriological discourses that have ancient theological pedigree and integrity. What has not been attempted here is the construction of a coherent systematic alternative understanding to the dominant Western discourse on salvation. Rather, multiple and various perspectives on salvation have been outlined above to demonstrate that there are many alternative, identifiably 'Christian' ways of speaking soteriologically. This more unsystematic representation of soteriological discourses reflects more accurately the multiple and sometimes conflicting approach to salvations that can be found in traditions that identify as 'Christian'. A number of these themes will be returned to in Chapters 5–7 as the second part of this book seeks to bring some of these understandings of soteriology into conversation with Christian thinking and praxis in a multi-faith world today. There will again be multiple ways of thinking about salvation as praxis presented there, that do not seek necessarily to speak to each other or to articulate a single coherent soteriology. This is again to reflect the multiple ways in which soteriology can be understood and practiced. In the next chapter, however, the case for needing such alternative approaches to soteriological thinking with regard to people of other faiths will be outlined.

3

Deconstructing historic practices of salvation

Introduction

The dominant soteriological discourse that has been central to Western Christianity, discussed in the previous chapter, provides just one way of speaking about and practising salvation. It is possible, it has been argued, to identify alternative understandings of salvation within Christian theology itself, many of which understand salvation to involve human and divine engagement in transformative praxis. In this chapter, it will be argued that a shift away from the dominant understandings of salvation is necessary, and not only because of the ways they have supported practices orientated toward the normalization of gender and people with disabilities. They have also been at the heart of a long history of a Christian 'presumption of superiority' towards people of other faiths. If at the heart of the Christian Gospel, as has been proposed, is a commitment to ending human suffering, fostering well-being, and seeking human liberation, freedom and equality, such an oppressive dominant discourse is necessarily deconstructed.

Four examples will be given from different periods of Christian history to illustrate why alternative soteriological understandings are necessary for shaping present and future Christian engagements with people of other faiths. First, it will be argued, soteriological beliefs and practices have been central to Christian anti-Semitic practices and this will be discussed with reference to the work of Rosemary Radford Ruether. Second, it will be argued that Christian theologies of salvation were used to justify the Crusades. Third, it will be argued that Western nations used soteriological discourses to justify colonialism that impacted on many indigenized faith communities and spiritual expressions. Fourth, it will be argued that predominantly Western developments in the twentieth and twenty-first centuries, such as practices that can be referred to as forms of neo-colonialism, use soteriological motifs, frameworks and language to defend Western political and economic agendas. It will also be argued that soteriological discourses can be found underpinning Western responses to the 'terrorist' attacks of 9/11 in New York and 7/7 in London. What emerges here is that the dominant Western soteriological discourse that promises a transformed reality in a future post-mortem world, served and continues to serve the imperialistic and colonizing agendas of Western nations, often with devastating consequences for people of other faiths.

Salvation and anti-semitic praxes

Christian soteriologies have informed and been expressed in anti-Semitic practices from as early as the period when the New Testament texts were written. Drawing on Rosemary Radford Ruether's work, *Faith and Fratricide*, it is argued that Christian discourses that claim universally exclusive truth for Christians about how God saves and how humans may attain salvation, have often been used to defend the proposition that Christianity supersedes and replaces Judaism. That Jewish people do not recognize this supposed Christian truth claim has been used to justify Christian anti-Semitic practices. It is also argued, however, that Ruether's alternative proposal, of a shared anticipation of a messianic age, is not an adequate soteriological alternative in response both to historic Christian praxes towards people of other faiths, or in responding to the needs of a contemporary multi-faith world.

Anti-semitic beginnings

Focusing on the theological roots of anti-Semitism, in response to the Holocaust, Rosemary Radford Ruether published *Faith and Fratricide*. In an introduction to a revised edition of this book, Baum notes that while the Church cannot be blamed directly for Hitler's anti-Semitism, nevertheless Hitler was able to draw on a 'heritage' of anti-Semitism, 'built up by Christianity'[1] to justify and defend the genocide of six million Jewish people. Ruether traces this Christian heritage right back to the period of the New Testament, where practices and subsequent texts began to lay the foundations for what would follow. She argues that in the very earliest period of the Church, those who identified themselves as Christians and Jews shared common Scriptures, but increasingly the two traditions began to interpret them differently.[2] A cursory reading of New Testament texts such as the Acts

---

[1]G. Baum, 'Introduction', in *Faith and Fratricide: The Theological Roots of Anti-Semitism* (ed. R. R. Ruether; Eugene, OR: Wipf & Stock, 1997), p. 8.
[2]R. R. Ruether, *Faith and Fratricide: The Theological Roots of Anti-Semitism* (Eugene, OR: Wipf & Stock, 1997), pp. 64–65.

of the Apostles and Galatians, for example, readily confirms that tensions between established Jewish communities and the newly emerging Christians were widespread, not least as increased numbers of Gentiles joined this new faith community. As the two interpretations of these Scriptures increasingly diverged, Ruether argues, the emergent Christian view was that the 'Church knew that it and it alone understood the real meaning of the Scriptures'.[3] That 'real meaning' involved a Christian reading of Jewish scriptures in which Jesus Christ was self-evidently the awaited messiah who would inaugurate a new messianic age, Ruether argues. Those who interpreted the Jewish scriptures in any other way, or who could not see who Jesus really was, were described as, 'hypocrites, blind fools, blind guides, whitewashed tombs, serpents, offspring of vipers, and children of hell'.[4] As for those who denied or questioned the messiahship of Jesus, 'God has made their hearts dull, their ears heavy and their eyes closed so that they will not be able to understand the message of redemption'.[5] Ruether argues, 'Even today, much of the anti-Judaic reading of the New Testament is based on the assumption that this distinction between the "inwardness" of the Church to really understand in their hearts who Christ was and the "hypocrisy" of the Pharisees was literally correct'.[6]

For Ruether, the implications of such a Christology of messiahship, that argued that Christianity rightfully superseded and replaced Judaism, also took on soteriological significance. The long-awaited messiah was a saviour figure whom it was anticipated would transform the context of Israel. Such a saviour would have been particularly significant during the Roman occupation of Jewish lands as one who would, once again, liberate Israel from oppression. But the followers of Jesus began to develop, Ruether argues, alternative understandings of the role of the messiah which were doubtless necessary if claims about Jesus as the messiah were to have meaning. Thus, belief in Jesus as a messianic figure began to replace Jewish practices and traditions that could lead to potential salvation:

. . . salvation was now found no longer in any observances – ritual or ethical – founded on the Torah of Moses, representing the covenant of the past. Rather, salvation was found solely through faith in the messianic exegesis of the Church about the salvific role of Jesus . . Only that community gathered around this cornerstone is God's true people.[7]

Thus soteriological discourses and practices in the early church began to justify Christian claims for the truth of what they believed about Jesus while disregarding Jewish practices themselves that had historically been

[3]Ibid., p. 72.
[4]Ibid., pp. 74–75. Ruether notes these terms in particular from Matthew's Gospel.
[5]Ibid., p. 74.
[6]Ibid., p. 78.
[7]Ibid.

understood to be soteriological. Jewish people could, therefore, not be saved, without conforming to Christian beliefs about the person of Jesus.

The ways in which those who denied Christian truth claims about Jesus, defending existing Jewish beliefs and practices described above is telling; Jewish people were insulted and their views discredited by referring to them as in some way disabled or animalistic. This is worthy of further comment than Ruether gives to it. Animals have, historically been interpreted as creatures that should be 'subject' to human 'dominion' and thus lesser forms of creation, reinforcing the superiority of human beings in creation.[8] The presence of disability has often been understood to be a consequence and sign of 'the fall', the representation of a lesser form of humanity than the ideal for which human beings were created.[9] Disabled people have been understood to be closer to animals than other humans in such a view. These perspectives on animals and disabled people have led to soteriologies in which their place in any future utopian reality, in this world or another, is at best ambiguous. In the New Testament, for example, it appears to be argued that salvation is only possible upon the removal of a person's disability; a form of 'normalization' of disabled bodies to conform to able-bodied ideals.[10] If Jewish persons, in particular those who challenged the authority of Jesus, are referred to using disabled and animalistic metaphors, the implications for how Jewish people should be viewed by Christians subsequently has proven to be that Christianity is superior to other religions, just as able-bodied people were of greater value than disabled people and humans of more importance than animals. In particular, Jewish people were to be regarded in the same way as animals and disabled people, those over whom the power of dominion could be exercised because they were not fully human or not human at all. Jewish people in some way represented a lesser form of humanity refusing to understand what is plain for the Christian to 'see' and as a result salvation for Jewish people, it was assumed, will only be possible through normalization and conformation to Christian norms.

Consolidating anti-semitism

Ariarajah argues that with the conversion of Constantine to Christianity, a united empire necessitated a unified religion and Christianity, with its emergent notions of its own superiority over other faiths, especially Judaism, would serve that purpose well.[11] If Christianity provided the emperor with

---

[8]This is often justified with reference to Gen. 1.26.

[9]See the discussion in R. McCloughry and W. Morris, *Making a World of Difference: Christian Reflections on Disability* (London: SPCK, 2002), pp. 94–110.

[10]See, for example, the healing narratives in the Gospels, discussed in more detail in Chapter 6.

[11]S. W. Ariarajah, 'Power, Politics and Plurality: The Struggles of the World Council of Churches to Deal with Religious Plurality', in *The Myth of Religious Superiority* (ed. P. F. Knitter; New York, NY: Orbis Books, 2005), pp. 176–93 (177–79).

the tool he needed to unite the empire, he provided Christianity with a new status in which its notions of its own superiority over other religions would develop, thus furthering Christian notions of its primacy over other faith traditions. With the conversion of Constantine, Ruether argues, 'It [Judaism] was [allowed] to continue to exist in a pariah status in history, both to testify to the present election of the Church and to witness the final triumph of the Church. At the return of Christ, Jews could either finally acknowledge their error or else be condemned to final damnation'.[12] Here, again, soteriological notions, informed by Christian self-perceptions of its own superiority shaped a view of Jewish people as in error and who could only be saved through 'normalization' and conformation to Christian paradigms. Ruether notes that for the next few centuries, new laws were introduced to further marginalize Jewish people politically, economically and socially. Examples of such laws included not being allowed to have 'lordship over Christians', which, in an economy dependent on slavery, meant Jews were effectively economically marginalized. Jews also could not marry Christians.[13] To convert from Christianity to Judaism meant a person had all their possessions confiscated, and some laws 'threatened [Jews with] capital punishment for proselytizing'[14] Christians.

Beliefs about Christ, translated into exclusive soteriological discourses in which it was thought that only Christians possessed the truth about Christ and only acceptance of that truth could lead to final salvation is, for Ruether, at the foundation of much Western, Christian anti-Semitic thought and practices throughout the ages. That, accompanied by the social and political status afforded to Christians from the conversion of Constantine onwards, provided Christians with the power to not only insist on the truth of their beliefs about Christ and salvation, but to insist that others either conformed to Christianity or suffered devastating consequences, either in this world or the next or both. It is this understanding of soteriology that has been dominant in Western Christianity until the twentieth century and expressed in Christian practices towards people of other faiths. As Christianity became the dominant religion of Europe, Ruether argues, Christianity increasingly insisted on a universalism for itself and engaged in an agenda of 'normalization' of all religious and spiritual pathways to Christian norms. She describes this as a 'pseudo-universalism which assumed that the culture of the dominant group was a universal culture, the culture of true civilization, against which all else was barbarism'.[15] Christological beliefs were at the heart of such universal claims and norms, acceptance of which determined one's salvation. Those who did not accept Christ could not be saved and must thus be converted (made to conform) or punished

---

[12]Ruether, *Faith and Fratricide*, p. 186.
[13]Ibid., p. 187.
[14]Ibid., p. 188.
[15]Ibid., p. 233.

for their unbelief (for causing offence to the God who wished to save them). Thus soteriology justified and was practiced in such a way as to ensure that Christianity was understood as normative and all other religious and spiritual expressions were deviant to that norm. Conformation to the Christian norm was, it could be argued, in the best interests of non-Christians as their future well-being would depend on it. As we shall see shortly, this same attitude of 'convert or persecute' people of other faiths was important in the Crusades of the medieval era too.

Ruether's alternative soteriology

Given the anti-Semitic implications and subsequent praxes of such Christological and soteriological formulations, Ruether has proposed a reconstructed Christology that is rooted in future eschatological soteriology. She proposes a Christology based on 'unfulfilled messiahship' that 'like the Exodus, the Resurrection represents an experience of salvation that is remembered by the heirs of that community which experienced it'. This remembrance becomes a 'foundation for continued and ultimate hope'.[16] It offers a 'foretaste' of the realization of this hope, but the messianic age remains in the future, 'the ultimate eschatological event . . . "when every tear will be wiped away"'.[17] Thus Ruether favours a Christology rooted in a future eschatology which is shared by Jews and Christians, both awaiting a new messianic age. Such a Christology, she argues, 'represents the way we should have read the New Testament'.[18] If both Christians and Jews are waiting for the same eschatological end in which the new age saves both alike, then, in turn, as the anti-Jewish nature of Christology that insists on interpreting the Hebrew Scriptures correctly and possessing the correct view of messiahship is eroded, so anti-Semitic attitudes and practices may be transformed.

Ruether's alternative salvation, located in an eschatological hope of a future messianic age may be useful in terms of reconstructing Christian perspectives on Judaism. No longer would Christianity view itself as superior to and replacing Judaism, but rather they could be viewed as equals, sharing in a common hope for a future possibility. However, Ruether's proposal is limited for our purposes here because it fails to address the role of soteriological thinking in Christian approaches towards people of other faiths beyond Judaism. There is no such common ground to be found with many other religions of the world for whom the notion of a messianic saviour is irrelevant. What Ruether potentially does, is widen the circle of the privileged few who have a normative understanding of what to hope

---

[16]Ibid., pp. 249–50.
[17]Ibid., p. 248.
[18]Ibid., p. 250.

and wait for in the future, and of what the final soteriological state is like but it does little to address directly how Christians may act more justly towards people of other faiths. It may be argued that this is not the remit of Ruether's work, that is, one seeking to speak theologically in a post-Holocaust context. However, widening the circle of privilege leaves many injustices enacted towards people of other faiths unaddressed. Given that within Christianity alternative salvations can be discovered that may help to reshape Christian perspectives of their own faith as well as people of other faiths, if there is a need for soteriologies that speak about a Christian participation in the transformation of unjust and discriminatory attitudes and practices in the present, Ruether's new soteriology falls short. This book proposes that there are more useful and appropriate alternative ways of thinking soteriologically about people of other faiths. If soteriological ideas have been used to justify anti-Semitic attitudes and praxes, so, as will be argued below, have they been used to justify further acts of violence towards people of other faiths too.

Salvation and the Crusades

The medieval Crusades began in the eleventh century with devastating consequences for both Jews and Muslims in Europe and especially in and around the region that included Jerusalem. While the Crusades were as much about political and economic ambitions for Western European powers as anything else, soteriological ideas were developed that not only suggested the Crusades were necessary, but also provided feudal and ecclesial powers with tools to persuade ordinary men and women to support and participate in these acts of violence and genocide. It was not so much the 'altruistic' desire to save the souls of Muslims and Jews that justified the Crusades, according to Brock and Parker, but rather through converting or shedding the blood of those who refused to be converted, Christian souls could be assured of their own salvation.[19]

In the previous chapter, we considered Brock and Parker's view that for much of the first thousand years of Christian history the dominant soteriological idea expressed in religious art and symbolism was of paradise established here on earth. However, they argue that by the tenth century the image of paradise as the dominant Christian symbol of salvation, was replaced by images of the cross. The cross, they argued, became a symbol of fear for ordinary Christians who were accused of killing Christ and who thus needed to find a means of penance. The eleventh century theologian Anselm of Canterbury only added to Christian anxiety. Humans were so sinful that nothing they could do could restore God's honour. Only the

---

[19]R. N. Brock and R. A. Parker, *Saving Paradise: How Christianity Traded Love of This World for Crucifixion and Empire* (Boston: Beacon Press, 2008), p. 270.

death of the 'God-man'[20] could satisfy that honour. Nevertheless, Brock and
Parker argue, Anselm maintained the position that humans would be barred
'from heaven unless they had performed sufficient penance to fulfil their
debt to God for their personal sins and their sinful nature'.[21] Christians
were thus encouraged to 'imitate Christ's self-offering in the cause of God's
justice',[22] that is, by shedding their own blood. Participation in acts that
caused non-Christians (such as Muslims and Jews) to shed the Christian's
blood was a way of imitating Christ that went some way to satisfying some
of the offence caused to God. As a result, by the Christian imitating Christ
through their own death at the hands of others, they could be assured of a
place in heaven; their future eschatological, post-mortem salvation. Further,
Brock and Parker argued that in light of Anselm's understanding of the
Eucharist and the atonement, anyone who did not participate in the body
and blood of Christ should of necessity be converted. Anyone who refused to
accept the Crusaders' message and conform to Christian beliefs and norms
again dishonoured God by rejecting what had been done in Christ. The only
course of action for the Christian confronted with such an 'affront' to Christ
was to shed the blood of the 'offender'. Brock and Parker explain thus that
both 'killing and being killed imitated the gift of Christ's death, the anguish
of his self-sacrifice, and the terror of his judgement'.[23]

There can be little doubt that the Crusaders believed that they were doing
the will and work of God in seeking to reclaim Jerusalem for the Latin
Church. As Delores Williams has argued, and was discussed in the previous
chapter, Anselm's approach to the atonement and how Christ saved the
world was one that made significant use of socio-economic-political practices
to articulate his understanding of how salvation was achieved. Given that
his theology was so radically informed by his medieval context, Brock and
Parker's analysis of his theology and how it was used to justify the imperialist
and expansionist agendas of the political and ecclesial elite of which he was a
part is evident in his work.[24] No doubt apologists for Anselm would invite us
to read him more carefully to understand the merits of his theology more fully,
but within his work, the notion that giving one's self over to death satisfies
God's honour, is not difficult to discover.[25] Whether or not Anselm intended
his theories of the atonement to be used to justify the acts of the Crusaders
is, anyway, secondary. The most important point is that his theology was
used for such purposes and therefore needs to be addressed. Anselm and
others who justified the Crusades through soteriological discourses have

---

[20]Ibid., p. 268.
[21]Ibid., p. 267.
[22]Ibid., p. 268.
[23]Ibid., p. 270.
[24]Ibid., pp. 265–70.
[25]See, for example, Anselm, *Why God Became Man and The Virgin Conception and Original Sin* (Albany, NY: Magi Books, 1969), pp. 136, 160.

built on the age-old traditions of a sense of Christian superiority over other faith traditions. The anti-Semitism that dates back to the New Testament era and subsequent anti-Jewish practices created a precedent and legacy of aggression towards people of other faiths expressed through the Crusades. Thus alternative salvations that can provide new norms to underpin new praxes are of paramount importance if such attitudes and practices towards people of other faiths of the past are to be transformed and not repeated in the present and future.

Salvation and colonialism

Thus far it has been argued that soteriological beliefs and practices have developed within Christianity from the first century onwards. These beliefs and practices have been used to justify anti-Semitism and the Crusades providing foundations for the principle ways in which Christians have engaged with people of other faiths historically. It has been proposed that Christian claims to have sole access to universal truths about the human condition and how it might be saved, with reference to its beliefs about God, has usefully supported religious and political agendas that have sought to force those who do not share such beliefs to conform and be normalized to Christian beliefs and practices. This has invariably had devastating consequences for people of other faiths and has led to wars, violence and the genocide of millions of people of other faiths in the name of Christianity. That is not to say that people of other faiths have not also at times sought to do the same to those who identify as Christian. However, this book is concerned to address the particularly Christian engagement with other faiths and to develop soteriological praxes that might improve such Christian practices in the future, conscious that often it has been Christian and Western nations that have been responsible for many devastating acts of violence and oppression towards people of other faiths historically. It is not only against Jews and Muslims, however, that the Christian 'presumption of superiority' and its use of soteriological discourse to justify the normalization of people of other faiths, has been used. Many other faith traditions and spiritual practices have similarly been suppressed. American-Indian theologian, George Tinker, has argued that soteriological discourses were used to justify European colonial expansion in contexts where local indigenous religions were practiced. Christian soteriology, he argued, was used to justify a Western supremacist agenda whereby universal truth claims such as the idea that salvation can only be obtained through Christ, were used to reinforce 'amer-european Christian triumphalism'.[26]

---

[26]G. E. Tinker, *American Indian Liberation: A Theology of Sovereignty* (Maryknoll, NY: Orbis Books, 2008), p. 129.

Robinson argues that 'for a thousand years, for much of the period from the eighth to the eighteenth century, the leading civilization on the planet in terms of spread and creativity was Islam'.[27] Robinson argues that, many scholars increasingly recognize 'how much through history Christian and Islamic civilizations have fruitfully interacted and played a part in shaping each other'.[28] The positive mutual impact of these two great faiths of the world has often been overlooked. Ahmed notes, for example that towards the end of the European medieval period, 'The Jews, Christians and Muslims living in Spain under Muslim rule until 1492 created a rich cultural synthesis which resulted in literature, art, and architecture of high quality. The library in Cordoba in al-Andalus had more books than all the other libraries of Europe put together'.[29] While the medieval period was also a time of particular conflict between Christians and Muslims, in particular in Europe and the Near East with the Crusades as was discussed above, it is of significance that Muslims and Christians occupying the same space did result in creative and positive outcomes too.

From the end of the eighteenth century onwards, however, Robinson argues that nations of predominantly Muslim peoples were 'overwhelmed by forces from the West, driven by capitalism, powered by the Industrial Revolution and civilized, after a fashion by the Enlightenment'[30] so that 'by the 1920s Afghanistan, Iran, Turkey, Central Arabia, and the Yemen were the only Muslim countries free from Western control, and even some of these were subject to influence'.[31] The period of European imperial colonialism has left many scars on many different peoples around the world as cultures and religious traditions were suppressed, people were enslaved and natural resources were exploited for the benefit of Western nations. The colonization of Muslim peoples by Western nations, as with the rest of Western colonial territories declined as increasingly nations declared independence beginning in the twentieth century, and picking up pace after the end of the Second World War. Nevertheless, Robinson explains it was not until the 1990s that declarations of independence by former states of the USSR were finally possible.[32]

It was not, however, only Islamic peoples and nations that suffered the consequences of Western colonialism. Among the religious and spiritual traditions discussed in many theologies of religions, perhaps the least

---

[27]F. Robinson, 'Islam and the West: Clash of Civilisations?', in *Islam and Global Dialogue: Religious Pluralism and the Pursuit of Peace* (ed. R. Boase; Farnham: Ashgate, 2005) pp. 77–89 (77).
[28]Ibid., p. 86.
[29]A. S. Ahmed, 'Islam and the West: Clash or Dialogue of Civilisations?', in *Islam and Global Dialogue: Religious Pluralism and the Pursuit of Peace* (ed. R. Boase; Farnham: Ashgate, 2005), pp. 103–18 (106).
[30]Robinson, 'Islam and the West', p. 78.
[31]Ibid.
[32]Ibid.

discussed is the approach that Christianity took to the many indigenous spiritualities and religions of peoples in colonized territories, the effects of which continue to have an impact to this day. Tinker, above, has noted the ways that soteriologies have been used to justify the suppression of indigenous faiths, spiritualities, cultures and languages in favour of what were considered to be superior, more civilized Western versions. In many parts of Africa, South and North America, and in Australasia, European nations were much more 'successful' in imposing their culture and religion on local peoples than in Muslim and Hindu contexts that they also colonized, for example. Where Western colonizers made their home in their newly discovered territories, such as in Africa and Latin Ameirca, it remains the case that among indigenous peoples in a good number of these contexts, many are among the poorest and often the most politically marginalized.[33]

Sugirtharahjah notes how in the nineteenth century, Christians were encouraged to become missionaries, arguing that if Christianity could have so many benefits for Britain, then it could also have the same impact in the newly colonized lands. He makes reference to an 1813 publication, the *Missionary Register*, to show how this case was made:

> Your own ancestors, in this very Island, once worshipped dumb idols: they offered human sacrifices; yea, their sons and their daughters unto devils: they knew not the truth: they had not heard of the name of Jesus . . . But mark now the contrast: you now are a favoured nation: your light has come: the glory of the Lord is risen upon you: all these heathen rites have ceased . . . an established Christian Church lifts its venerable head: the pure Gospel is preached: ministers of the sanctuary, as heralds of salvation, proclaim mercy throughout the land.[34]

Sugirtharajah comments: 'The intention was to turn the former waywardness of the British and their present state of maritime power into an irresistible argument for the spread of the gospel'.[35] Colonialism was thus justified as having benefits to colonized peoples, giving them the opportunity to experience the temporal transformation from living in a state of 'savagery' and 'barbarity' to a new and improved state of 'civilization' and military prowess. The soteriological underpinnings and practices that date back to the early church that justified a sense of Christian superiority over people of other faiths could once again be found in colonial practices. But perhaps most notably here, salvation is understood as a possibility that

---

[33]This can be seen in the ways that people of European descent possess most of the wealth and power in contexts such as Australia and North and South Americas.

[34]R. S. Sugirtharajah, *The Bible and the Third World: Precolonial, Colonial and Postcolonial Encounters* (Cambridge: Cambridge University Press, 2001), p. 62.

[35]Ibid.

can be realized in this world. Soteriology was used to justify missionary activity and colonialism because it was believed Christianity had 'saved' Britain from its assumed 'wicked' and 'uncivilized' past. When present earthly understandings of salvation have served political agendas, theology, churches and governments have not been prevented from using them despite the dominant model of salvation outlined in Chapter 2.

Salvation and neo-colonialisms?

While the influence of Christianity during the twentieth century in many Western nations has been in decline, a sense of superiority over others has not left the Western mindset. The legacy of Christian beliefs and practices towards people of other faiths, shaped by soteriological discourses continues to pervade and influence contemporary Western attitudes and practices towards people of other faiths, cultures and nationalities. The agenda of striving towards the normalization and conformation of people of other faiths and cultures to Western paradigms thus continues.

Emmanuel Lartey argues that globalization 'happens when, in whole or in part, the lifestyle, world view, values, theology, anthropology, paradigms and forms of practice developed in North America and Western Europe are exported or imported into different cultures and contexts'.[36] Based on such an understanding, globalization is not about a mutual sharing and encounter between cultures and peoples but rather represents what Lartey terms as 'a flow from the West to the rest'.[37] Globalization has variously been referred to as a 'Western Project',[38] 'Americanization',[39] 'McWorld'[40] reflecting the particularly political and economic nature of globalization and its origins in broadly Western and especially American ideologies. It is assumed that Western economic and political systems that have so successfully delivered economic prosperity and political freedom represent the ideal state for every person and society. While military power has been used to impose Western capitalist and democratic systems onto non-Western nations, such Western expansionism in politics and economics has often been realized without armed conflicts.

Fukuyama described the end of the Cold War as 'the end of history as such: that is, the end point of mankind's [sic.] ideological evolution and the universalization of Western liberal democracy as the final form of

---

[36] E. Y. Lartey, *Pastoral Theology in an Intercultural World* (Peterborough: Epworth, 2006), p. 43.
[37] Ibid., p. 44.
[38] A. Giddens, *The Consequences of Modernity* (Cambridge: Polity Press, 1990), p. 174.
[39] T. Friedman, *The Lexus and the Olive Tree: Understanding Globalization* (London: HarperCollins, 2000), p. xix.
[40] Term from Benjamin Barber quoted in J. Sacks, *The Dignity of Difference: How to Avoid the Clash of Civilizations* (London: Continuum, rev. edn, 2003), p. 30.

human government'.[41] For many like Fukuyama, the end of the Cold War seemed to demonstrate that Western liberal democracy, the free market and the capitalist way of life had triumphed over its opponents, most notably communism, and that the Western way of life would prove to be universally and '*completely satisfying* to human beings'.[42] This assumed rightness of the Western economic and political systems is reflective of the 'presumption of superiority' that has for centuries shaped the mindset of especially Western nations and peoples. The promise that by conforming to such Western paradigms will deliver a transformed and improved state – economic prosperity and political freedom – also looks suspiciously soteriological and not unlike the colonial discourses we have just reviewed. Globalization itself has, then, attracted the critique that it is a form of neo-colonialism or 'empire'.[43]

The soteriological promises of globalization, like those of the Crusades and colonialism, have not often delivered, however, for those persuaded to conform to Western norms. Sacks notes that countries that have embraced capitalism, though some nations have not embraced it wholeheartedly and uncritically, such as 'Singapore, South Korea, Taiwan, Thailand, China, the Dominican Republic, India, Mauritius, Poland and Turkey – have seen spectacular rises in living standards'.[44] However, globalization appears not to have led to a redistribution of wealth but rather has perpetuated and increased wealth inequalities. Leonardo Boff argues, 'This process [of globalisation] appears to be based on relations of interdependence. In truth, however, the process is based on relations of dependence on large global conglomerates and on speculative capital, which destabilize and dominate peripheral economies in their pursuit of their own particular interests'.[45] Sacks further argues that, 'In eighteen countries, all African, life expectancy is less than 50 years. In Sierra Leone it is a mere 37 years. Infant mortality rates are higher than one in ten in 35 countries, mostly in Africa but including Bangladesh, Bolivia, Haiti, Laos, Nepal, Pakistan and Yemen'. Sacks proposed, by the year 2000, 'the top fifth of the world's population had 86 per cent of the world's GDP while the bottom fifth had just one per cent. The assests of the world's three richest billionaires were more than the combined wealth of the 600 million inhabitants of the least developed countries'.[46] Sacks' predictions were not far off the mark.

---

[41]F. Fukuyama, 'The End of History?', *The National Interest*, 16 (Summer), (1989), pp. 3–18 (4).

[42]F. Fukuyama, *The End of History and the Last Man* (London: Hamish Hamilton, 1993), p. 136.

[43]See, for example, M. Hardt and A. Negri, *Empire* (Cambridge, MA: Harvard University Press, 2001).

[44]Sacks, *The Dignity of Difference*, p. 28.

[45]L. Boff, *Fundamentalism, Terrorism and the Future of Humanity* (London: SPCK, 2006), p. 23.

[46]Sacks, *The Dignity of Difference*, p. 29.

The inequality of wealth is not only between the developed nations and others, but within Western nations too. Sacks notes in '1996 Britain had the highest proportion in Europe of children living in poverty with 300,000 of them worse off in absolute terms than they had been 20 years before'.[47] The globalized capitalist economy is, according to Sacks, good at making money, but not good at distributing it,[48] while Boff notes that 'large conglomerates and speculative capital do not show any regard for the well-being of people or for the sustainability of the planet, and this fact gives rise to millions and millions of excluded people'.[49] The salvific power of capitalism and Western democracy does not, therefore, seem to have delivered the transformed and improved lives it promises to those whom it affects. However, the legacy of Christian soteriological beliefs and practices that underpinned the Christian 'presumption of superiority' and justified all kinds of atrocities with the promise of an improved existence through conformation to Christian norms can be seen underpinning and being practiced in globalization agendas and an ongoing imposition of Western paradigms on other parts of the world. This has further been the case since the events of 9/11.

Salvation discourses in a post 9/11 context

On 11 September 2001, two hijacked planes flew into the twin towers of the World Trade Center in New York and 2,752 people in those buildings were killed. The World Trade Center symbolized the Western capitalist system and was significant not only in the number of deaths but as an attack on capitalism itself. Given Fukuyama's philosophy that had pervaded much of the West's mindset, that capitalism was the ultimate and final form of human government and society (the saved state?), this attack undermined the foundations of Western civilization itself. As Ahmed explains, the events of 9/11 left 'buried in the rubble of the World Trade Center in New York and in the smoking ruin of the Pentagon in Washington: that of triumphant globalization as an irresistible, irreversible process, and the idea of America as an impregnable fortress'.[50] Since 2001, other similar such attacks have taken place in the West, most notably in the United Kingdom, the London bombings of 7 July 2005, in which 52 people were also killed. Following the events of 9/11, Ahmed notes that 'The news and discussions in the media were broadcast under the heading "America under attack". "Why do they hate us?" asked Americans. War was declared on "terrorists" and in early October, the bombing of Afghanistan began'.[51]

---

[47]Ibid., p. 29.
[48]Ibid., p. 87.
[49]Boff, *Fundamentalism*, p. 23.
[50]Ahmed, 'Islam and the West', p. 103.
[51]Ibid., p. 104.

Forrester argues that, 'we need to attempt to understand, for instance, why young Palestinians were dancing and singing in the streets for joy when they heard the news of the attacks on the twin towers and the Pentagon'.[52] Instead of seeking to understand why America in particular and the West in general has become an object of hatred by some, the Western response was rather one framed in historic soteriological language of cosmic battles between good and evil. Historic soteriological and eschatological motifs were utilized once again to speak about these events in which the West understood itself as the good, innocent, superior civilization that the evil Eastern nations wanted to attack. According to El Fadl, following 9/11, 'President Bush invited the world to choose sides: one had either to join the forces of good in the world, the upholders of civilization and civility, or conversely, be counted among the evildoers'.[53]

El Fadl comments that dividing the world into two, between good and evil, is a way of 'perpetuating an old and well-established colonial habit'.[54] Western nations already understood themselves, according to Fukuyama's philosophy, as in a saved state, the new and transformed reality of capitalism that provided so much. Any challenge to this state must, therefore, be interpreted as an attack by evil on the good. El Fadl argues, 'when one examines the arguments of Western proponents of the clash of civilizations, one finds that they invariably ascribe most of what they find positive to be good and desirable to the West, and most of what they find distasteful or objectionable to Islam or Islamic civilization'.[55] The response of Western powers to 9/11 and 7/7 resonated strongly with the ancient discourses of the Crusades and of the colonial era and the Christian, now Western 'presumption of superiority'. Invasion of lands like Iraq was justified as being in the best interests of the people, liberating them from the powers of evil so that they can live the good life that the West already experienced but, as with many nations in the colonial era, this saved state has not been realized. Even further, however, Bush's rhetoric not only reflected colonial ideals, he also drew on the Crusades to justify his ends. Speaking in September 2001, Sudworth notes George Bush's words: 'this is a new kind of . . . a new kind of evil. And we understand. And the American people are beginning to understand. This crusade, this war on terrorism, is going to take a while'.[56] To evoke the Crusades only serves to reinforce in Western

---

[52]D. Forrester, *Apocalypse Now? Reflections on Faith in a Time of Terror* (Aldershot: Ashgate, 2005), pp. 6–7.

[53]K. A. El Fadl, 'The Orphans of Modernity and the Clash of Civilisations', in *Islam and Global Dialogue: Religious Pluralism and the Pursuit of Peace* (ed. R. Boase; Farnham: Ashgate, 2005), pp. 179–88 (179).

[54]Ibid., p. 179.

[55]Ibid., p. 182.

[56]R. J. Sudworth, 'Toward a Theology of Mission Amongst Muslims in Post July 7th Britain', *Practical Theology* 2(2), (2009), pp. 161–204 (162).

mindsets that there is a civilization 'out there' that seeks to infiltrate and destroy the West and so the West must resist it and make it like itself, and if that fails, then destroy it. Sudworth argues 'From a backdrop of 1095 and Pope Urban II's edict that brought about the first crusade, to the capture of the Muslim city of Granada in 1492, a consciousness of Western Christian aggression towards Islam has pervaded the popular imaginations of Muslims'.[57] George Bush's words reflect and perpetuate that ancient legacy.

Using soteriological discourses resonant with those used during Crusades and colonialism was not restricted to politicians. Duncan Forrester describes a public letter published in 2002 in response to the events of 9/11 and signed by 60 'leading American intellectuals'.[58] He explains, 'The Letter seeks to make clear the reasons for which America has gone to war against "Terror"'.[59] In a book published subsequently by Elshtain,[60] which unpacked and explained the letter further, Forrester notes Elshtain's defence of the 'war on terror' as an 'ideological conflict, in which the unambiguously good confronts the totally evil'.[61] The letter, Forrester argues, does not draw on Christianity explicitly or on any insights from the Gospel. 'As a consequence, it throws little light on why 9/11 happened, or how it is to be understood, except as an unqualified and unintelligible evil'.[62] The letter was signed by many prominent theologians and church leaders[63] and despite the absence of any explicit use of theology, its tenor is very much couched in Christian notions of struggles between good and evil and a missionary zeal to spread the good and the virtue of Western 'Christian' democracy at the expense of Islamic traditions. What this suggests, along with the language used by politicians such as Bush to defend the 'war on terror', is that Christian theological notions and language have been used to justify and defend Western actions in response to 9/11 and 7/7. As a consequence, Sudworth rightly acknowledges that 'it should be no surprise to encounter the common misunderstanding by Muslims that the actions of Western governments in military expansion and globalizing greed are in fact the actions of Christians and the "New Crusaders"'.[64]

---

[57]Ibid., p. 177.
[58]Forrester, *Apocalypse Now?*, p. 2.
[59]Ibid., p. 3.
[60]J. B. Elshtain, *Just War Against Terror: The Burden of American Power in a Violent World* (New York, NY: Basic Books, 2004).
[61]Forrester, *Apocalypse Now?*, p. 3.
[62]Ibid., p. 4.
[63]Ibid., pp. 2–3.
[64]Sudworth, 'Toward a Theology of Mission', p. 192.

The need for alternative soteriological praxes: Concluding remarks

Seeking ways of living together better is not only something happening at the level of politics, institutions and organizations, but also between communities and individuals. Malcolm Torry and Sarah Thorley have edited a remarkable little book titled, *Together & Different: Christians Engaging With People of Other Faiths*,[65] which provides examples of the way people of faiths at local levels are seeking to understand each other better, to exchange ideas, to share cultures and traditions, to live together better and to create a better future. Among the examples, they include accounts from participants involved in multi-faith hospital and prison chaplaincies, a Muslim and Christian women's group, teacher's working in schools consisting of people from faith traditions other than their own. Such engagements of Christians with people of other faiths, that seek to transform past and present beliefs and practices by searching for better ways of living together exemplify alternative soteriological praxes to those that have dominated the past and shape the present in the ways described above. No doubt greater theological reflection on such practices are important so that not only are alternative soteriological discourses developed, but so that practice speaks to and critically engages with those discourses.

There have also been significant developments at the levels of church institutions since the middle of the twentieth century. Writing in 2003, Jonathan Sacks recalls standing at Ground Zero in New York in 2002 with a range of people from different faith traditions. Sacks reflects:

> I found myself wondering at the contrast between the religious fervour of the hijackers and the no less intense longing for peace among the religious leaders who were there. The juxtaposition of good and evil, harmony and conflict, global peace and holy war, seemed to me a fitting metaphor for the century we have just begun.[66]

This is just one of an increasing number of examples of faith communities recognizing that a continuation of the past in terms of inter-faith relationships can only result in millions more deaths. There are many other signs of hope that people of faiths can and are willing to contribute to creating a better world for all. In Britain, following the bombings of the London Underground in 2005, a number of 'Faith Leaders' met together to discuss ways forward and to show solidarity in condemning such devastating acts.

---

[65]M. Torry and S. Thorley (eds), *Together & Different: Christians Engaging with People of Other Faiths* (London: Canterbury Press, 2008).
[66]Sacks, *The Dignity of Difference*, pp. 1–2.

Notably church leaders have shifted thinking and practices too. The Ecumenical Patriarch of Constantinople acknowledges that 'during the last few decades, there has been a particular effort for the development of interreligious dialogues, especially among the three great monotheistic religions' and he welcomes this development.[67] In 2002, Pope John Paul II convened a second[68] 'Day of Prayer for Peace in the World', including representatives and leaders of many faith traditions in the world and in his address to them, alluding to 9/11 and subsequent events he said, 'It is the duty of religions, and of their leaders above all, to foster in the people of our time a renewed sense of the urgency of building peace'.[69] Such events and statements were only possible because of generally theological and especially soteriological developments of the Second Vatican Council that indicated a significant shift in Roman Catholic perspectives on people of other faiths. Further, the World Council of Churches has made moves to engage with the world's Muslims alongside other religions evidenced in documents such as its report in 2006, *Religious Plurality and Christian Self-understanding*.[70] So there is a hope for alternative soteriological praxes at the initiative of church leaders expressed in a desire to create a transformed and better world through inter-faith engagement and expressed in greater respect of people of other faiths and other religious and spiritual traditions. In this spirit of seeking alternative soteriological praxes as new 'sources and norms' for 'gracious living together', this book is offered because, what has been described in the most part of this chapter has been a history of attitudes and practices towards people of other faiths that have led to the most devastating acts of violence. This history must not be allowed to be the present and future too.

---

[67]Bartholomew (Ecumenical Patriarch), 'The Necessity and Goals of Interreligious Dialogue – A Speech Given By His All Holiness Ecumenical Patriarch Bartholomew to the Plenary of the Parliamentary Assembly of the Council of Europe – Strasbourg, France' www.patriarchate. org/documents/speech-of-his-all-holiness-ecumenical-patriarch-bartholomew-to-the-plenary-of-the-parliamentary-assembly-of-the-council-of-europe-strasbourg-france, last accessed on 1 February 2013.
[68]The first was held in 1986 also in Assisi.
[69]John Paul II 'Address of His Holiness Pope John Paul II to the Representatives of the World Religions', www.vatican.va/holy_father/john_paul_ii/speeches/2002/january/documents/hf_jp-ii_spe_20020124_discorso-assisI_en.html, last accessed on 1 February 2013.
[70]World Council of Churches, *Religious plurality and Christian self-understanding* (Geneva: World Council of Churches, 2006).

4

Salvation in contemporary theologies of religions

Christian theological and soteriological reflection on people of other faiths is not a recent phenomenon. As we have already seen, Christianity can locate its beginnings in the multi-faith and multi-cultural context of Roman-occupied Palestine, and the New Testament provides a number of accounts of encounters between Christ and his followers and people of non-Jewish faith traditions. Among the significant people of other faiths in the New Testament are the Magi, various Samaritans and a number of adherents of ancient Roman and Greek religious traditions. As has already been argued, developing within Judaism, Christianity itself became a distinct faith tradition among the many of the ancient near eastern world. From its modest beginnings, right throughout its history, Christianity has found itself to be one religion among many, though at different periods of its history, Christianity has occupied more privileged and dominant positions, especially in Europe, than at others.[1] From the earliest periods of Christianity, therefore, theological reflection on its relationships with, and attitudes and practices towards other faith traditions has been necessary and in Chapter 3 we have seen the consequences of some of these theologies.

In a survey of the Catholic tradition of *nulla salus extra ecclesiam (no salvation outside the church)* Sullivan notes how the interpretation of this 'mantra' has changed across the centuries according to the changing contexts in which Catholicism was located.[2] For example, when Western Christianity was the dominant religion of Western European nations, and the Christian world was more or less synonymous with the known world, or

---

[1]G. D'Costa, *Christianity and World Religions: Disputed Questions in the Theology of Religions* (Oxford: Wiley-Blackwell, 2009), pp. 5–6.
[2]See F. A. Sullivan, *Salvation Outside the Church? Tracing the History of the Catholic Response* (London: Geoffrey Chapman, 1996).

when Christianity was involved in a conflict with another religious tradition, the Catholic Church operated with particularly exclusivist soteriologies. Subsequently, the thirteenth century pope, Boniface VIII, made clear that only baptized and obedient Catholics could be saved, asserting that 'it is a matter of necessity for salvation to be subject to the Roman Pontiff'.[3] However, such exclusivist soteriologies were, according to Sullivan, reformulated when Catholic European nations discovered continents, such as South America, where people who inhabited those lands had never heard of Christ or Christianity. Could the innocent, who had never heard of Christ, be condemned just as easily as the person who had consciously chosen to reject Christ? Departing from insisting that salvation was dependent on being subject to the Roman Pontiff, who symbolized the church, Catholicism drew on Aquinas' notion of baptism by desire (*in voto*), whereby a person could be associated with the church by desiring a form of 'sub-conscious' baptism into the church, but without hearing the Gospel. *Actual* baptism and *conscious* obedience to the Pope were no longer emphasized as being necessary for salvation in this new context.

Since Christianity's beginning, through to the many different forms of Christianity that exist in the world today there has never been a single consistent view that can be traced throughout Christian history, no fully ecumenical conciliar statements, regarding who will or will not be saved. The revelation of God in the three persons of the Trinity, and in particular, the incarnation of Christ have, in various ways, been seen as central to the Christian understanding of salvation. There is no agreement, however, on whether faith is necessary for salvation, or indeed what faith means, whether it is conscious and explicit or not. There is no agreement on who is saved and through what action or response, if any, persons achieve salvation. Those views that have been dominant in the churches throughout the ages, as Sullivan provides some examples above, have been developed in response to the issues and concerns generated by the contexts in which the churches have historically found themselves, and while Church traditions have endeavoured to be faithful to what has gone before – its received theologies (*nulla salus extra ecclesiam* is still a part of formal Catholic teaching) – various churches' teachings on soteriology have ranged from predominantly narrow exclusivism to almost complete universalism.

As the world underwent and emerged from two globally significant wars in the twentieth century, this generated new theological questions that emerged out of the new multi-faith contexts locally and globally that, as in previous centuries, demanded critical theological reflection in response. This context and the subsequent theologies concerning other faiths that emerged continue to be important and to shape Christian beliefs, attitudes and practices towards people of other faiths today. As shall be discussed shortly,

---

[3]Ibid., pp. 64–65.

the discourses that have developed have involved for many theologians further reflection on specifically soteriological questions. However, it is important to note that in the post-war period, theologians were engaging with questions such as:

1 To what extent was Christianity responsible for the Holocaust and how should it subsequently respond?

2 What should theology have to say about other faiths in a context of nuclear proliferation and 'cold war'?

3 In a post-colonial era, should Christianity review its claims of superiority over other religious traditions, in particular the major world religions of formerly colonized nations?

4 With the migration of people affiliated to many different faith traditions to Europe, how should the encounter of Christians in that context with people of other faiths shape their theology, and how might theology inform Christian beliefs, attitudes and praxis in these new multi-faith and multi-cultural contexts in formerly predominantly Christian nations?

All of the above provided a context for perhaps the event that marks the most important ecclesial and theological development to influence Christian theology of the twentieth century regarding people of other faiths, the Second Vatican Council. Convened in 1962, among the many conciliar documents produced and decisions made, were important statements about other Christians and people of other faiths, in particular members of Jewish and Muslim faith traditions. Regarding people of other faiths, commenting on Vatican II, Sullivan notes that in no way does the Roman Catholic church suggest that other religions might mediate salvation, but that salvation does nevertheless include all who acknowledge the creator, especially Jews and Muslims. It is through grace that the creator is made known and is therefore able to be acknowledged, and so, wherever there is grace there is salvation.[4] Indeed, *Lumen Gentium* says,

> Nor is God far distant from those who in shadows and images seek the unknown God, for it is He who gives to all men *[sic.]* life and breath and all things, and as Saviour wills that all men *[sic.]* be saved. Those also can attain to salvation who through no fault of their own do not know the Gospel of Christ or His Church, yet sincerely seek God and moved by grace strive by their deeds to do His will as it is known to them through the dictates of conscience.[5]

---

[4]Ibid., pp. 153–55.
[5]Second Vatican Council, *Lumen Gentium*. www.vatican.va/archive/hist_councils/iI_vatican_council/documents/vat-iI_const_19641121_lumen-gentium_En.html, last accessed on 1 February 2013.

The period that led to Vatican II, and the Council itself inspired a plethora of theologies regarding people of other faiths to emerge from Catholic theologians in the twentieth century. Among them are Karl Rahner, Hans Kung, Gavin D'Costa, Paul Knitter, Tissa Balasuriya, Rosemary Radford Ruether and Gerald O'Collins. Vatican II also impacted on theological thinking beyond Catholicism, being influential in shaping Protestant theologians' discourses regarding people of other faiths, such as Clark Pinnock. These Catholic and Catholic-inspired theologies represent a range of perspectives on soteriology from exclusivism (D'Costa) to full universalism (O'Collins) to pluralism (Knitter).

In addition to the development of Catholic theologies of religions, important trends were emerging in other traditions as well. In the modern period, since Schleiermacher, Protestant theologians had been engaging with questions regarding how to think about other faith traditions, and other particularly important figures in this debate included Karl Barth and Paul Tillich. However, the most influential development to emerge from a Protestant context, that had a major impact across many different traditions, as Vatican II did, was the development of pluralist discourses. Although some trace the beginnings of pluralism back to an earlier period,[6] the most significant theologian and philosopher to develop a pluralist theology and philosophy of religions was John Hick. Schmidt-Leukel notes that many subsequent theologians and philosophers who advocate pluralism at least 'partly build on Hick's ideas, or complement them or present alternative versions of pluralistic approaches'.[7] Pluralists influenced by Hick have included Gordon Kaufman, Paul Knitter, Rosemary Radford Ruether, Raimundo Panikkar, Marjorie Suchocki, Ursula King and Alan Race among others. Hick's significance for theological discourse is further demonstrated in the amount of time Hick's opponents spend arguing why Hick has got it wrong including the likes of Gavin D'Costa, along with many other exclusivist theologians, for example. Given these developments, let us now turn to consider the main debates surrounding soteriology and people of other faiths that have emerged since the second half of the twentieth century.

Dominant soteriological models in twentieth century discourse

By the early 1980s, a number of different writers across various traditions were proposing contributions to thinking about people of other faiths,

[6]P. Schmidt-Leukel, 'Pluralisms', in *Christian Approaches to Other Faiths* (eds A. Race and P. M. Hedges; London: SCM Press, 2008), pp. 85–110 (88–90).
[7]Ibid., p. 90.

in particular, in response to the questions raised by the post-war context described above. Such theologies focused on questions of the uniqueness of Christ, the role of the church in salvation, the possibility of salvation in or through other faiths, whether the deity that Christians refer to as 'God' was particular to Christianity or present in other faith traditions, or whether the activity of the Christian third person of the Trinity could be discerned in other faiths. In 1983, Alan Race categorized the main theological positions held by theologians concerned with issues regarding people of other faiths under three main headings: pluralism, inclusivism and exclusivism.[8] By 2009, D'Costa describes Race's 'threefold typology' as the 'dominant model'[9] for articulating the main perspectives on the so-called Christian theologies of religions. Recent textbooks continue to use this model to articulate the main theologies of religions of the twentieth century.[10] Further, the significance of Race's model can be seen in the way theologians of religions are often located under one of these three headings, as well as by the way many still use this 'dominant model' as a framework for engaging with the main approaches to theologies of religions. The main Christian soteriological questions and discourses concerning people of other faiths largely fell into one of these three categories. While there is a considerable body of literature that has outlined, reviewed, deconstructed, rejected, reconstructed and adapted at length both Race's typology as a framework, and the content of many of the theologies that fall into that framework, my task here is to outline the main arguments from this threefold typology on soteriology. I will do so drawing on the reflections on Race's initial threefold typology developed by D'Costa in 2009.

'Classical' pluralisms

D'Costa identifies three 'types' of pluralism that he refers to as 'unitary pluralism', 'pluriform pluralism' and 'ethical pluralism'. The second of these sub-categories, 'pluriform pluralism', is used by D'Costa to refer to the works of Raimundo Panikkar, Mark Heim and William Placher among others. Grouping together such diverse approaches to theological thinking about people of other faiths is not appropriate. Heim and Placher, while clearly a development of earlier pluralisms, argue for theological positions that mark a significant enough departure from the pluralisms of Hick and, indeed, Panikkar, that they deserve separate discussion. In this section, therefore, we will consider only unitary pluralism and ethical pluralism, saving both

---

[8] A. Race, *Christians and Religious Pluralism: Patterns in the Christian Theology of Religions* (London: SCM Press, 1983).

[9] D'Costa, *Christianity and World Religions*, p. 3.

[10] See 'Section B' of Race, A. and Hedges, P. M. (eds), *Christian Approaches to Other Faiths* (London: SCM Press, 2008), pp. 36–110.

Panikkar and the new pluralisms of Heim and Placher for a later section in which I will discuss developments in soteriological discourse that, it is here argued, stand outside of the 'dominant model'. Unitary pluralisms and ethical pluralisms are similar enough to be discussed together here and provide examples of an early form of pluralism. These earlier forms of pluralisms will here be referred to as 'classical pluralisms' to make a distinction between them and the 'new pluralisms' of Heim, Placher and others.

As already argued, John Hick is perhaps the most influential 'classical pluralist' and D'Costa refers to Hick's particular approach to pluralism as 'unitary pluralism'. His theology of religions initially developed in response to important contextual and theological concerns that arose as a result of living in the multi-cultural and multi-faith context of Birmingham, United Kingdom.[11] It was out of this context that he began to question his assumption that it was 'God's will that the whole world be evangelised and that humanity was in fact slowly but surely becoming Christian'.[12] His experience of people of other faiths caused him to question traditions within his own faith so as to ask: 'Is it compatible with the limitless divine love that God should have decreed that only a minority of human beings, those who have happened to be born in a Christian part of the world, should have the opportunity of eternal life?'[13] He argued that in most instances, 'we *inherit* our religion along with our nationality, our language, and our culture'.[14] In response to the changing multi-faith context in which he lived as a result of migration to the United Kingdom after the Second World War, this raised questions for Hick about the nature of a God of love who refused to save the majority of people because they were either not born into or did not inherit a Christian faith. In addition, Hick also noted the urgency of dialogue between the world faiths and, with Kaufman, argued that 'the threat of the mushroom cloud impels all religions to dialogue and cooperation'.[15]

Hick resisted theologies of salvation that insisted on a Christian superiority over other faith traditions, or that only Christians had the truth and others, at best, had only a part of the truth.[16] Hick argued that in a volatile world, such a position could make a sustainable future extremely vulnerable. Instead, Hick argued, experience showed that people of other faiths were not 'on a different moral and spiritual level from Christians'[17] and so in response to his experience and the important theological and practical questions that he raised, he developed a pluralist hypothesis. On salvation, he articulated a pluralist understanding of soteriology as, 'a

---

[11]J. Hick, 'A Pluralist View', in *Four Views on Salvation in a Pluralistic World* (eds S. N. Gundry, D. L. Okholm and T. R. Phillips; Grand Rapids, MI: Zondervan, 1996), p. 37.
[12]Ibid.
[13]Ibid., p. 45.
[14]J. Hick, *The Metaphor of God Incarnate* (London: SCM Press, 2nd edn, 2005), p. 7.
[15]J. Hick, and P. Knitter (eds), *The Myth of Christian Uniqueness: Toward a Pluralistic Theology of Religions* (Eugene, OR: Wipf & Stock, 2005), p. ix.
[16]Hick, 'A Pluralist View', p. 39.
[17]Ibid., p. 39.

gradual transformation from natural self-centredness . . . to a radically new orientation centered in God and manifested in the "fruits of the Spirit"'.[18] Defined, thus, he concluded, 'it seems clear that salvation is taking place within all of the world's religions'.[19] Therefore, he claimed, that if

> we distinguish between the Real/Ultimate/Divine in itself and that Reality as humanly perceived, recognizing that there is a range of modes of human cognition, we can at once see how there is a plurality of religious traditions constituting different, but apparently more or less equally salvific, human responses to the Ultimate. These are the great world faiths.[20]

In response to the claims of most traditions of Christianity that the life, death and resurrection of the incarnate Christ is necessary for salvation, he argued that the incarnation should be understood as a 'metaphor' or 'myth' that needed to be deconstructed.[21] D'Costa refers to Hick's pluralism as 'unitary pluralism' because of the way Hick aims to articulate an essential unity between all of the world's religions in which all share common ideals and beliefs, even if they are articulated and practiced differently. In seeking unity, Hick does not stand back from challenging fundamental beliefs within Christianity and re-configuring the beliefs of all religions so as to show unity between them. Such an approach to belief has caused considerable offence not only to Christians but to people of other faiths too for his lack of regard to differences between faith traditions on matters of belief and practice such as soteriology.

An important development beyond Hick's 'unitary pluralism' is what D'Costa refers to as 'ethical pluralism'. By this, D'Costa refers to a pluralist perspective that holds that 'all religions are related to the divine insomuch as they contain certain ethical codes and practices, and religions should not be judged according to the conceptual pictures of divine reality they profess'.[22] This approach to pluralism is perhaps best exemplified in much of the earlier work of Paul Knitter but also in the work of Tissa Balasuriya, Aloysius Pieris, Marjorie Hewitt Suchocki and Rosemary Radford Ruether. Knitter's earlier soteriology had been one that drew on liberation theologies. He argued that pluralistic discourse needed to move from the 'theocentrism' of Hick et al., to a form of new 'soteriocentrism'. Writing from a Sri Lankan context, Balasuriya argues for the primacy of such a soteriology:

> 'Without radical changes in the world political and economic system, in our cultural values and our attitude towards populations and living space,

---

[18]Hick, 'A Pluralist View', p. 43.
[19]Ibid.
[20]Ibid., p. 47.
[21]For example in Hick, *The Metaphor*, pp. 184–86.
[22]D'Costa, *Christianity and World Religions*, p. 6.

poverty and hunger in Asia will not remedied. Therefore, participation in such a mental, cultural, and social revolution is incumbent on the followers of Christ. No other issue can come before it.[23]

Soteriology then is understood as a transformation of the present, politically, socially and economically, but further, that this understanding of soteriology must have priority over all other religious concerns across all faith traditions.

In addition to insisting that this particular notion of soteriology should have primacy in thinking about religious questions, ethical pluralists go further still. Ruether and Suchocki both engage with questions of religions drawing on feminist methodologies, describing Christian claims to superiority over other religions as 'an outrageous and absurd religious chauvinism'.[24] Suchocki argues 'My feminist rejection of absolutizing one religion as the norm for all others accepts the uniqueness and self-naming quality of each religion'.[25] But in seeking to reject any notion of one religion being the measure against which others are judged, Suchocki, surprisingly, suggests that one's particularity must be transcended in order to establish another norm by which one's own and other religions might be judged: 'That norm is justice'.[26] Despite acknowledging that the meaning of justice will be understood contextually, Suchocki insists that notions of justice can be found in all religions (of any worth) and that justice should remain the norm against which any religion can be legitimately measured. While Knitter speaks of 'soteriocentrism', he applies the same principle, that criteria can be established – the extent of a religion's commitment to the values and practice of justice/salvation – which can be an objective measure of the validity of each religion. Such propositions demonstrate that ethical pluralisms are also unitary pluralisms in that they seek to identify and articulate common goals and ideals between religions. Like Hick, they are not afraid to challenge, even reject the fundamental beliefs of a faith tradition, while using ideas from the particularity of one context (a Western liberal form of Christianity) to speak about, even judge, the values and practices of all religions, including Christianity. However, in contrast to Hick, they argue for a shift away from focusing on finding common ground in matters of belief, to finding common ground in the struggle for justice/salvation. This work, while seeking to articulate a form of ethical soteriological praxis, does so without asserting

---

[23]T. Balasuriya, *Planetary Theology* (London: SCM Press, 1984), p. 135.

[24]R. R. Ruether, 'Feminism and Jewish-Christian Dialogue: Particularism and Universalism in the Search for Religious Truth', in *The Myth of Christian Uniqueness: Toward a Pluralistic Theology of Religions* (eds J. Hick and P. Knitter; Eugene, OR: Wipf & Stock, 2005), pp. 137–48 (141).

[25]M. H. Suchocki, 'In Search of Justice: Religious Pluralism from a Feminist Perspective', in *The Myth of Christian Uniqueness: Toward a Pluralistic Theology of Religions* (eds J. Hick and P. Knitter; Eugene, OR: Wipf & Stock, 2005), p. 150.

[26]Ibid., p. 154.

that such an understanding should be the most important question for all faith traditions and neither do I propose that a faith tradition is of any value unless it conforms to such an understanding of ethical soteriology.

Inclusivisms

Gavin D'Costa suggests that the second category in Race's typology, inclusivisms, can be divided into two sub-categories which he describes as 'structural inclusivism' and 'restrictivist inclusivism'.[27] According to D'Costa, both structural and restrictivist inclusivists both affirm that Christ's incarnation is necessary for the salvation of anyone, distinguishing inclusivisms from pluralisms that mostly suggest that Christ is only one pathway to salvation among others. The main difference between the two forms of inclusivism is that structural inclusivists, according to D'Costa, 'affirm non-Christian religions as "salvific"' in that the religion provides a framework or *structure* through which salvation may be possible, while restrictivist inclusivists reject such a notion, insisting on the necessity of an 'epistemological relationship to Christ'[28] for salvation. Restrictivist inclusivists, while rejecting the salvific possibilities of other faiths may see other religions as no more than 'preparations for the gospel'.[29] This essentially amounts, not to a form of inclusivism, but soteriological exclusivism. Karl Rahner is perhaps the best example of a structural inclusivist and one which D'Costa engages with. It is important to note that Rahner does not, however, refer to himself either as an 'inclusivist' or as a 'structural inclusivist'.

Rahner's theology concerning people of other faiths began, like Hick's, as a result of a conflict between his exclusivist soteriology, belief in a God of love and the realization that there are many good people who belong to other faith traditions. Rahner argues that 'The Christian is convinced that in order to achieve salvation man [sic.] must believe in God, and not merely in God but in Christ'.[30] While he affirms this, he also argues that at the same time the Christian 'must reject'[31] any notion that the 'overwhelming mass' of people in the world should be condemned 'to eternal meaninglessness'.[32] The Second Vatican Council, like Rahner, argued that God's grace could be active in other faiths and that through grace people of other faiths were moved to do God's will. Further, however, Rahner suggests that other faiths might provide structures through which they may come to salvation and that those who respond to the saving grace of Christ, discovered in their religion, without naming it as such, are 'anonymously Christian'. An anonymous

---

[27]D'Costa, *Christianity and World Religions*, pp. 19–25.
[28]Ibid., p. 24.
[29]Ibid.
[30]K. Rahner, *Theological Investigations: Volume Six* (London: DLT, 1969), p. 390.
[31]Ibid., p. 391.
[32]Ibid.

Christian therefore, is a person of another faith who, inspired by grace (from the God of Christians), knowingly or unknowingly responds to that grace by doing God's will. It is not faith that saves (or at least an explicit faith, though Aquinas notion of baptism by desire is surely influential on Rahner), but acting according to and in response to God's will. In developing his notion of the 'anonymous Christian', Rahner is finally careful to reject a universal notion of salvation saying, 'Anyone who in his [sic.] basic decision were really to deny and to reject his [sic.] being ordered to God, who were to place himself [sic.] decisively in opposition to his [sic.] own concrete being, should not be designated a "theist", even an anonymous "theist"'.[33] Perhaps Rahner saw universalism as too much of a reduction of Christian notions of salvation.

Other inclusivists, beyond Rahner, include such theologians as Clark Pinnock, Daniel Strange and Amos Yong. According to Pinnock, inclusivisms argue that,

> because God is present in the whole world (premise), God's grace is also at work in some way among all people, possibly even in the sphere of religious life (inference). It entertains the possibility that religion may play a role in the salvation of the human race, a role preparatory to the gospel of Christ, in whom alone fullness of salvation is found.[34]

The connection between grace and salvation in Pinnock's definition reflects the influence of *Lumen Gentium* (above) that it is possible to be saved by grace without an explicit faith. D'Costa rejects any suggestion that official Catholic teaching is inclusivist. It is noteworthy, however, that Pinnock's understanding of inclusivism may go beyond the salvation of persons adhering to faith communities other than Christianity, to the salvation of any person who responds to God implicitly or explicitly. Inclusivisms, therefore, are open to the possibility that other religions may provide pathways or structures to salvation, but insist that, finally, salvation is possible only in and through Christ. They acknowledge that the second or third persons of the Christian Trinity – Christ and/or the Holy Spirit – or the grace of the Christian God may be at work in other faiths, and maybe even in all people, inviting them to respond to God. Whosoever responds to that invitation either through their own faith tradition or by some other means, by acting according to the will of God, could be saved.

Exclusivisms

As with inclusivism, D'Costa divides Race's third category for speaking about theologies of religions, exclusivisms, into two distinct strands:

---

[33]Ibid., pp. 394–95.
[34]C. H. Pinnock, 'An Inclusivist View' in *Four Views on Salvation in a Pluralistic World* (eds S. N. Gundry, D. L. Okholm and T. R. Phillips; Grand Rapids, MI: Zondervan, 1996), p. 98.

'restrictive-access exclusivism' and 'universal-access exclusivism'.[35] D'Costa argues that exclusivism was 'mainstream Christian orthodoxy until the nineteenth century',[36] a view that is not uncontested, even within D'Costa's own Roman Catholic tradition.[37] Sullivan's survey of Roman Catholic interpretations of the notion of *nulla salus extra ecclesiam* shows clearly how this once exclusive notion has been re-interpreted according to the context in which the Church found itself as discussed. The lack of a fully ecumenical conciliar statement on salvation, together with the ambiguity of the Bible on this matter and the multiple understandings of salvation that be found in traditions that identify as Christian, makes any assertion of what effectively constitutes soteriological orthodoxy dubious. Nevertheless, various forms of exclusivism have been and remain a major and significant way of speaking soteriologically across many Christian traditions both historically and today.

'Restrictive-access exclusivism' is D'Costa's label for the Calvinist tradition that salvation is only for the elect. It is rooted in the view that all human persons, because of their sin, deserve to be damned. Despite what all humans deserve, God in his graciousness determines to save some, the 'elect'.[38] The question of the goodness of a God who creates all human persons to be deserving of damnation, and then saves only a few, resulted in both Hick and Rahner determining that exclusivist theologies of salvation needed to be reconstructed as they were incompatible with God's goodness and love. According to D'Costa, such reconstruction of soteriology is not necessary for restrictive-access exclusivists, as the goodness and love of God is maintained because God graciously saves some, despite what all deserve. The damnation of those who never have the chance to 'hear' the Gospel, according to one Calvinist at least, is also not considered to be problematic. Those who do not have the opportunity to 'hear; the Gospel do not do so because they would have refused the Gospel anyway, so all those who are destined for salvation have a chance to 'hear' the Gospel.[39] Based on such a view, Hick's concern about one's faith being largely dependent on where a person happens to be born (discussed above) remains largely unresolved unless it is accepted that historically God has only chosen to save, and so favour, only white Europeans (where Christianity happened to be predominant).

While D'Costa only really deals with Calvinism as the principle form of restrictive-access exclusivism, this is not the only manifestation of

---

[35]D'Costa, *Christianity and World Religions*, pp. 25–32.

[36]Ibid., p. 25.

[37]In Sullivan, *Salvation Outside the Church?*, Sullivan traces developments within Roman Catholic soteriologies with regard to people of other faiths. This suggests that there was not one single static view even prior to the nineteenth century, but rather a changing and evolving view on this subject within Roman Catholicism as it sought to respond to new contexts and challenges.

[38]D'Costa, *Christianity and World Religions*, pp. 26–27.

[39]Ibid., p. 26.

this understanding of salvation. Geivett and Phillips, for example, while describing themselves as 'particularists',[40] define their essentially exclusivist position on soteriology as follows: 'except perhaps in very special circumstances, people are not saved apart from explicit faith in Jesus Christ, which presupposes that they have heard about his salvific work on their behalf'.[41] Such a position, not uncommon in many conservative evangelical traditions, emphasizes the importance of faith for salvation, mostly, a faith expressed during a human person's earthly life. In some instances this view draws on traditions of election, but in other instances is influenced by other Protestant traditions such as 'justification' and the importance of the principle of *sola fides*. Some conservative evangelical traditions, like that in which Hick first found himself believe not in election, but that slowly and surely the entire earth will be evangelized and the task of the Christian is to 'save as many souls as possible'. Further, in Sullivan's examination of Roman Catholicism, restrictive-access exclusivism describes well the notion that only those subject to the Roman Pontiff will be saved. Restrictive-access exclusivism, which emphasizes the necessity of a conscious faith in this life has implications that extend beyond the question of relationships between faiths which, as I have argued elsewhere, condemn a whole range of people to 'eternal meaninglessness' who will never have the opportunity to express an explicit faith in Christ or to 'hear' the Gospel, because of the nature of their disabilities.[42]

The second form of exclusivism, with which D'Costa identifies himself and contemporary Catholic soteriological teaching, is 'universal-access exclusivism'. D'Costa suggests that, like the restrictive-access exclusivists, 'hearing' the Gospel and responding to it are necessary for salvation. The principle difference between this and restrictive-access exclusivism is that 'hearing' the Gospel and responding to it in faith is something that can happen either in this life or in some kind of 'post-mortem' state such as limbo or purgatory.[43] Because 'hearing' the Gospel does not need to happen in this life, everyone will have the opportunity to 'hear' the Gospel before being condemned or saved (depending on their response) thus making salvation *universally accessible* but not necessarily *universally realized*. D'Costa, like Rahner, is keen to reject the possibility of universal salvation given to everyone whether or not they 'hear' the Gospel, and he does not even give such a proposition of universalism the consideration that Rahner

---

[40]R. D. Geivett, and W. G. Phillips, 'A Particularist View: An Evidentialist Approach', in *Four Views on Salvation in a Pluralistic World* (eds S. N. Gundry, D. L. Okholm and T. R. Phillips; Grand Rapids, MI: Zondervan, 1996), pp. 213–45.
[41]Ibid., p. 214.
[42]W. Morris, 'Transforming Tyrannies: Disability and Christian Theologies of Salvation', in *Transforming Exclusion: Engaging Faith Perspectives* (eds H. Bacon, W. Morris and S. Knowles; London: T&T Clark, 2011), pp. 121–40 (127).
[43]D'Costa, *Christianity and World Religions*, p. 29.

gives it, but rather dismisses the very notion simply because, he claims, 'it is disallowed by the church'.[44] Some Roman Catholic theologians, however, do hold a universalist position and find this to be consistent with their denominational affiliation.[45]

Summary: The 'Dominant Model'

Thus far, I have outlined the background to the three main approaches of the twentieth century to soteriological discourses regarding people of other faiths: classical pluralisms, inclusivisms and exclusivisms. While each of the three main discourses, in what became the predominant model of the twentieth century for categorizing the way theology constructed understandings of people of other faiths, offer distinctive contributions to soteriological thinking, it would not be appropriate to maintain that the three categories are each mutually exclusive. There is sometimes overlap between those who locate themselves in different perspectives (e.g. inclusivists and exclusivists agree on the necessity of Christ for salvation) and sometimes one may be exclusivist about one topic (e.g. Christology) and inclusivist about another topic (e.g. soteriology). Further, D'Costa notes that all three perspectives may be said to be exclusivist. He argues that classical pluralism imposes an absolute of 'agnostic liberalism' that 'stops religions pursuing their own agendas on their own terms' while inclusivists are invariably exclusivist in the way they insist on the 'exclusive truth of Christ'.[46] So the three categories may perhaps best be understood as three overlapping circles making distinct contributions but each, in various ways, responding to similar contexts and sharing or contesting particular methodologies and arguments.

John Reader, in a study on practical theology, draws on Ulrich Beck's notion of 'zombie categories'. Reader defines them as 'the living dead' that is, 'the tried and familiar frameworks of interpretation that have served us well for many years and continue to haunt our thoughts and analyses, even though they are embedded in a world that is passing away before our eyes'.[47] The three approaches in the dominant model of the theologies of religions are such 'zombie categories', familiar and often-rehearsed, but increasingly dated. With the exception of exclusivism, they often claim to be able to see and understand what is happening in other faith traditions, and use Christian discourse (such as salvation) to make universal claims. They emerge out of and genuinely seek to respond to the urgent crises of

---

[44]Ibid., p. 172.
[45]For example, G. O'Collins, *Salvation for All: God's Other Peoples* (Oxford: Oxford University Press, 2008).
[46]D'Costa, *Christianity and World Religions*, p. 35.
[47]J. Reader, *Reconstructing Practical Theology: The Impact of Globalization* (Aldershot: Ashgate, 2008), p. 1.

the period in which they were developed but, as we saw earlier, key voices such as Rahner were accused of arrogance and an imperialistic approach to faith communities, allegations that could just as easily be made against exclusivists and unitary pluralists who seek to homogenize contrasting religious beliefs and practices as though they could stand outside of culture and their particular religious tradition. Further most of the proposals for thinking about salvation in this threefold typology, with the exception of ethical pluralists, understand salvation as something realized in a future post-mortem state or define salvation in such a way that most Christians would not even recognize it. As a result, there is often an absence of any reflection on how these approaches to salvation might shape praxis or concretely transform Christian practices towards people of other faiths. Given these limitations, and that other approaches to soteriological discourses and people of other faiths have emerged, let us turn to consider some of these later developments.

Perspectives on soteriology: Moving beyond the 'Dominant Model'

In what follows, therefore, I would like to add four further circles to the picture of Christian soteriological discourses regarding people of other faiths that are additions and developments to Race's three categories. These are: (1) universalism, (2) new pluralisms, (3) the notion of 'multiple belongings' and indigenized soteriologies, and (4) practical soteriologies. These, together with the threefold typology outlined above, provide a more complete and comprehensive overview of the main soteriological responses to thinking about people of other faith traditions.

Universalism

Universalist understandings of salvation can be found in many different traditions. A collection of essays edited by Parry and Partridge, for example, discuss the possibility of universal salvation from an evangelical perspective.[48] Roman Catholic theologian Gerald O'Collins proposes universalism as the best way to understand salvation in the Catholic tradition,[49] while Kallistos Ware has explored the possibility of holding a universalist position within Eastern Orthodoxy.[50] Further, Keith Ward, an Anglican priest suggests that universalism is a proper understanding of the biblical view of salvation,

---

[48]R. Parry and C. Partridge (eds), *Universal Salvation? The Current Debate* (Carlisle: Paternoster, 2003).
[49]O'Collins, *Salvation for All.*
[50]K. Ware, *The Inner Kingdom* (New York, NY: SVS Press, 2000), pp. 193–215.

indeed, 'what the Bible really teaches'.[51] Some have developed a universalist theology of salvation specifically in response to thinking about people of other faiths (e.g. Gerald O'Collins and Tom Greggs[52]), while others have reflected on the question for different reasons (e.g. Keith Ward).

Plantinga has suggested that universalism is akin to pluralism and in light of this suggestion, it can be argued that there are at least two approaches to understanding a universalist theology of salvation: 'pluralist universalism' and 'particularist universalism'. Both types of universalism argue that all people will experience salvation, and some may even argue that salvation is not only for humans but, indeed, for the entire universe. The two approaches, however, define salvation differently and argue for different processes by which salvation can be achieved. Pluralist universalism defines salvation in a way akin to Hick's definition of salvation above. It does not emerge out of any religious tradition in particular, but is a generic soteriology that can arguably be found in all religions and spiritualities. Salvation is achieved, by following the religious or spiritual pathway a person chooses to take, and each pathway provides an equally valid route to salvation to all others. While Hick speaks about salvation mainly in the great world religions, the way he defines salvation as the 'gradual transformation from natural self-centredness . . . to a radically new orientation centered in God'[53] or the Ultimate, suggests that, for Hick, it is possible for anyone who goes through this experience of transformation to be saved. Pluralist universalism, therefore, suggests that salvation is possible for all, and can be realized through many different means, including it being open to those who do not experience the kind of transformation that Hick suggests.

Particularist universalism speaks specifically from a place of Christian particularity and is exemplified in the work of Greggs and O'Collins.[54] Like pluralist universalists, this understanding of universalism argues that salvation is for everyone, indeed, some will argue that it is for the entire cosmos. However, particularist universalisms, such as Greggs, like many forms of inclusivism, argue that salvation is only possible because of and through Christ.[55] Soteriology is defined and understood as a particularly Christian discourse but with universal significance. Such universalisms are not concerned, in the main, with making any claims about the possibility of salvation through any other faiths, principally because it is not the agenda of such particularist theology to speak about any tradition other than one's own. Instead, O'Collins, for example, proposes that 'all human beings are

---

[51]See K. Ward, *What the Bible Really Teaches: A Challenge for Fundamentalists* (London: SPCK, 2004).
[52]See O'Collins, *Salvation for All*, and T. Greggs, *Barth, Origen and Universal Salvation: Restoring Particularity* (Oxford: Oxford University Press, 2009).
[53]Hick, 'A Pluralist View', p. 43.
[54]Greggs, *Barth, Origen and Universal Salvation*, and O'Collins, *Salvation for All*.
[55]Greggs, *Barth, Origen and Universal Salvation*.

"in" Christ and the Holy Spirit is "in" all human beings'[56] and therefore salvation is open to everyone.

This kind of universalism contrasts sharply with many forms of exclusivism in claiming that salvation is for all, irrespective of faith, whether it is acquired in this world or in some post-mortem state. It is different to classical pluralisms and inclusivisms because it is principally concerned with speaking about a Christian perspective on salvation, without necessarily making claims about the possibility of salvation through other faith traditions. Particularist universalism goes beyond inclusivism to make much stronger claims about the salvation of all, rather than simply being open to the possibility that others might be saved. Finally, some particularist universalisms move beyond all three categories in Race's threefold typology, being willing not just to speak about the salvation of all human persons, but of the entire cosmos.

Particularity and multiple truths: New pluralisms

The second approach to salvation and the world religions that goes beyond the dominant model is here referred to as 'new pluralisms'. In his discussion of pluralism, D'Costa identifies what he calls 'pluriform pluralism' a category under which he locates the work of Panikkar, Heim and Placher. In discussing pluriform pluralism, D'Costa focuses on the work of Panikkar whose theology is much more akin to the classical pluralisms described above. According to D'Costa, 'Panikkar is content to allow the reality of each tradition to fructify and transform the others, while recognizing that none has the whole truth, all have some truth, a truth that is pluriform, not unitary'.[57] In some ways, Panikkar exhibits the characteristics of the more recent notion of comparative theology, allowing each tradition to speak to the other 'on its own terms'[58] and to develop a theology that emerges from the process of dialogue.[59] Further, to suggest that religions and traditions should be seen to have value on their own terms is a departure from many classical pluralisms. However, Panikkar, like Hick, seems to suggest that while different religions may not have the whole truth, nevertheless, there is a whole truth 'out there' which each religion has in part. Panikkar's pluralism is still dependent, therefore, on an underlying notion that there is a unity to truth, some sort of overarching metanarrative, and that he is able to see that each religion is, in part, working towards it.

Mark Heim, however, departs from this kind of classical unitary pluralist approach arguing that 'these theologies are not religiously pluralistic at all.

---

[56]O'Collins, *Salvation for All*, p. 208.
[57]D'Costa, *Christianity and World Religions*, p. 14.
[58]Ibid., p. 41.
[59]Ibid., pp. 37–45.

Difference in religious aims and ends is what they bend their impressive efforts to deny'.[60] For Heim, classical pluralists do not affirm a plurality of different approaches to salvation, but rather seek to homogenize profoundly different religious beliefs and practices into a singular discourse. In contrast, on the question of salvation, Heim proposes what he terms a '"more pluralistic hypothesis": the contention that there can be a variety of actual but different religious fulfilments, salvations',[61] to retain the particularly Christian terminology. Pluralistic notions of salvation are thus redefined, not as different pathways to the same reality, partial perspectives on a single truth, alternative routes to one ultimate end, shared visions of justice and liberation, but as a way of speaking about multiple realties, multiple truths and multiple ends. Knitter's later work has in many ways embraced this new kind of pluralism, recognizing in his own work that he 'did not make sufficient room for the real, deep distinctive, perhaps irreducible differences among the religions'.[62] He argues that if God is ineffable, 'all religions can accept the pluralists' invitation to come to the table of dialogue without claiming to have the full, final, or definite hold on revelation or truth' alone, and that even his own church, Roman Catholicism, 'can still admit that it has more to learn about what this fullness [of God] really contains'.[63] While this may be so, there is still an air of arrogance in Knitter, in his implied suggestion that the table of dialogue was in some way created, or is owned by pluralists, or that pluralists are the only ones who are able to initiate, and so invite others to engage in genuine dialogue.

The new pluralisms of Heim, Placher and others demonstrate many similarities with the 'comparative theology' approach to religions, which is 'grounded on the assumption that one cannot speak in generalized ways about religions'.[64] Comparative theologies, however, go beyond asserting that religious traditions are simply different, to seek 'theological engagement with the other'.[65] The purpose of such engagement would be to 'see what Christianity learns from engagement with'[66] those traditions. Such comparative theological projects are often focused around the study of sacred texts and religious practices. They are consciously open to the possibilities of change as a result of the encounter with religious others. Particularity is also key, that one can only speak from a particular religious tradition, not for any other religion and not, like classical pluralists, all religious traditions.

---

[60]S. M. Heim, *Salvations: Truth and Difference in Religion* (New York, NY: Orbis Books, 1995), p. 129.
[61]Ibid., p. 131.
[62]P. F. Knitter, 'Is the Pluralist Model a Western Imposition: A Response in Five Voices', in *The Myth of Religious Superiority: A Multifaith Exploration* (ed. P. F. Knitter; Maryknoll, NY: Orbis Books, 2005), pp. 28–42 (37).
[63]Ibid., p. 35.
[64]D'Costa, *Christianity and World Religions*, p. 38.
[65]Ibid.
[66]Ibid., p. 8.

The problem with some notions of particularity in many theologies of religions, including comparative approaches, is that when the term 'particularity' is used, it seems to refer to whole religious or faith traditions.[67] This helpfully acknowledges that there are fundamental differences between faith traditions, but not necessarily within each faith tradition. From a Christian perspective, 'particularism' should be a term that reflects the notion that perspectives on salvation and religions, like all theologies emerge from a tradition (e.g. liberal Anglican) within a tradition (such as Christianity) as well as from a particular socio-economic, political location, shared history and culture, shaped by one's gender, sexuality, disability and so on. All aspects of a person's or community's particularities affect the way that theology is approached. So while Heim speaks of salvations between religions, it is also right to suggest, as Chapter 2 argued, that there is a plurality of salvations within Christianity itself. Some differ so significantly within Christianity, it may even, it could be argued, be appropriate to speak about 'Christianities' [68] (plural) perspectives on salvation.

'Multiple Belongings' and indigenized soteriologies

It is noteworthy that one important development in theologies of religions has been the notion of what D'Costa calls 'multiple belongings'[69] but only refers to in passing. Panikkar exemplifies this notion when he describes himself as a 'Christian-Hindu-Buddhist', someone who inhabits multiple religious traditions. This notion is not unique to Pannikar, and is perhaps more widespread in many non-Western contexts where there are multiple, deep-rooted religious traditions. It is not unusual in many parts of Africa, for example, for people to identify themselves as Christians, go to church and lead a life committed to many Christian values, while also continuing to believe in and participate in aspects of African traditional religions.[70] Further, while in Bolivia in 2007, I met a man who was an ordained deacon in the Roman Catholic Church who was also a 'priest' or 'shaman' in the indigenous religion of which he was a part. Such practices of multiple belonging are not uncommon among many formerly colonized peoples and nations, not least as the chains of colonization have been thrown off, what is good in indigenous cultures has been rediscovered (for some it was arguably

---

[67]See, for example, the discussion in P. Hedges, 'Particularities: Tradition-Specific Post-modern Perspectives', in *Christian Approaches to Other Faiths* (eds A. Race and P. M. Hedges; London: SCM Press, 2008), pp. 112–35.
[68]This terms is used by P. Gifford, *African Christianity: Its Public Role* (London: Hurst & Company, 1998), p. 325.
[69]D'Costa, *Christianity and World Religions*, p. 38.
[70]M. Engelke, *A Problem of Presence: Beyond Scripture in an African Church* (Los Angeles: University of California Press, 2007), p. 38 notes this among some Christians in Zimbabwe.

never lost), while what is perceived to be good from Western Christianity has continued to be embraced.

If it can be accepted that there are multiple ways of understanding, articulating and practicing the ideals and ends, even ultimate ends, of a faith tradition or spiritual pathway, and that the concern of the theologian is not to make judgements or claims about other faiths (the new pluralisms), it is not inconceivable, therefore, as a next step, to note that some people may choose to participate in and belong to more than one faith tradition. Many soteriological perspectives, particularly exclusivist views, have historically demanded that to be 'saved' meant to give up any allegiances to other faith commitments of any kind. Writing from an 'American Indian' perspective, George Tinker notes that the missionary message of 'salvation in Jesus alone' led to the 'unequivocal disavowal of the beliefs, experiences, ceremonies, community connectivity, and religious traditions of one's own culture'.[71] Such an understanding of salvation in Christianity derived from and reinforced 'amer-european Christian triumphalism'[72] and served to affirm the Christian sense of superiority and grasp of the truth over other faith traditions. The practice of 'multiple belongings' subverts such a sense of Christian superiority by suggesting that faith traditions, including Christianity, can co-exist in one context and even be practiced by the same people in that context. Holding one set of beliefs and practices on soteriology does not automatically deny the validity of other religions which may or may not have something to say about soteriological questions as Christians understand this notion. What multiple belongings means for soteriology is that, as the new pluralisms recognize there may be many different salvations, so it is possible to practice more than one tradition, with potentially contrasting ideals and goals, without producing an interior or spiritual conflict or the need to deny one tradition in favour of another tradition.

While traditions may co-exist, and people belong to multiple traditions, soteriologies that are named as Christian have also emerged out of indigenous experience. For some, a conflict remains between colonial Christianity and indigenous religious traditions not least because, as Tinker notes, 'the controlling impetus of every [Christian] denomination is loath to allow Indians to move very far away from the denomination's central doctrinal focus'.[73] Instead, an indigenization of theological concepts is required that insists that 'Indians who have converted to the colonizer's religion must be free to interpret the gospel for themselves, even constructing an interpretation of Jesus on the "old testament"[74] foundation of ancient tribal

---

[71]G. E. Tinker, *American Indian Liberation: A Theology of Sovereignty* (Maryknoll, NY: Orbis Books, 2008), p. 130.
[72]Ibid., p. 129.
[73]Ibid., p. 139.
[74]Ibid., p. 138, Tinker suggests that the 'old testament' of American Indians is not the text of the Hebrew Bible, but rather the traditions they have inherited that have been given to them by their 'Creator'.

religions'.[75] Thus, particularized soteriological concepts such as 'liberation', for example, are indigenized to break away from colonial notions of salvation as liberation from individual or original sin. Indeed, liberation is interpreted to mean a 'break away [liberation] from the way language is used so easily and comfortably by our colonizer'.[76] It involves such decisive action as when 'Larry Sellers, decided some years ago to bring the Sun Dance back to the Osage people after a seventy-seven year absence, that was a clear liberative act with deep theological implications for the Osage nation'.[77] So, while in some contexts, peoples belong to multiple faith traditions, there is also a process of soteriological indigenization, whereby colonial notions of salvation are deconstructed and indigenous notions of salvation are constructed in light of colonial Christianity's encounter with indigenous religions and spiritualities. Tinker provides one example of such indigenization though there are many others.[78] This development in soteriological discourse is one that is often overlooked in many discussions of soteriology[79] in light of thinking about living in a multi-faith world and reflects a shift towards the possibility of the construction of new soteriological praxes.

Practical soteriology

The final approach to soteriology and religions that will be discussed here is that of 'practical soteriology'. Amos Yong argues, 'Christians need to give much more sustained reflection to the implications of their theologies of religion for Christian attitudes and actions regarding other faiths'.[80] That is not to say that most theologies of religion, are not, at least in some way, concerned with practice and attitudes, but rather that the focus of many such theologies, especially those in the 'dominant model', have often been concerned with primarily defending, amending, deconstructing and/or reconstructing Christian orthodoxy with the notable exception of ethical pluralisms. Praxis then becomes little more than an application or a set of consequential actions that emerge out of and result from such theologies. This form of 'applied theology', which is concerned with belief before praxis is not an adequate way of engaging with such an important question as that of the relationship between Christianity and other religions. Yong argues

---

[75]Ibid., p. 139.
[76]Ibid.
[77]Ibid., p. 137.
[78]Engelke, *A Problem of Presence*, provides one example of theological indigenization using similar methods to those of Tinker. Engelke notes especially the indigenization of understandings of the Bible and the Holy Spirit.
[79]That is, it does not really appear in D'Costa, *Christianity and World Religions*, and only receives attention in one chapter of Race and Hedges (eds), *Christian Approaches*.
[80]A. Yong, *Hospitality & The Other: Pentecost, Christian Practices, and the Neighbour* (New York, NY: Orbis Books, 2008), p. 38.

that right from the beginnings of Christianity, 'Doctrinal affirmations . . .
were second order reflections emerging out of Christian practices . . . .
Theologians are now beginning to retrieve this linkage of beliefs and
practices long after they had been sundered in many ways by early modern
rationalism, individualism and positivism'.[81]

In response, Yong does not develop an explicitly soteriological discourse,
but focuses instead on the theme of hospitality. 'Hospitality', however, can
be understood soteriologically. Yong focuses, for example, on the parable of
the Good Samaritan, a parable told in response to the question 'what must
I do to inherit eternal life'? The response is to love God and your neighbour
as yourself. Future salvation is dependent on present attitudes and actions
towards God and one another, expressed in the parable, according to Yong,
through acts of hospitality.[82] Of significance in this approach to thinking
about soteriology with regard to religions is the way that Yong connects
the future with the present and the present with the future, a more holistic
picture of soteriology in the Christian tradition. Further, Yong reconnects
praxis with belief, noting how what is believed transforms praxis and how a
person acts reflects and shapes beliefs. It is this approach to theology, taken
by Yong that I also take in this book in the construction of a more explicit
soteriology that seeks to transform praxis through a dialogue between
received theologies and the contemporary context so that belief and praxis
might both be transformed. To date, there has been too little of this practical
thinking with regard to people of other faiths.

Summary

Thus far, I have identified the 'dominant model' of soteriological discourse
regarding people of other faiths of the twentieth century in which there are
three main perspectives: 'classical' pluralism, inclusivism and exclusivism. I
have suggested that these three perspectives on soteriology are best understood
as three overlapping circles, each sharing something in common with the
other while making distinctive contributions to soteriological thinking. I
have then added four further overlapping circles to the so-called dominant
model to complete the picture of the main perspectives on soteriological
discourse regarding people of other faiths in recent times. Finally, as argued in
Chapter 1, I have again argued that context and experience must be allowed
to engage in a questioning and, if necessary, reconstructive engagement with
received theologies, to argue for a soteriology that treads the path between
theological integrity and practical relevance for the multi-faith and global
context of today. Indigenous soteriologies provide one example of how
this has worked in other contexts. Having identified seven approaches to

---

[81]Ibid., p. 46.
[82]Yong, *Hospitality & the Other*, p. 103.

soteriological reflection regarding people of other faiths, in the final part of this chapter, as a prologue to the second part of the book, I will use the above to identify what I perceive to be the main problems and the main strengths of these approaches and, in so doing, to articulate some principles for the construction of an alternative soteriology: salvation as praxis.

Shaping a practical theology of salvation for a multi-faith world

Qualifications for any soteriological proposition

Kallistos Ware tells the story of a question he once put to a Greek Archbishop:

> If it is possible that the devil, who must surely be a very lonely and unhappy person, may eventually repent and be saved, why do we never pray for him? To my disappointment (for I could not at the moment think of other topics of conversation), the archbishop settled the matter with a sharp and brief rejoinder: 'Mind your own business'.[83]

A document on inter-faith dialogue from the World Council of Churches (WCC) puts the Archbishop's point to Ware in a different and less forthright way:

> ... salvation belongs to God, God only. We do not possess salvation; we participate in it. We do not offer salvation; we witness to it. We do not decide who would be saved; we leave it to the providence of God. For our own salvation is an everlasting 'hospitality' that God has extended to us. It is God who is the 'host' of salvation (Rev. 21:3).[84]

Both Ware's story and the WCC statement articulate important points about soteriology. It is, of course, the task of any theologian to seek to further understand something of soteriology, but it is also necessary to acknowledge the limitations of human understanding and the nature of mystery in all theological questions. The Christian theologian can only speak from their own particularity, their own context. The theologian can argue a case, based on the best evidence they have, but the absolute truth of their arguments can never be known. As the Roman Catholic theologian Paul Knitter acknowledges, 'All Catholics, even the pope, is still "on the way" to understanding the "finality" or "absoluteness"

---

[83]K. Ware, *The Inner Kingdom* (New York, NY: SVS Press, 2000), pp. 202–03.
[84]World Council of Churches, *Religious plurality*.

of their God-given revelation'.[85] Any claims about soteriology must acknowledge the particularity and context from which they emerge and the partiality with which they speak. If this is true even in one's own faith community, it must be even more true when speaking about other faith traditions. This book does not aim to speak about or for any other faith tradition, in contrast to many existing theologies of religions. In light of the particularity and partiality of all theology, any soteriologies that speak arrogantly or with condescension should be avoided.

Many theologies of salvation regarding people of other faiths, including most of those discussed in this chapter, appeal to various authoritative sources to evidence and support their case. Exclusivists, Geivett and Phillips and universalist, Keith Ward, each appeal to the Bible to evidence their soteriological argument and claim that their respective soteriologies are faithful to the biblical tradition. D'Costa makes greater use of the Magisterium of the Catholic Church to make his case for 'universal-access exclusivism'. O'Collins rightly notes, however, that many theologians engaging with questions of religions 'adopt a position and then rustle up some biblical evidence in its support'.[86] A thorough survey of the Bible and many received theologies do not, however, provide much clarity on questions about who will or will not be saved, not least because they are often ambiguous or else often provide a number of conflicting views. The lack of any fully ecumenical conciliar statement only adds to the ambiguity. Exclusivisms in particular will re-assert their received traditions on soteriology and people of other faiths, often without a real engagement with the questions and the issues that the multi-faith and globalized world of the twenty-first century. Sullivan's review of *nulla salus extra ecclesiam* (described earlier) and the indigenous soteriologies outlined above show clearly how important context is in shaping soteriological perspectives. As contexts change, so soteriology changes. Theology is never simply some abstract articulation of an idea, but a response to contextually relevant questions and concerns. Likewise, this practical theology of salvation aims to address a particular context, and to be relevant to it, but it is not proposed as a soteriology that should have new universal and timeless significance of any kind.

On the other hand, one particular characteristic of classical pluralisms that demands attention is the problem of reductionism. Like many other 'classical' pluralists, Hick's response to the challenges that Christian soteriologies present in thinking about people of other faiths is to reduce the notion of soteriology, and subsequently the incarnation in Christianity, along with aspects of other traditions. Hick's definition of salvation as 'a gradual transformation from natural self-centredness . . . to a radically new orientation centered in God and manifested in the "fruit of the Spirit"'[87] does

---

[85]Knitter, 'Is the Pluralist Model a Western Imposition', p. 35.
[86]O'Collins, *Salvation for All*, p. vi.
[87]Hick, 'A Pluralist View', p. 43.

not do justice to or reflect most Christian soteriologies. It is vague, ignores much of the language of sin, does not speak of the role of Christ in salvation so central to Christian perspectives, and does not speak either of the future eschatological nature of salvation or the difference soteriology might make to the transformation of this world. As Bernhardt notes, 'Theologically, Christians wonder if Hick's understanding of pluralism does justice to the integrity of their own faith; philosophically, they ask whether Hick's revolution does justice to the integrity of other faiths'.[88] With D'Costa, I argue that, 'the outcome of his [Hick's] escape from particularity leads to nothing in particular'.[89] Reducing aspects of belief or praxis to the lowest common denominators is not helpful for living in a multi-faith world. It serves only to cause offence to the tradition from which a theologian writes and potentially causes offence to people of other traditions too.

So there is an important balance to be achieved between being open to constructing theologies that are practically relevant and not simply asserting what has been useful for past generations, but there is also a need to bring that desire alongside the need for some kind of theological integrity, depending on what that means for each theologian and Christian community. Reducing key beliefs, or pretending they do not matter, in the end will not persuade most Christian persons of the value of an argument. While the Bible and traditions are ambiguous, it does matter practically, that any soteriological proposal can demonstrate some theological and practical credentials.

Finally, it is important to reiterate that when addressing questions of people of other faiths, many theologians unhelpfully operate with incomplete understandings of soteriology, focusing mostly on future eschatological aspects. Alastair McGrath, for example, recognizes that salvation means many things in the New Testament. He says, 'The controlling images used in the New Testament to articulate its [salvation's] various aspects include terms and concepts drawn from personal relationships, physical healing, legal transactions and ethical transformation'.[90] He acknowledges in Greek religions that salvation was conceived in terms of 'temporal deliverance from a present threat rather than any notion of eternal salvation'.[91] He writes, however, as though this does not echo a Christian understanding of salvation at all, but rather, prefers to sum salvation up as centring 'on a relationship, inaugurated in time and to be consummated beyond time, with none other than the "God and Father of our Lord Jesus Christ"'.[92]

---

[88]R. Bernhardt, 'The *Real* and the Trinitarian God', in *The Myth of Religious Superiority: a Multifaith Exploration* (ed. Maryknoll, NY: Orbis Books, 2005), pp. 194–207 (194).

[89]D'Costa, *Christianity and World Religions*, p. 11.

[90]A. E. McGrath, 'A Particularist View: A Post-Enlightenment Approach', in *Four Views on Salvation in a Pluralistic World* (eds S. N. Gundry, D. L. Okholm and T. R. Phillips; Grand Rapids, MI: Zondervan, 1996), pp. 151–80 (163).

[91]Ibid., p. 163.

[92]Ibid., p. 169.

When inclusivists and exclusivists discuss soteriological questions with regard to people of other faiths, they are generally concerned with soteriology as a future eschatological possibility in which human persons may or may not have the opportunity to participate. Classical pluralists often try to move away from such notions of soteriology, as we have seen, either by talking about salvation as some kind of reorientation to transcendence, or else homogenize differences by describing salvation as a concern common to most religions, such as the liberation of the oppressed and a commitment to justice. Inclusivists and exclusivists therefore generally speak only of salvation as a future hope and reality, ignoring how salvation in the Christian tradition is not only concerned with the life of the soul or resurrected body in the afterlife, but also with salvation from the tyrannies of the present. Some pluralists, Knitter, Suchocki, Balasuriya and others have recognized the present aspects and significance of soteriology that is so central, as this book argues, to Christian notions of salvation, but then impose such a view of salvation onto other religions, even suggesting that all religions might be measured against a Christian notion of salvation as some form of liberative justice.

This work does not claim to offer a complete soteriology but rather seeks to redress a balance in debates about salvation and people of other faiths. It seeks to re-orientate the soteriological gaze of theologians and the churches away from future eschatological ends to present concrete realities. This book also aims to pay greater attention to questions of practice rather than exercising a concern to ensure that any new proposal is logically and philosophically coherent above all else. In contrast, it considers how soteriology has contributed to the destructive ways Christian communities have engaged with people of other faiths in the past, with a view to constructing alternative soteriological praxes. Three approaches to salvation as praxis follow, each one offering a distinct perspective on how salvation might be differently understood by Christians as a form of praxis, and it is to these we now turn.

PART TWO

Salvation as praxis

5

'Communion and Otherness':
Salvation as deification

Introduction

In the first of three ways of thinking about salvation as a form of praxis, and in bringing that into conversation with Christian practices in a multi-faith world, this chapter will specifically focus on the notion of salvation as 'deification' or 'theosis'. While this is an established view of soteriology predominantly found in Eastern Orthodox traditions, it is not unique to Orthodoxy. Deification as a form of soteriological praxis will be constructed, however, by drawing on received traditions that have shaped Orthodox and other understandings of this soteriological discourse. This understanding of salvation is developed so as to provide an alternative to the dominant Western discourse described in Chapter 2, while also representing a form of soteriological praxis that may affect positively Christian engagement with people of other faiths in this world. It will be guided by the principle established earlier that the Christian Gospel is orientated towards ending human suffering, fostering well-being, and seeking human liberation, freedom and equality. First, therefore, it will be argued that deification is a way of thinking about salvation that not only speaks about a promise regarding a future eschatological existence for human beings, but that also speaks about salvation in, and therefore, transforming this world. Second, if salvation can be understood as being concerned with a process of 'becoming God', then the best way to understand what that means, it is proposed, is to turn to a Trinitarian understanding of God. Third, drawing on social and ecclesiological models of the Trinity, this chapter will consider how this notion of deification may or may not be useful for practising salvation in a multi-faith world.

Salvation as deification

Becoming G/god: Exploring origins

Deification, becoming God, is by no means a particularly Christian idea
and neither is it a notion only referring to Christian understandings of
soteriology. Norman Russell notes that the idea of deification itself can be
found in the 'ruler-cults' of the ancient world. He notes that the 'origins
of the imperial cult go back to the practices of the Hellenistic kingdoms'[1]
where it had become a custom to attribute 'divine honours' on royal and
imperial rulers. Similar traditions, he argues, could also be found in ancient
Egypt. Russell explains: 'The Ptolemaic dynasty cult dates from 271 BCE
when images of Ptolemy II and Arsinoe were incorporated into the temple
of Alexander next to the *sema* as the Brother and Sister Gods'.[2] Further, in
the later Roman Empire, Julius Caesar was likewise 'deified' by the Senate
in 42 CE and 'Octavian, as he then was, became known as the divi filius',
the son of a god.[3] That gods disguised themselves as human, or that humans
might be in some way divine either during their life or after their death,
was common in the ancient world, in particular among rulers who styled
themselves and their predecessors in this way, no doubt in order to secure
and defend their positions and power. Russell argues that as the tradition
of deification developed, it also democratized and popularized. Therefore,
while not all emperors in the Roman Empire were deified,[4] for example,
it did also become common for 'apotheosis' to be used as a term for 'the
solemn burial' of 'ordinary citizens'.[5]

The idea of deification, however, according to Russell, in ancient
philosophical religion did not compromise the unity of God. Drawing on
Platonic and Aristotelian perspectives, God is understood as the 'perfect,
living and intelligent being' and that 'below God in this absolute sense are the
heavenly bodies, the "moved movers", which are also alive and divine. And
below them on a descending scale are the gods, human beings, animals and
plants'. In this tradition, therefore, it was possible to be deified, to become
a god, without compromising the fundamental unity of God as 'immaterial,
eternal substance whose only activity is a direct intuitive knowledge not
of anything external, because that would imply change, but of himself'.[6]
Russell argues that the ruler cults, the democratization of deification and
the ways in which deification was understood in the philosophical traditions

---

[1] N. Russell, *The Doctrine of Deification in the Greek Patristic Tradition* (Oxford: Oxford
University Press, 2004), p. 19.
[2] Ibid.
[3] Ibid., p. 21.
[4] Ibid., p. 25.
[5] Ibid., p. 27.
[6] Ibid., p. 36.

were largely rejected in ancient Jewish and early Christian traditions. They were content to pray for the emperor, for example, and would be loyal to him, but they would not worship him, they worshipped the Judeo-Christian God alone.[7]

Deification in the Bible?

Russell argues that a Christian soteriological perspective on deification cannot really be found in the New Testament, or in particular, as it is often argued, in the Pauline corpus. Paul (and Pauline psuedopigraphers) speaks of the importance of participation in Christ (e.g. 1 Corinthians 15), putting on Christ (Romans 13.14) adoption as children and heirs of God (e.g. Romans 8) and becoming one with Christ in the sharing of the Eucharist (e.g. 1 Corinthians 10.17). That Paul had a developed soteriology of deification articulated as a form of human communion with Christ is, however, contested, because not until much later was it widely accepted that Jesus Christ was also fully God and that therefore to speak of becoming one with Christ was also to speak about becoming one with God. Christ's divine status was only fully confirmed, and therefore no longer debateable for the Church, at the Council of Nicaea in 325 CE (although Pauline texts such as Colossians 1.15–20 and Philippians 2.5–11 may suggest this understanding of Christ was present early on, if not formal doctrine).[8] Perhaps as Russell suggests, 'Paul simply gives us a hint of what is to come in the writings of Clement, Origen, and their successors'.[9]

If Pauline literature suggests that Jesus might have divine qualities in Colossians and Philippians, certainly by the time John's Gospel had been written it was not unthinkable to suggest that the human Jesus might also be divine: 'If you know me, you will know my Father also. From now on you do know him and have seen him' and 'Have I been with you all this time, Philip, and you still do not know me? Whoever has seen me has seen the Father' (John 14. 7 and 9). While the deification of emperors may have been offensive to early Christians, and a Christian theology of deification hardly developed in the New Testament, the possibility of humans having divine qualities, and not just Jesus Christ, was not anathema to them. Russell argues that 'evidence of superhuman power could suggest a human being who joined the gods as well as a god in human form. This is why Paul was credited with divine power in Malta when he was bitten by a viper without coming to any harm (Acts 28: 1–6)'.[10]

[7]Ibid., p. 25.
[8]Ibid., pp. 79–85.
[9]Ibid., p. 85.
[10]Ibid., p. 16.

Russell indicates that in Hebrews there is a discourse regarding becoming 'partakers of Christ' (e.g. Hebrews 3. 14) and that in the Johannine literature, 'participation through faith and the sacraments in the life of God makes believers "children of God"'.[11] These have also been used to suggest biblical allusions to notions of salvation as deification. 2 Peter 1.4 has further often been used to defend deification as a 'biblical' soteriology: 'Thus he has given us, through these things, his precious and very great promises, so that through them you may escape from the corruption that is in the world because of lust, and may become participants in the divine nature'. Finlan and Kharlamov also cite numerous biblical passages that reflect the idea of deification expressed through themes in the Bible such as 'imitation of God', 'Taking on God's nature', being 'indwelt by God', 'being re-formed by God', 'being con-formed to Christ' and the 'final divinization of the kosmos'.[12] Thus, while Kärkkäinen cites 2 Peter 1.4, and Psalm 82.6 as evidence of a biblical soteriology of deification, Finlan and Kharlamov suggest that passages such as Matthew 5.48, Ephesians 4.25 and 1 Corinthians 15.28 are also widely interpreted to be allusions to deification.

Perhaps, however, the most that can be said about the origins of deification as a soteriological motif in the New Testament is as much as can be said of the doctrine of the Trinity: there are undeveloped allusions to what is later interpreted to be deification in the New Testament, but specific discourses about salvation as a process of becoming divine itself develops fully much later on. This should not be understood to undermine this as an approach to salvation. There are many Christian beliefs that are not explicitly found in the Bible. That is not to say, however, that because complex and carefully worked out and articulated doctrines are not directly in the Bible, that passages from the Bible have not informed and shaped the development of such doctrines, they have. The absence of their full articulation in the Bible is not a justification for suggesting such theologies are of any less significance. Indeed, most Christian soteriological understandings only take a partial and selective account of biblical perspectives, including those that claim of themselves to be authentically 'biblical'. Salvation as deification draws heavily, therefore, on the biblical traditions described above even if it is not a fully articulated doctrine in the Bible.

Deification in western theologies

Deification is one of the principal ways in which Christians have understood and spoken about salvation from its beginnings though it has been developed considerably since. As we have seen, it is a perspective on soteriology that

---

[11]Ibid., p. 89.
[12]S. Finlan and V. Kharlamov (eds), *Theosis: Deification in Christian Theology* (Eugene, OR: Wipf & Stock, 2006), pp. 2–3.

is dominant in Eastern Orthodox[13] understandings of salvation and is most commonly referred to as 'deification', 'divinization' or 'theosis'. In Western traditions, deification has not been as prevalent in Christian soteriological discourses as the notions of justification, sanctification or even liberation. Indeed, Finlan and Kharlamov suggest that the notion of deification all but disappeared in 'Western Christendom . . . for over a thousand years'.[14] In Western Christianity, they further suggest that 'in lay theology the term is usually perceived as either blasphemous or absurd'.[15] According to Russell, however, for the last century, Western perspectives on deification were shaped by the work of Adolf von Harnack who viewed deification as contradictory to the message of the Gospels.[16] Nevertheless, there has been a renewed interest in the notion of deification as a way of thinking about salvation in Western traditions, shown by the work of, among others, Norman Russell,[17] Veli-Matti Kärkkäinen,[18] Emil Bartos[19] and Hans Urs von Balthasar.[20]

While notions of deification have been less familiar in Western traditions, Finlan and Kharlamov argue that deification can be found in the work of Augustine, perhaps the most influential of the Church Fathers on the Western tradition.[21] It is not absent from Western theologies, however. In the Church of England's most recent liturgical text, *Common Worship*, the collect for the first Sunday after Christmas reads '. . . grant that, as he [Jesus] came to share in our humanity, so we may share the life of his divinity'[22] while the collect for the 'Sunday next before Easter' in the *Book of Common Prayer* reads, 'Almighty and everlasting God, who, . . . hast sent thy Son our Saviour Jesus Christ to take upon him our flesh . . . mercifully grant, that we may both follow the example of his patience, and also be made partakers of his resurrection'.[23] The *Catechism of the Catholic Church* says, 'The Beatitudes teach us the final end to which God calls us: the Kingdom, the vision of God, participation in the divine nature, eternal life, filiation, rest in God'.[24] Further as Olson notes, while many Protestant theologians have

---

[13] C. Carlton, *The Life: The Orthodox Doctrine of Salvation* (Salisbury, MA: Regina Orthodox Press, 2000).

[14] Finlan and Kharlamov, *Theosis*, p. 8.

[15] Ibid.

[16] Russell, *The Doctrine of Deification*, p. 6.

[17] Ibid.

[18] V. M. Kärkkäinen, *One with God: Salvation as Deification and Justification* (Collegeville: Liturgical Press, 2004).

[19] E. Bartos, *Deification in Eastern Orthodox Theology* (Eugene, OR: Wipf & Stock, 2006).

[20] See Kärkkäinen, *One with God*, p. 9 who notes German texts written by von Balthasar on this subject.

[21] Finlan and Kharlamov, *Theosis*, p. 8.

[22] Church of England, *Common Worship: Services and Prayers of the Church of England* (London: Church House Publishing, 2000), p. 381.

[23] Church of England, *The Book of Common Prayer* (Cambridge: Cambridge University Press, rev. edn, 1968), pp. 95–96.

[24] United State Catholic Conference, *Catechism of the Catholic Church* (Vatican City: Libreria Editrice Vaticana, 2nd edn, 1997), p. 429.

'been reluctant to speak of real deification',[25] Kärkkäinen acknowledges discussions of deification can also be found in the works of Martin Luther[26] and John Wesley.[27]

Recognizing that deification is a principally Eastern Orthodox understanding of salvation with historically minimal significance in the West for the past thousand years, deification provides an alternative way of speaking about salvation in contrast to the predominant Western soteriological view. It is important to note once again that as this is developed, it is done so by seeking to tread Campbell's difficult path 'between theological integrity and practical relevance'. With the tradition of Orthodox theology that seeks continuity with the past, this chapter too seeks to draw on established and received theological traditions, but also to deconstruct and reconstruct those traditions as appropriate, a departure from the methods of established Orthodox theologies and the ways deification may be articulated within them. What, therefore, does a Christian soteriology of deification look like?

Salvation as deification: Towards an understanding

Salvation as deification is an ancient soteriological perspective that has been widely engaged with across the centuries. It is not a single homogenous view of salvation to which a whole series of Christians subscribe in precisely the same way. Olson, for example, outlines some of the contemporary debates on deification[28] while many scholarly works have been devoted to the study of deification and the various articulations of this theology that have emerged across the centuries.[29] It is not my intention to engage in that kind of study here. Rather, the purpose here is to provide a brief outline of some of the major and most significant aspects of deification that have developed, focusing in particular on its potential for developing an approach to soteriological praxis in a multi-faith world.

The saved state: 'Becoming God'

The notion of salvation as deification in the Christian tradition is rooted first and foremost in the doctrine of the incarnation. According to Kärkkäinen,

---

[25]R. E. Olson, 'Deification in Contemporary Theology', *Theology Today* 64(2), (2007), pp. 186–200 (187).
[26]See Kärkkäinen, *One with God*, pp. 37–66.
[27]See ibid., pp. 72–81 and Olson, 'Deification'.
[28]Olson, 'Deification'.
[29]For example, Russell, *The Doctrine of Deification*.

both St Athanasius and St Irenaeus are the two Church fathers whose work is most commonly associated with soteriological understandings of deification.[30] The link between salvation and the doctrine of the incarnation in the work of Athanasius is no surprise given his work on Christology and the significant contributions he made to the construction of the Nicaean formulae. However, Kärkkäinen also acknowledges that the notion of salvation as deification is to be found in the work of Origen, Gregory of Nyssa, Gregory of Nazianzus, Basil and many others from the patristic era, including Augustine.[31]

Finlan and Kharlamov rightly note that 'Of course, Christian monotheism goes against any kind of literal "god-making" of believers'[32] as a description of the final state of salvation. To speak about deification in the Christian tradition is not to speak about the creation of lots of other gods who are precisely the same as the God defined as Trinity. God is totally other to humans and such a transformation would not only compromise the divinity of God, but the humanity of human beings too. Zizioulas aims to clarify the notion of the potential for humans to 'become God' explaining that theosis 'means participation not in the nature or substance of God, but in His [sic.] personal existence'.[33] Ware provides further clarification explaining that 'although "ingodded" or "deified", the saints do not become additional members of the Trinity. God remains God ... The distinction between Creator and creature still continues: it is bridged by mutual love but not abolished'.[34] Thus Finlan and Kharlamov note that a number of terms are used to refer to the ways in which human persons share in the divine life including, participation or partaking in the divine life, communion with God,[35] or 'taking on godly qualities' rather than becoming a 'godlike being',[36] and so there are marked contrasts with such a Christian approach to deification and those found outside Judeo-Christian traditions in the ancient world.

The state from which salvation is necessary

Deification, as a soteriological perspective, is deeply connected with the notion of *imago dei* and a distinction between being made in God's image and growing into God's likeness. What is the state of existence, therefore, that human beings are in, that necessitates their salvation into a new and transformed reality? Kärkkäinen notes, as discussed in Chapter 2, that

[30]Kärkkäinen, *One with God*, p. 26.
[31]Ibid., pp. 17–36.
[32]Finlan and Kharlamov, *Theosis*, p. 1.
[33]J. D. Zizioulas, *Being as Communion* (London: Darton, Longman & Todd, 1985), p. 50.
[34]K. Ware, *The Orthodox Way* (New York, NY: St Vladimir's Seminary Press, rev. edn, 1995), p. 125.
[35]Finlan and Kharlamov, *Theosis*, p. 6.
[36]Ibid., p. 7.

in the Eastern tradition there is no Augustinian notion of original sin.[37] Kärkkäinen argues that 'inherited guilt is impossible' in the Eastern tradition as it is understood that the sin of Adam is a personal sin, meaning that the consequences of the fall for Adam was, 'physical death and the obscuring or distortion of the image of God'.[38] In a study of the work of the Orthodox theologian Stăniloae, Emil Bartos suggests that in the Eastern tradition that even after the sin of Adam, human beings did not lose the image of God; they are not completely lost to original sin. To be in the image of God is to be in receipt of a gift from God that cannot be taken away. However, in contrast, to be in the *likeness* of God is a 'mission' which human persons must work to expedite.[39] Notions of humanity being created in the image of God and growing into the likeness of God are thus distinguished so that to speak about the 'image' of God is to speak about human dignity, while to grow into the likeness of God is to speak about an 'ethical duty'.[40] After the fall, the image of God in human persons is not lost but 'dimmed'.[41] While the fall 'weakened' human beings relationship with God, it was not broken altogether, and human beings maintained a 'will to do good, but not the power'.[42] Death, corruptibility and those things historically associated with deserved and subsequently inherited punishment for sin in the Western tradition are understood rather, according to Kärkkäinen, as pedagogy. In other words, suffering and death are present to teach the human person the way back to God. We will return to this point shortly. The state of the human condition, as it is articulated in the traditions described above, is arguably constructed more positively in this approach to salvation than in the dominant Western discourse. Although the condition of humans is one of separation from God because of sin, something of the inherent goodness of every human person is affirmed. This understanding of the state from which salvation is necessary so that humans can become like God encourages the Christian to engage in purposeful activities that will realize salvation.

Realizing salvation

Therefore, while human beings retain the 'dimmed' image of God, the human life is designed to grow more fully into the likeness of God and this becomes possible because of the incarnation. Deification is based on the principle that God, in Christ, became human so that human persons could become divine. The very purpose of the incarnation was to enable human persons to grow more fully into the likeness of God. Again, commenting on

---

[37]Kärkkäinen, *One with God*, p. 22.
[38]Ibid.
[39]Bartos, *Deification*, p. 136.
[40]Ibid.
[41]Ibid., p. 138.
[42]Ibid.

the work of Stăniloae, Bartos argues that the notion of deification is bound up with the Chalcedonian definitions of the two natures of Christ.[43] Christ is both fully human and fully divine. Made in the *imago dei*, believers aspire to grow into the likeness of God. Bartos explains that 'Jesus Christ becomes the linking chain that brings together [hu]mankind as a whole with God'.[44] The incarnate Christ therefore makes deification possible by bringing together divine and human natures into God's self, but Christ also provides a vision of the potential in human persons. As Kärkkäinen notes, '. . . the destiny of humanity is to be found in Christ'.[45] As Finlan and Kharlamov explained (see earlier), the way to deification then is to imitate Christ, to take on Christ's nature, to be indwelt by God and to be con-formed to Christ.[46] To be deified is to become like Christ but, as Maximos the confessor argues, 'not by nature or by relation but by [divine] decree and grace'.[47]

Commenting on the theology of Vladimir Lossky, Olson argues that Orthodox Christians understand deification as a gift rather than something that can be achieved through human endeavour. But while it is a divine gift to human beings, it is nevertheless a gift that requires a response from human beings. Olson comments that deification 'is, then, a synergistic process that includes divine initiative and human response in an endless cycle until its completion, when the person is fully perfected in union with God'.[48] Deification, therefore, it can be argued, is concerned not only with the attainment of a future possibility, but with the process of the transformation of the person in the present. Likewise Zizioulas speaks of theosis as a doctrine of salvation that has its roots in the future; humanity is being called to grow more and more into the likeness of God. But if the roots of theosis are in the future, its branches reach out into the present, transforming the present and inviting human persons to live out and work towards such future possibilities;[49] Zizioulas therefore speaks about the 'already, but not yet'[50] of soteriology. Thus, while growing into the likeness of God in this understanding of salvation is a process completed in a new future life, it is nevertheless a process begun in this life. To be saved is to grow more and more into the likeness of God, to become like God, in response to the invitation of God to the person to work towards deification. Deification, therefore, involves a transformation of persons in the present, it is lived, in the present, and it is a form of praxis: committed action towards one final end, the eschatological communion of the individual, humanity, and maybe the entire cosmos with God. Before considering further what it

---

[43]Ibid., p. 168.
[44]Ibid.
[45]Kärkkäinen, *One with God*, p. 25.
[46]Finlan and Kharlamov, *Theosis*, pp. 2–3.
[47]Quoted in Kärkkäinen, *One with God*, p. 27.
[48]Olson, 'Deification', p. 190.
[49]Zizioulas, *Being as Communion*, p. 59.
[50]Ibid., p. 62.

may mean to speak about salvation as a process in which Christian persons, humanity more broadly or, indeed, the entire cosmos might become God, it is important to recognize some limitations with this understanding of salvation at this point.

Notes of caution on salvation as deification

While the distinction between the image and likeness of God is not one that is familiar to most Western theological traditions, that every human being is made in the image of God, and that this constitutes not only their essential personhood but their value before God, has been an important theme in Western traditions. Such perspectives have been criticized however, for their tendency to draw on anthropological characteristics that reinforce certain types of normativity. For example, as we saw in Chapter 2, in seeking to determine what God is like, it has often been suggested that God is a rational being which draws on human characteristics that have been historically attributed more to men than women. Discourses have then been developed that serve to dehumanize those who are supposed not to conform to such notions of God's being. It is important, therefore, to construct an alternative way of speaking about what God is like and so what it means to grow into God's likeness that disrupts any discourses that reinforce, in relation to the example given, oppressive practices such as patriarchy.

It is further important to recognize the difficulties posed with the proposition that becoming like God can be realized through the imitation of an able-bodied male, Jesus Christ. Those opposed to the ordination of women to the priesthood, for example, often cite the maleness of Jesus, whom the priest is thought to represent, as being essential to the nature of who Jesus was and therefore to those who represent Jesus in priestly ministry.[51] Likewise in many Orthodox traditions, the priest is thought in some way to visually represent Christ and that, together with Levitical laws barring people with a 'blemish' from priestly activities, has been used to justify the exclusion of people with disabilities from this particular ministry. While there have been attempts to construct images and use language that suggests that Christ can be understood as female and disabled in recent times,[52] and as we saw in Chapter 2, some have argued that the maleness of Jesus was incidental or insignificant, nevertheless, the maleness and able-bodiedness of Christ prevails as central to understanding Christ's identity in many contexts. Thus any theology that argues that salvation involves some form of imitation of Christ is in danger of being rooted in images of and

---

[51]An overview of this perspective is provided in T. Ware, *The Orthodox Church* (London: Penguin Books, rev. edn, 1997), p. 293.
[52]For example, S. McFague, *Models of God: Theology for an Ecological, Nuclear Age* (London: SCM Press, 1987) and N. L. Eiesland, *The Disabled God: Toward a Liberatory Theology of Disability* (Nashville: Abingdon Press, 1994).

language about Christ that reflect and reinforce the presumed superiority of patriarchal, able-bodied and, indeed, Christian paradigms of normativity. Any theology that seeks to develop alternative Christian practices towards people of other faiths cannot at the same time support the marginalization and social exclusion of women and disabled people. Therefore, any use of deification needs to find an alternative way of thinking about what it means to be deified.

To suggest that corruptibility, suffering and death are used by God for pedagogical purposes, or what Irenean theodicy terms as 'soul-making', has been shown to be particularly problematic in many pastoral contexts where clearly human beings are not improved as a result of their suffering, and nor are they brought closer to God through that suffering.[53] To suggest that the process of becoming God might involve humans engaging in suffering and hardship in order to expedite this process could further serve to justify the perpetuation of historic acts of violence, war and genocide towards people of others faiths. For the sake of the future of humanity, and for consistency with the proposal here that the Gospel is concerned with human liberation, freedom and well-being, including the transformation of human suffering, any such notion of what it means to 'become God' must be resisted.

Given the difficulties of notions of the *imago dei* and focusing solely on Christ as the likeness of God to which the believer should strive, is there another way of speaking about what it could mean to become God? If salvation is to be understood as deification or theosis, and this means growing more into the likeness of God, what alternative images of God can be used? Only by asking this question can we get a sense of what theosis as a future possibility might mean for humans and how in turn such future possibilities might reach into the present to transform it for the better. It has already been argued that to say that Christ is the best likeness of God to which a believer may conform or imitate is potentially problematic, and therefore below, it is suggested that to speak of deification as salvation is best understood by arguing that to become like God is to become like God as Trinity. This is preferable to a process of deification rooted in Christology, and the reasons for this are discussed below.

Becoming God: A trinitarian perspective

God as Trinity

Since Jürgen Moltmann's landmark work, *The Trinity and the Kingdom of God*,[54] in which he articulated a particularly 'social' understanding of the

---

[53]J. Swinton, *Raging with Compassion: Pastoral Responses to the Problem of Evil* (Grand Rapids, MI/Cambridge: Eerdmans, 2007), pp. 17–21.
[54]J. Moltmann, *The Trinity and the Kingdom of God: The Doctrine of God* (London: SCM Press, 1981).

Trinity, a number of subsequent 'social' and 'ecclesial' models of the Trinity have emerged, transforming the theological landscape and reinvigorating this doctrine with new contemporary relevance. Perhaps, after Moltmann, of greatest significance was Leonardo Boff's work, *Trinity and Society.*[55] Other studies have also emerged along similar lines that have argued for the merits of thinking about the Trinity as a model for the ways that societies and churches might operate in more egalitarian and just ways. Other significant works include those by Paul Fiddes,[56] Colin Gunton,[57] Catherine Mowry LaCugna,[58] Hannah Bacon[59] and Miroslav Volf[60] among others. On the whole, these works have suggested that the doctrine of the Trinity provides a useful and positive model for ecclesial practice and societal relationships. However, some feminist theologians have viewed the Trinity less favourably such as, for example, Mary Daly who called for an abandonment of the doctrine because it is, in her view, irredeemably patriarchal,[61] while Sallie McFague, critical of the androcentric terminology used in the Niceno-Constantinopolitan doctrine, proposed alternative language.[62] While such ways of thinking about the Trinity in relation to practice are relatively recent in origin, Bacon acknowledges that in the Orthodox tradition there has always been what she describes as an 'ethical-pastoral' dimension to Trinitarian discourse.[63]

If the state of salvation involves human persons in some way being deified, then what does it mean to become 'like God' or perhaps even more basic is the question, 'what is God like'? In order to avoid the dangers of the Christocentric understanding of deification that have emphasized traditionally anthropocentric notions of the *imago dei,* an alternative understanding is necessary, hence the turn to the Trinity here. Of greater import, however, for turning to the doctrine of the Trinity is that it has been the one central doctrine of most Christian traditions, through which they have sought to articulate their deepest understanding of the nature of the Godhead in which most people who identify as 'Christian' believe. While interest in the doctrine of the Trinity has grown in recent times, belief in a

---

[55]L. Boff, *Trinity and Society* (Eugene: Wipf and Stock, 2005).

[56]P. Fiddes, *Participating in God: A Pastoral Doctrine of the Trinity* (London: Darton, Longman & Todd, 2000).

[57]C. E. Gunton, *The Promise of Trinitarian Theology* (London: T&T Clark, 2nd edn, 1997).

[58]C. M. Lacugna, *God for Us: The Trinity and Christian Life* (New York, NY: HarperCollins, 1991).

[59]H. Bacon, *What's Right with the Trinity? Conversations in Feminist Theology* (Aldershot: Ashgate, 2009).

[60]M. Volf, *After Our Likeness: The Church as the Image of the Trinity* (Grand Rapids, MI: Eerdmans, 1998).

[61]M. Daly, *Beyond God the Father: Toward a Philosophy of Women's Liberation* (Boston: Beacon Press, 1985).

[62]S. McFague, *Models of God: Theology for an Ecological, Nuclear Age* (London: SCM Press, 1987).

[63]Bacon, *What's Right with the Trinity?*, p. 59.

Trinitarian God has remained central to Christian belief since the fourth century. It is used by ecumenical organizations to determine membership,[64] it is the first of the thirty-nine articles of religion of the Church of England,[65] it is at the heart of the Catechism of the Roman Catholic Church,[66] central to Eastern Orthodox belief in God[67] and the Niceno-Constantinopolitan definitions represent a point of unity between Monophosyte churches and other parts of Christianity.[68] So central is this belief in God, to ask in Christianity 'what is God like?' is virtually synonymous with asking 'what is God the Holy Trinity like?'

Orthodox theologian, Kallistos Ware, concurs with the general principle proposed here that understanding God as Trinity is key to understanding deification, becoming God. He explains, 'salvation is social and communal more particularly because of our faith in the Holy Trinity'.[69] The doctrine of the Trinity is not a description of what God is like as such, but is rather the best articulation of the divine being that we have. In the Orthodox tradition, Trinitarian discussion should be understood in light of the apophatic tradition: 'the final word, then, of theology is silence'.[70] In Trinitarian discourse, likewise, all that can be said about God ultimately is silence for God is always other, above and beyond. Yet, in the economy of revelation, God can be glimpsed through experience. In this light, Niceno-Constantinopolitan definitions provide a framework for Zizioulas' Trinitarian discussions regarding deification to which we will now turn as he provides a way of bringing a social and ecclesiological understanding of God as Trinity into conversation with soteriology.

Trinity as communion and otherness

Zizioulas argues that in reflection on what it means to be a human being, and what it means to speak of God as Trinity, it is necessary to distinguish the concepts of nature and personhood. By nature, Zizioulas is referring to what he describes as the 'mode of existence', the *what* of existence.[71] On human nature, he explains we,

> refer it to all human beings; there is nothing unique about having a human nature. Furthermore, all the 'natural' characteristics of human nature

---

[64]World Council of Churches, *Constitution*.

[65]Church of England, *The Book of Common Prayer*, pp. 611–12.

[66]United State Catholic Conference, *Catechism*, p. 62.

[67]Ware, *The Orthodox Way*, pp. 27–41.

[68]Ware, *The Orthodox Church*, pp. 25–26.

[69]K. Ware, *How are we Saved? The Understanding of Salvation in the Orthodox Tradition* (Minneapolis: Light and Life Publishing, 1996), p. 68.

[70]Bartholomew (Ecumenical Patriarch), *Encountering the Mystery: Understanding Orthodox Christianity Today* (New York, NY: Doubleday, 2008), p. 51.

[71]J. D. Zizioulas, *Communion & Otherness* (London: T&T Clark, 2006), p. 165.

such as dividedness – and hence individuation leading to decomposition and finally death – are all aspects of human 'substance' and determine the human being as far as its nature is concerned.[72]

Perhaps Emmanuel Lartey explains this a little more clearly when he says, as we saw earlier, that all humans are in some ways like all others, like some others and like no other.[73] That human beings have a 'nature' is to say that all human persons are in some ways like all others. Zizioulas' use of the language of the 'nature' or 'substance' of human being, however, clearly resonates with the concept of 'substance' found in Trinitarian language; that is, the very quality that the three persons of the Trinity share and thus unites them in the one Godhead. Zizioulas does not really say much about what this human 'nature' is, other than that it is divided through procreation and individuation and finally leads to death.

The key to Zizioulas' distinction between 'nature' and 'personhood' in his book, *Communion & Otherness*, is to argue that the human nature or substance, as it has just been described, and the divine nature or substance are wholly and always other to one another.[74] He is not concerned with describing or defining what human nature is, it is simply that God's nature and ours are not the same. They are wholly other and so, he argues, to be deified does not mean that human nature is changed into the divine nature or in anyway absorbed into the Trinity so that the human nature is lost or the divine nature compromised. In salvation as deification, humans remain human and God remains God, including in the human's renewed eschatological saved state. The only point at which the human and the divine natures fully meet, though without merging into one nature, is in the incarnation (according to Chalcedonian definitions). Humans can, however, become God by modelling and participating in the personhood of God, not the nature of God. A distinction is thus made between nature which is the unchanging and wholly other essences of humanity and God, and personhood, to which we now turn.

Zizioulas argues that there is an important distinction to be made between nature, the *what* of existence, and personhood, the *how* of existence.[75] If *nature* is that which is common to all humanity and is that which distinguishes us from God whose nature is other to that of humans, to be a *person* means to '*be truly and be yourself*'.[76] He is swift to argue that he does not understand personhood to be the same as individuality. Zizioulas argues that an individual is someone with an 'identity conceivable in itself, "an axis of consciousness" and a concurrence of natural or moral

---

[72]Ibid.
[73]Lartey, *In Living Colour*, p. 12. (See discussion in this book's 'Introduction').
[74]Zizioulas, *Communion & Otherness*, p. 165.
[75]Ibid.
[76]Ibid., p. 166.

qualities, or a number that can be subject to addition or combination'.[77] Zizioulas rejects any idea that the persons of the Trinity can be thought of as individuals 'either in the psychological sense of a centre of consciousness, or in that of a combination and concurrence of natural or moral qualities'.[78] God does not exist as three individuals, but three persons in communion: 'The three constitute such an unbreakable communion . . . that none of them can be conceived apart from the rest'.[79] Personhood is dependent then on a combination of 'communion and otherness'.[80] A person, he argues, 'is thus defined through properties which are absolutely *unique*'.[81] To use Lartey's framework again, all persons, human and divine, are in some ways like no other.[82] Personhood is present in the uniqueness of each person and makes each person 'other' to another. But this 'otherness', this uniqueness, is only discovered and realized in communion between unique persons. In God the Trinity, the three persons each have 'properties' which are absolutely unique and yet that personhood is not realized or possible without the absoluteness of communion. If to be deified is to become God by growing into the likeness of God the Holy Trinity, then, Zizioulas argues, to be like God is to mirror the way that God exists as three persons – other to one another – yet sharing one substance or nature in full communion. The nature is common to the three, but the personhood of each remains unique. Reflecting this likeness of God is possible in this world. The end state of salvation, however, is a place in which human beings can enter into personal communion, not only with each other but also with God. Humanity and God always remain other to one another in nature and substance, but can participate in *personal* communion.

Deification is not only about a future eschatological hope but about a process of becoming God in the present – a form of praxis for those who believe to seek to grow more and more into the likeness of God. The significance of the Trinity for salvation is that to speak of humans becoming God is to speak about unique human persons acknowledging that they share the same nature with each other yet are always other to one another personally. For the Christian, soteriological praxis therefore involves human persons striving to be in loving communion with other persons as they will be in the world to come, while respecting the integrity of their otherness, just as the persons of the Trinity exist in communion with one another. This is a utopian vision rooted in future eschatological possibilities, but with transformative potential for the present. Deification is not simply a description of heaven, but a vision for the earth in which humans persons

---

[77]Ibid., p. 171.
[78]Ibid.
[79]Ibid., p. 159.
[80]Ibid., p. 166.
[81]Ibid., p. 160.
[82]Lartey, *In Living Colour*, p. 12.

strive to live 'according to the image of God' and for Zizioulas this means 'living in the way God exists', in the *how* of God's existence, 'as an image of God's personhood':[83] otherness in communion. In so doing, human communion with the Trinity is fostered as human persons become more like God, and the hope of an alternative existence in heaven is made real and concrete on earth.

Summary: Becoming God, becoming Trinity

Thus far in this chapter, the concept of deification as a way of speaking about salvation within Christian traditions has been explored. It has been proposed that if it can be argued that soteriology is concerned with a human (or cosmic) growth into the likeness of God, then it is important to ask 'what, then, is God like?' for humans to be able to strive to grow into that likeness. It has been argued that a Trinitarian understanding of God, for most traditions that identify as 'Christian', provides the most appropriate response to this question. In particular, the Trinitarian theology of one Orthodox scholar, for whom deification is central to his understanding of salvation, has been outlined. It has been proposed that Zizioulas' suggestion that the Trinity should be understood in terms of communion and otherness and so if to be saved is to become like God, this provides a model for Christian soteriological praxis. This chapter has further so far raised some concerns both about some of the ideas that underpin notions of God and deification, such as *imago dei*, tendencies to Christocentrism, notions that suffering is intentional pedagogy and difficulties with Trinitarian language. Conscious of these critiques and not losing sight of them, it is proposed that the Trinitarian discourse of communion and otherness as a metaphor for a Christian understanding of future eschatological possibilities, and therefore of earthly soteriological praxes, can usefully be brought into conversation with real concrete questions regarding Christian participation and practice in a multi-faith world in the twenty-first century.

Practising deification in a multi-faith world: Further conversations

It has been argued that to speak of 'becoming God' as a Christian theological discourse is to speak about a form of soteriological praxis: committed action that seeks to realize the future utopian vision of an alternative way of living alongside and with people of other faiths to those of the past. This understanding of soteriology is rooted in the future, as Zizioulas explained,

---

[83]Zizioulas, *Communion & Otherness*, p. 166.

but reaches into and is transformative of the present. To what extent does deification, understood as a praxis that seeks to model the Trinitarian God, provide a paradigm for an alternative form of Christian soteriological belief and practice in multi-faith contexts? It is to this question that the remainder of this chapter now responds.

Subverting agendas of normalization

In Chapters 2 and 3, the dominant Western soteriological discourse that has been worked out in Christian belief and practice has been used, it was argued, to seek the normalization of people of other faith traditions and forms of spiritual expression. Given this history, what does the soteriological praxis of deification as a realization of a Trinitarian view of communion and otherness have to offer that might subvert such historic and contemporary agendas of normalization? As we have seen, to speak of the 'otherness' of people of other faiths has become common in many contemporary theologies of religions, in contrast to the homogenizing discourses of the mid twentieth century.[84] In an attempt to define terms in the 'Introduction' to this book, the difficulties of using such terminology was outlined, reflecting on the way 'othering' people of other faiths can dehumanize and depersonalize them. It can also serve to homogenize large groups of people by creating a category of 'otherness' suggesting that people of other faiths are all the same and are also entirely different (other) to those who identify themselves as Christian. The Trinitarian theosis of Zizioulas serves as an important reminder that while otherness matters and should be affirmed, this should be accompanied by praxes that seek communion between persons.

Further if 'otherness' does indeed affirm the 'uniqueness' and 'irreplacableness' of every human person,[85] then the homogenization of people of other faiths into large religious groups or into a single category of 'otherness' to Christianity means that differences between people who identify with the same faith and spiritual traditions are also largely lost; 'otherness' is a quality of all human persons, including those who identify as 'Christian'. Every person is different, every community is different and the affirmation of that difference within and outside the Christian community provides an important corrective to the homogenizing tendencies of many theologies of religions and, indeed, to the rhetoric of any who stereotype one faith tradition as evil and another as good. Human beings and faith traditions are too complex for such generalizations and so 'otherness' in the language of theologies of religions should be redefined in terms of absolute uniqueness rather than as broad homogenizing categories of difference.

---

[84]For example, this is term used in T. Greggs, *Barth, Origen and Universal Salvation: Restoring Particularity* (Oxford: Oxford University Press, 2009).
[85]Zizioulas, *Communion & Otherness*, p. 167.

This recognition of absolute uniqueness, otherness, is the beginning of an expression of soteriological praxis that seeks to model the life of the Trinitarian God in a multi-faith world; it is, in a Christian sense, to strive to become like God.

Trevor Phillips is the former chair of the Commission for Racial Equality[86] in the United Kingdom. Writing in *The Guardian* in 2004, he commented on the state of multiculturalism in Britain in the 1970s and 1980s arguing that 'Too many institutions have seized one half of the integration equation – recognition of difference – while ignoring the other half: equality'.[87] Integration suggests the conformation of a group or groups to a particular set of norms established by a dominant group, but that is not the kind of society that Phillips argues British people should be striving to create. Instead, he proposes, 'Our ideal should be one nation of many faces; one culture integrating many faiths and traditions'.[88] Thus, his vision of an integrated society includes the presence and recognition of difference. Reflecting on the integration of more recent immigrants into the United Kingdom, he proposes, 'Integration only works if it both recognizes newcomers' differences and extends complete equality. Celebrating diversity, but ignoring inequality, inevitably leads to the nightmare of entrenched segregation.'[89] Legal and public affirmations and celebrations of diversity do little to transform the injustices that many people experience, but addressing inequality is necessary for the creation of a fair and just society. He notes, 'Half a century after legal segregation was outlawed in the US, nine out of 10 African-American children are in black-majority schools; nine out of 10 whites live in areas where the black population is negligible. Guess whose schools underachieve, and whose districts are poorer'.[90]

To recognize the personhood of every human being as that which is utterly unique to them must, for Phillips, go beyond the mere affirmation and celebration of otherness to an active seeking of a more egalitarian society. Perhaps this is where Zizioulas' understanding of communion is so important. The nature or substance of the three persons of the Trinity is that which holds the three together in loving communion with one another. Personhood, difference, otherness is thus only fully discovered in full and loving relationship with other persons, through seeking communion with them, in their difference and otherness. If this notion of communion and otherness provides a way of speaking about the Trinity, and the future

---

[86]This body no longer exists in the United Kingdom and has been replaced by the Equality Commission. Its function was to ensure the implementation of racial equality legislation in the United Kingdom.

[87]T. Phillips, 'Multiculturalism's Legacy is "Have a Nice Day" Racism', *The Guardian*, 20 April 2008, www.guardian.co.uk/society/2004/may/28/equality.raceintheuk, last accessed on 1 February 2013.

[88]Ibid.

[89]Ibid.

[90]Ibid.

eschatological saved state is one in which humanity reflects the divine life, and if this future utopia provides a paradigm for Christian living and practice in the present, then this has the potential to provide an alternative framework for understanding and engaging with people of other faiths to those provided by the historic dominant soteriological understanding.

Such a way of thinking about otherness challenges members of the Christian community from within to perceive people of other faiths and spiritual pathways not as a threat, but as people with whom relationships are essential, so that people of all faiths can discover how to '*be* truly and to *be yourself*'.[91] The desire to seek to normalize people of other faiths, to insist on their conformation to the norms of Christian belief and practice in order to ensure their own and the Christian's salvation is arguably subverted by such a view. Instead, in the affirmation of difference and otherness of people of different faith and spiritual pathways becomes a way of making the future eschatological vision of the saved state a present possibility. In the encounter with one another we discover the uniqueness and irreplaceableness of ourselves and others do the same and so we all potentially learn to value ourselves and every other person more fully. It is important, however, not to forget Phillips' concerns about the way societies can celebrate difference while ignoring inequality. When the affirmation and valuing of otherness as essential to human personhood is accompanied by a commitment to communion, to model the Trinitarian God, this must be practiced in relationships where persons see others' as different yet equal. In turn, this should involve the Christian affirmation of the value of all human life and in so doing influence Christian persons to speak out against and resist the homogenization and stereotyping of people of other faiths that can lead to their depersonalization, dehumanization and even demonization. Such a way of operating may be understood as a praxis of salvation, becoming like God on earth.

Neither the notion of 'communion' nor 'otherness' is consistent with the homogenization that can result from many pluralist discourses. Rather the import of seeking 'communion' allows the other to be and to remain other, in fact this is crucial for the relationship between persons to flourish. Experience would no doubt testify that relationships between people of different faiths are more likely to flourish where differences are accepted rather than one trying to convert the other to their norms. But communion recognizes the need for relationship, for dialogue, for friendship, for hospitality, for a spirit of love towards, between and from the other. So, if otherness calls members of the Christian community to speak out against and resist the homogenization and stereotyping of people of other faiths, communion challenges the Christian community to strive to construct a new, just and fair context for living. To construct a world in which the

---

[91]Zizioulas, *Communion & Otherness*, p. 166.

humanity of every person is affirmed and every life is valued because it is unique and irreplaceable. To work to know and to understand people who are different, and to form relationships with them, but relationships based not on hierarchy, injustice or inequality, but the kind of mutuality and reciprocity we glimpse in the Trinitarian God. This is perhaps what salvation as deification can mean for living in a multi-faith world; affirming otherness but seeking communion. This all may seem idealistic but perhaps soteriology is always finally about idealism. It can be easy to talk about dreams of future ideals, but this vision of salvation as deification has the potential to guide practice and challenge the Christian community to work for and to realize living and modelling the life of the Trinitarian God in the present.

Avoiding Christian impositions

Any model of Trinitarian community with practical significance must be tested against practice and, in this instance, it will mean testing the model contextually. I have been asked, 'what would such a model of Trinitarian community look like?' and the response to such a question must simply be that the model may provide some guiding principles, but the actual construction of such communities must be worked out contextually. Respecting otherness, but seeking communion may, for example in contexts of multifaith dialogue mean faith communities collaborating on an issue of justice. In another context, it may mean disagreeing with one another and learning to accept and live with difference. It is, however, underpinned by an understanding of the Christian Gospel as being orientated towards ending human suffering, fostering well-being, and seeking human liberation, freedom and equality. There are many ways in which members of Christian communities might engage in this sort of soteriological praxis. However, this approach differs from pluralism because it does not wish to identify religious universals, but rather its point is always to respect otherness and allow that to have an equal importance alongside the desire for communion. This ultimately takes priority over any desire to normalize or convert people of other faiths to Christianity; salvation is lived and experienced now, without normalizing everyone in this world in the hope of accessing another future world.

To suggest that a Christian vision of a future saved state is one of communion and otherness that can lead to an alternative soteriological praxis towards people of other faiths, while potentially transformative could also become imperialistic. Some qualifications of this approach to soteriological praxis are thus essential. First, this should not be understood as a Christian claim to have all the answers to questions regarding how to shape multi-faith contexts – including the global context – for the better. Such an approach to people of other faiths is potentially open to the criticisms of postcolonialists such as Sugirtharajah who challenge the 'major narratives' of colonizing powers, while reclaiming those narratives that have been marginalized in decolonized contexts.[92] Leonardo Boff argues that the former US President, George Bush

> interpreted the Barbarism of September 11th as a war against humankind, a war between good and evil, a war against democracy and against the globalization of the market economy that, according to Bush's understanding, so much benefited humankind. Whoever is against this interpretation is an enemy, is the other, is the foreigner, who must be fought and eliminated.[93]

Boff here interprets the actions and words of President Bush as reflecting a metanarrative that assumes its own rightness and therefore superiority over other conflicting views. Past experiences have shown that such an approach to people of other faiths does not foster good relationships between people of different faiths, but also begins relating to people of other faiths from a position of assumed superiority. Whether it be the concept of globalization, capitalism, Western democracy or indeed, Christian models of communion and otherness, the *particularity* of such worldviews must be maintained and not imposed on others. They can be presented to others, suggested as good ideas, but when they become universals, metanarratives, to which everyone must conform then there are dangers of a form neo-colonialism rearing its ugly head, setting human persons against one another as 'us' and 'them' and not being prepared to seek either otherness or communion, but rather annihilation of the 'enemy'.

This approach to salvation as praxis is intended as a way of re-orientating particularly Christian engagement with people of other faiths away from a destructive past towards a more hopeful future, and provides an alternative Christian theological approach to shaping that future. However, it is not proposed as the only way that people of different faiths might live together in community, it is a particular Christian contribution to a much wider debate. Its usefulness may only be determined by the contribution it makes to transforming the future engagement of Christians with people of other faiths for the better.

Conclusion

One way of speaking about salvation in the Christian tradition has been as 'deification', that is to become God or perhaps more specifically, to grow

[92]R. S. Sugritharajah, *The Bible and the Third World: Precolonial, Colonial and Postcolonial Encounters* (Cambridge: Cambridge University Press, 2001), p. 246.
[93]L. Boff, *Fundamentalism, Terrorism and the Future of Humanity* (London: SPCK, 2006), pp. 42–43.

into the likeness of God. Zizioulas understands this process of becoming
God as a process of becoming God as Trinity, to grow into the likeness of
God as a relationship of persons (others) in loving communion with one
another. This can provide, it has been argued, an alternative soteriology to
that which has shaped and been expressed in Western Christian practices
towards people of other faiths historically. It has been proposed that thinking
about salvation in this way can lead to alternative soteriological praxes in
which the desired normalization of people of other faiths to conform to
Christian norms is subverted by a soteriology that affirms differences in
expressions of faith and spirituality as essential to the human capacity to be
truly persons and truly in communion. There is thus arguably no room for
the Christian 'presumption of superiority', but only places in which human
persons view each other equally. If that is one way in which salvation as
praxis in a multifaith world might be understood, we now turn to a second
approach to salvation as praxis: salvation as healing.

6

Embodied well-being:
Salvation as healing

Introduction

Christian practices of normalization have included violence towards and the colonization of people of other faiths, and theologies of salvation have helped to justify these practices. It could be argued that such acts have been driven by altruistic motives to save the soul of the non-Christian for fear that they may be condemned for all eternity. However, it is much more likely that these practices of 'mission' reveal a deep-rooted suspicion of difference, a sense of Christian religious and spiritual superiority, and political wills to dominate and suppress others. In Chapter 2, examples from feminist theologies and disability theologies were outlined to highlight how Christian soteriological beliefs and practices have been used to justify a normalization agenda with regard to gender and people with disabilities. In this chapter, salvation as healing will be explored as a way of thinking and acting soteriologically that has the potential to subvert and transform normalization agendas and practices. It is a marginalized understanding of salvation within Christian traditions though one that can trace its origins back to the New Testament.

In most historic and contemporary theologies, the notion of salvation as healing has often been used to reinforce socially constructed understandings of able-bodiedness as the social and religious norm for human existence.[1] This can be evidenced in the many practices of so-called healing ministries in which people who are ill or disabled are thought to be in need of a cure

---

[1]W. Morris, 'Transforming Tyrannies: Disability and Christian Theologies of Salvation', Bacon, H., W. Morris and S. Knowles (eds), *Transforming Exclusion: Engaging Faith Perspectives* (London: T&T Clark, 2011), pp. 121–28.

for their particular condition.[2] When a person's condition is invariably not cured, those who have become the objects of this ministry are accused of having insufficient faith or unrepented sin.[3] The language of 'faith' and 'sin' at once associates healing with salvation in relation to the dominant Western soteriological discourse, identifying disability or illness with a state of sinfulness and able-bodiedness or health with repentance and faithfulness. Such discourses have served to marginalize and dehumanize many people who have been ill or disabled by blaming them for their condition. They have been accused of being sinful and considered to be unworthy of entering into communion with God without first becoming well or able-bodied. The healing narratives have thus been used abusively towards people who are ill or disabled with a view to reinforcing their places at the margins of religious and social structures and practices essentially because they are unable to conform to particular notions of normativity. Thomas Reynolds describes this in relation to people with disabilities as 'the tyranny of the normal'.[4]

Such approaches to and interpretations of the healing narratives in contemporary Christian practices have been deconstructed by a small number of disability theologians.[5] This chapter draws on their work of deconstruction and reconfiguration of the notion of salvation as healing, not as a practice of normalization, but as a praxis of commitment to the embodied well-being of human persons. It is proposed that salvation as healing is concerned with the well-being of the whole person, body, mind and spirit, and seeks to subvert practices that push people who are ill or disabled to the margins of society by calling for their restoration to full participation in society. This concept of 'salvation as healing' will be brought into critical conversation with questions of Christian engagement with people of other faiths in the twenty-first century, with a view to developing possible alternative Christian soteriological praxes towards people of other faiths.

Salvation as healing

Swinton argues that 'the Bible has no word for health' and that the 'closest approximation to contemporary understandings of health is the Hebrew word *shalom*' a word he translates as 'peace'.[6] However, in the New

---

[2]See the discussion in R. McCloughry and W. Morris, *Making a World of Difference: Christian Reflections on Disability* (London: SPCK, 2002), pp. 94–110.

[3]Ibid., pp. 96–101.

[4]T. Reynolds, *Vulnerable Communion: A Theology of Disability and Hospitality* (Grand Rapids, MI: Brazos Press, 2008), p. 69.

[5]See, for example, K. Black, *A Healing Homiletic: Preaching and Disability* (Nashville: Abingdon Press, 1996) and McCloughry and Morris, *Making a World of Difference*, pp. 94–110.

[6]J. Swinton, 'From Health to *Shalom*: Why the Religion and Health Debate Needs Jesus', in *Health to All Their Flesh: Jewish & Christian Perspectives on Spirituality, Theology & Health* (eds J. Levin and K. G. Meador; West Conshohocken, PA: Templeton Press, 2012), pp. 219–41 (233).

Testament there are at least two other words or concepts that refer to health, both of which are probably closer to the contemporary understanding of this concept: *therapeuw*, to cure or heal, and *swzw*, 'to save' or 'to be made well'. *Therapeuw* is the term that is closest to contemporary notions of health, as health is understood to be more focused on bodily conformation to a particular understanding of normativity. *Swzw*, however, has a much broader meaning and refers to the well-being of the person in their body, mind and spirit, conscious that such well-being is determined not only by biological and physical health, but also the extent to which a person is able to be in communion with other people and with God. This understanding of salvation can be further discovered, as it was noted in Chapter 2, by the English word 'salvation' which itself derives from the Latin *salve*, also meaning health.

In most English translations of the New Testament, *swzw* is not translated as 'to save' when it appears in the narratives in which a disabled, ill or demon-possessed person is 'cured' of their particular condition. Where *swzw* appears in the healing narratives, it is usually translated as 'made you well'. Notably this is in contrast to the translation of the term elsewhere in the New Testament.[7] Translators have made a hermeneutic decision about what precisely these texts mean, but the decision to translate *swzw* in this way has been informed by an underlying bias towards able-bodied normativity. In other words, it has largely been inconceivable to the translators that what Jesus was about in these texts was anything other than curing people of their various conditions rather than with the salvation of the person more broadly. This has led to a cycle of oppression where the translation is informed by able-bodied normativity and subsequently the text reinforces able-bodied normativity; and so it continues in perpetuity. When these texts have been considered to have soteriological significance, they have usually been interpreted as suggesting that if salvation means anything for disabled people, first they must enter a state of able-bodied normativity before they have even a chance of participating in a future post-mortem state of salvation. In developing an understanding of salvation as healing as a form of soteriological praxis, in what follows, it is necessary to resist these interpretations and instead try to recover something of the broader meaning of this approach to salvation in the New Testament as a concept concerned with holistic human health and well-being on earth, biologically, socially and spiritually.

The state from which salvation is necessary

Healing provides a way of speaking soteriologically that is rooted in the New Testament's so-called healing narratives. This term is used here to

---

[7]See for example the way the following uses of the verb are translated explicitly as 'to save' rather than 'to heal' or 'to make well' across a range of translations: Mark 13.20, Luke 23.35, John 12.27 and Acts 2.47.

refer to those narratives in which either Jesus or the apostles engage in acts whereby people who were thought to be ill, disabled, or demon-possessed experience embodied change. These stories occur in all of the four Gospels as well as in the Acts of the Apostles. Those who are shown to be in need of such a transformed existence include, 'all who were sick, those who were afflicted with various diseases and pains, demoniacs, epileptics, and paralytics' (Matthew 4.24). Others included people with leprosy (Matthew 8.2–4), a woman suffering with repeated haemorrhages (Matthew 9.20–22) 'two blind men' and 'a demoniac who was mute' (Matthew 9.27–34) another two blind men (Matthew 20.29–34), and a man who was Deaf (Mark 7.31–37).[8] These various conditions may be categorized under three broad headings: illness, disability (a contemporary way of referring to some of the conditions described) and demon-possession. Conditions that the New Testament describes as 'demon-possession' are not easily compared to any contemporary conditions. While much scholarship has suggested demon-possession was a way of speaking about particular forms of mental illness, care should be exercised in making such comparisons.[9] It is from one or more of these states that, it can be argued, the healing narratives suggest salvation is necessary.

While it is not clear how a twenty-first century audience should interpret and recognize conditions described as 'demon-possession', and while salvation from forms of suffering and pain that are caused by many illnesses seems uncontroversial, the concept of salvation as healing looks particularly problematic when the healing narratives are read in light of contemporary understandings of disability. New Testament narratives themselves suggest that disability was understood to be a punishment from God for the sin of the individual or even that of their parents, and often led to religious and social marginalization. The Bible is, of course, not clear but rather ambiguous on this point as these perspectives are both challenged in the New Testament (e.g. John 9.3) as well as endorsed (e.g. Mark 2.10–11). Because these texts also form part of the biblical canon for Christians, however, they have been understood to have timeless and universal significance by many, so that, read in light of a twenty-first century Western understanding of disability, the state of salvation appears to be constituted by a state of able-bodied normativity that many disabled people today would not welcome

---

[8]Other accounts of 'healing narratives' can be found in Matthew 8.28–9.8; 9.18–20 and 23–26; 17.14–23; Mark 1.29–34; 2.1–12; 5.1–43; 8.22–26; 9.14–32; Luke 4.31–44; 5.17–26; 7.1–17; 8.26–55; 9.37–45; 13.10–17; 17.11–19; 18.35–43; John 5.1–15; 9.1–12; 11.38–44; Acts 3.1–10; 5.12–16.

[9]It has often been assumed that demon-possession was a way of trying to understand mental illness, although H. J. Toensing '"Living among the Tombs": Societym Mental Illness, and Self-Destruction in Mark 5:1–20', in *This Abled Body: Rethinking Disabilities in Biblical Studies* (eds H. Avalos, S. J. Melcher and J. Schipper; Atlanta: Society of Biblical Literature, 2007), pp. 131–43, rightly warns of the dangers of equating contemporary diagnoses of mental illness with ancient understandings of demon-possession.

or desire. However, many people with disabilities, especially those born with a disability or those who's disability does not cause particular forms of physical pain and suffering, often interpret their disability as something that is not only positive, but is central to their understanding of their identity and humanity just as much as their gender or race. The saved state of salvation, therefore, could be understood as little more than transformation into a state of able-bodied normativity. Amos Yong argues, 'for mainstream Christian belief and piety, then, heaven represents the final overcoming and healing of disability once and for all'.[10] Thus the concept of salvation as healing is, for some, a theology that suggests that only through conformation to particular accepted norms can a person be saved.

As it was argued in Chapter 2, seeking normalization is not always an entirely negative notion. If a person with a body that does not have cancer, for example, is defined as 'normal', actively seeking to 'normalize' the person with cancer in this world or, at the very least hoping the cancer will be removed in some future eschatological world seems logical. Historically, the normal human being has, however, been much more narrowly defined. Indeed, it has been the white, European, Christian, heterosexual (or celibate), able-bodied male that has been determined as normative, an image that reflects those who construct such notions of normativity. Thus, as we have seen variously in this book, soteriological discourses of many kinds have been used to reinforce the normative human by insisting that in some way or other salvation will involve conformation to that notion of normativity. If salvation as healing is nothing more than a discourse that reinforces conformation to particular forms of normativity, be they of able-bodiedness for disabled people, or of Christian identity for people of other faiths, then this approach to salvation is itself a practice of normalization and so problematic for shaping alternative Christian praxes in a multi-faith world. It is precisely the agendas of normalization of people of other faiths that has been so catastrophic historically, resulting in much suffering, oppression and even deaths.

Rowan Williams, however, while recognizing that in the healing narratives, Jesus does indeed heal people and 'that's wonderful and everyone is very glad', he goes on to argue that 'the act of healing in these contexts is, again and again, subtly connected with different kinds of isolation, different kinds of alienation'.[11] Williams explains that 'in all these stories and in many, many more, what we have in Jesus' healings seems to be restoration of relation, inclusion in community'.[12] Thus it is arguable that the cure of the illness or disability was incidental to, or at least secondary to, the primary significance

---

[10]A. Yong, *Theology and Down Syndrome: Reimagining Disability in Late Modernity* (Waco: Baylor University Press, 2007), p. 267.
[11]R. Williams, 'A theology of health for today', in *Wounds that Heal: Theology, Imagination and Health* (ed. J. Baxter; London: SPCK, 2007), pp. 3–14 (6).
[12]Ibid., p. 7.

these stories have in the Gospels as narratives in which marginalized persons are restored to full participation in community.

Certainly many conditions now defined as disabilities or illnesses as well as conditions less easily identifiable in today's terms such as demon-possession would have led to social and religious marginalization and isolation. Many would have been understood to have not only been of little value to society economically, politically, or useful for the purposes of work, warfare or for the production of children,[13] but many would also have been understood to be ritually impure, untouchable, and therefore necessarily living outside of towns and villages and communities for fear of 'contamination'.[14] Because illnesses and disabilities were understood as more than biological or physiological conditions, if the acts of healing in these narratives were soteriological in nature, they were as much concerned with the transformation of the place of individuals in society as they were with the transformation of bodies to able-bodied norms. In healing, restoring the body so as to be socially 'acceptable' and ritually clean, full participation in society was possible for those who would otherwise have remained on the margins indefinitely. Salvation was thus from social isolation and marginalization as much as it was from physiological and biological conditions that the ancient world understood prevented human beings from living full lives. If healing can be considered to be not primarily about normalization, and such an understanding of salvation that seeks normativity is to be rejected, then what else might the healing narratives suggest about the state from which salvation is necessary? What is proposed here is that salvation as healing is concerned with addressing states of suffering and pain in the body, mind and spirit that resulted from a complex mix of physiological and biological conditions. Because of the way such conditions have been constructed socially and religiously, people living with these conditions were socially isolated and marginalized, so salvation as healing is concerned with the transformation of such constructed practices of oppression. This approach to salvation is further concerned to name and resist the systemic and institutional sins that, to varying degrees, may be responsible for both the physiological suffering experienced and social and religious practices of exclusion, conscious that often the two are not mutually exclusive to one another.

The saved state: Embodied well-being

The notion of 'healing' as an approach to thinking about salvation has shaped Christian soteriological practices towards people of other faiths, so

---

[13]C. R. Fontaine, '"Be Men, O Philistines" (1 Samuel 4.9): Iconographic Representations and Reflections on Female Gender as Disability in the Ancient World', in *This Abled Body: Rethinking Disabilities in Biblical Studies* (eds H. Avalos, S. J. Melcher and J. Schipper; Atlanta: Society of Biblical Literature, 2007), pp. 61–72.

[14]Yong, *Theology and Down Syndrome*, p. 23.

that mission practice, the propogation of a Christian gospel, has become a practice of insistent conformation to Christian normativity in matters of belief, culture and practice. If the healing narratives do nothing more than suggest that to be saved is to be conformed to the likeness of a white, Western, Christian, heterosexual, able-bodied male, then this approach to salvation takes us in the very direction from which this book seeks to move away. Williams' proposal for an alternative reading and interpretation of the healing narratives is therefore necessary if this approach to salvation is to have currency and relevance for Christian engagement with people of other faiths in the world today.

The healing narratives may indeed be interpreted as Williams proposes, and he is not alone in seeking to reinterpret these texts.[15] However, in his 'Introduction' to Ruether's book, *Faith and Fratricide*, Baum rightly cautions against the way theologians will sometimes seek to reinterpret problematic texts and traditions that pose problems for contemporary understandings of aspects of human life and experience to make them more palatable to contemporary audiences.[16] Such an apologetic approach to the Bible too readily ignores the realities that sometimes certain texts and traditions are offensive, and no amount of reinterpretation will resolve that. Conscious of this, any alternative reading of the healing narratives should not seek to downplay the very real offence that has been caused to some people with disabilities who read them. That Jesus always removes a person's disability when encountering a disabled person cannot really be refuted. Notwithstanding that these ancient texts written in another context can cause offence in the present context, is there any way in which the notion of healing might be developed constructively as a form of soteriological praxis? If Williams is right that the healing narratives, read at a deeper level, are much more concerned with the transformation of social isolation and marginalization, albeit by misguided means, then what might an alternative saved state of salvation look like in this approach? In formulating a response to these questions, it is argued that reinterpreting the healing narratives is no mere biblical apologetic, but an attempt at a more faithful and careful re-reading of these texts.

As we have seen, it is certainly the case that many of the people whom Jesus heals were isolated and marginalized both socially and religiously and there is considerable evidence of this in the healing narratives themselves. When Jesus stands up in the temple and reads from Isaiah a text that is thought to be significant for interpreting the remainder of Luke's Gospel (Luke 4.17–19), blind people are singled out alongside captives, the oppressed and the poor, suggesting that blindness could be understood as akin to captivity, oppression and poverty, experiences of social and religious

---

[15]For example, ibid, pp. 21–27.
[16]G. Baum, 'Introduction', in *Faith and Fratricide: The Theological Roots of Anti-Semitism* (ed. R. R. Ruether; Eugene, OR: Wipf & Stock, 1997), pp. 2–3.

marginalization and isolation. In Luke 5.1–13, a man thought to be demon-possessed is completely socially isolated, living among tombs on the other side of the lake and whom others had sought to restrain with chains. Jesus' liberation of this man was as much from captivity as from the possession by a demon. The blind man of John 9.1–12 and the physically disabled man in Acts 3.1–10 are both described as 'beggars' while the woman with haemorrhages in Luke 8.43–48 is said to have spent everything she had on seeking a cure. We can assume, therefore, that living with disability invariably meant living in a state of poverty. John 5.1–15 describes a man who has no one to help him to enter a pool, while people around him step over him to get into the pool themselves. This man is invisible to others in society. Others who are healed include children (e.g. Matthew 17.14–23), a (probably) non-Jewish servant of a Roman Centurion (Matthew 8.15–13) and people with leprosy, a condition that demanded isolation because it was thought to be especially contagious.

In these passages, therefore, healing is characterized not by becoming able-bodied, but by full participation in social and religious practices, opportunities to be in relationship with other human beings, an end to economic poverty and to be viewed as a full human being rather than as someone to be ignored or stepped over. Perhaps in an Ancient Near Eastern context, where 'disability' would have been understood differently, the only conceivable way of achieving this kind of transformed reality for those who were isolated and marginalized was through the removal of the condition that was seen to be the cause of their religious and social exclusion. However, if the healing narratives can be understood as concerned principally with marginalization and isolation, and the removal of an illness or disability was a means by which such situations were transformed, then the healed, saved state of salvation is not one of 'cure' but of social and religious participation. The removal of the condition was simply the way that this new saved state was realized. That saved state is a condition in which human beings are able to be in full, loving and equal relationships with others that lead to human flourishing, where those historically at the margins are brought to the centre, where false justifications for marginalization and poverty are subverted and economic equality is sought for all. Understood in this way, the saved state of salvation as healing might have an alternative and constructive contribution to make to thinking about Christian soteriological praxis in a multi-faith world as will be discussed shortly.

It is not appropriate, however, to limit the interpretation of the healing narratives only to questions of social marginalization and isolation and to pretend the transformation of the body did not matter at all. We will return to this point further in relation to the way Jesus engages with the people he heals or saves in a moment. It is important to note, here, however that while the healed state involves the establishing of practices whereby human beings can live more fully in community, that is arguably realized through paying attention to the earthly, concrete, embodied well-being of the persons involved. The health and well-being of the body and mind matter as much as the restoration of the person to full participation in society, and so a body and mind that is 'well' and a person that can participate fully in society is a person whom we can describe as 'healed' or 'saved'. The wellness of the body and the wellness of the person in relation to other embodied persons are mutual characteristics of salvation as healing. However, it is not simply in making ill people well and in making disabled people able-bodied that this care for the body is expressed in these narratives but rather in the soteriological praxes of Jesus.

Realizing salvation

The healing narratives represent a particular concern for the embodied well-being of the person. Indeed, to be 'well', however understood, is a part of the New Testament's presentation of the notion of salvation. Given that it is Jesus who is the 'healer', the ways in which he engages in the practices of healing are paradigmatic for thinking about a model of soteriological praxis. This resonates with the way Delores Williams and Rosemary Radford Ruether, discussed in Chapter 2, have both focused on the life and work of Jesus as having soteriological significance over the death on the cross, noting that the life and actions of Jesus can serve as a model for Christian practices of salvation.

It is noteworthy that some interpretations of the healing narratives, read from the perspectives of people with disabilities, recognize that while the normalization of disabled bodies is problematic in these texts, the praxis of Jesus reveals a particular care and concern for the needs of the person in front of him. One example can be found in a contemporary Deaf woman's reading of the healing of a Deaf man in Mark 7.31–37. Vera Hunt explains that in her readings of this narrative her attention is drawn not to the removal of the man's lack of hearing, but to the way Jesus attends to the man's needs. She explains that when Jesus spits on the ground and touches the man's ears she observes 'a physical touch of love and compassion – an acknowledgement that deaf people should be accepted'.[17] Visual acts and interaction through touch are very much part of the way that Deaf people communicate with one another. Hunt interprets Jesus' actions as emerging out of an understanding of Deaf people's needs and a willingness to meet with and communicate with the Deaf man on his terms. Others have noted the way that Jesus removes the Deaf man from the crowd in this narrative.[18] Because most Deaf people have some residual hearing, noisy environments

[17]V. Hunt, 'The Place of Deaf People in the Church', in *The Place of Deaf People in the Church* (eds International Ecumenical Working Group; Northampton: Visible Communications, 1996), pp. 20–33 (24).
[18]See discussion in W. Morris, *Theology without Words: Theology in the Deaf Community* (Aldershot: Ashgate, 2008), pp. 103–04.

can be extremely uncomfortable for Deaf people. In taking the Deaf man away from the crowd, the man is less distracted by the indecipherable noises around him and able to focus visually on who is in front of him, Jesus. Remarkably, Mark then records Jesus' use of the word 'Ephphatha', an Aramaic term presented and translated in a text that is otherwise written in Greek. It has been noted that this could be easily lip-read, unlike the Greek *dianoichtheti*, where all the sounds are created at the back of the mouth.[19] Such insights as these into the text could only come from a Deaf person. What is transformative – soteriological – is not, I argue, the act of removing the man's Deafness, but the praxis of Jesus. Jesus recognizes the specific context and circumstances of the person in front of him and responds to embodied needs of the Deaf man. Jesus treats the Deaf man as a human being, as someone different but equal, and as someone worthy of attention in the man's Deaf state. This attention and care to the specific needs of the Deaf man is transformative perhaps not only of the Deaf man himself as he encounters treatment he would have not often received, but perhaps these actions were transformative of the entire crowd observing the scene. Jesus removes the Deaf man's social and religious marginalization and isolation and restores him to a place of full participation in community. Read in this way, the praxis of Jesus becomes central to the story and the removal of the man's Deafness is merely incidental, a culturally specific means of achieving a particular end.

Elsewhere, Jesus' praxis can be interpreted as the focus of at least some of the healing narratives. There are a number occasions in the healing narratives, for example, when Jesus appears to make a link between disability and sin, and healing and forgiveness.[20] In John's Gospel, however, Jesus rejects the link between sin and disability in the narrative of the healing of a man who is born blind. In John 9.2–3, the disciples of Jesus are reported to have asked 'Rabbi, who sinned, this man or his parents, that he was born blind?' Jesus responds, saying, 'Neither this man nor his parents sinned; he was born blind so that God's works might be revealed in him'. That the disciples ask this question in such a 'matter-of-fact' way suggests that it was widely accepted that disability was caused either by an individual's or their parents' sin. Jesus, however, makes an explicit disconnect between the condition of blindness and sin in this passage so that Jesus' words, at least here, reject any idea that a person is disabled because they are being punished for sin. Jesus subverts the socially constructed and accepted norms surrounding disability that the disciples assume to be matters of fact. These words, this radical praxis in contrast to accepted conventions and understandings reinterprets how disability can be understood as something good and positive; salvation is not dependent on normalization but, instead, the man's blindness, his

---

[19]Ibid., pp. 103–04.
[20]Luke 5.20–24 tells the story of the healing of a paralysed man and a strong link appears to be made here between the man's inability to walk and sin.

difference from socially and religiously constructed normativity, is a vehicle through which God's glory is 'revealed' (John 9.3).

John 9 is not without its difficulties for disabled people, just like most of the healing narratives. Not only is the man's blindness taken away which would not be desirable for many blind people, the image of blindness is then used as a metaphor for stubbornness and ignorance while the image of sight implies understanding and insight. John Hull has developed an important critique of this use of the metaphor of blindness in the Bible and in Christian traditions more broadly.[21] In this story, however, the praxis of Jesus does in some ways resonate with that of the healing of the Deaf man in Mark 7. Once again, Jesus engages in a physical tangible act of communication with the blind man who is in front of him. It can often be disorientating for a blind person to be in a crowd without contact with anyone or anything, unsure of what is happening around them. Locating someone you know or finding the person that you have been seeking out provides a significant amount of reassurance. Jesus engages with the man who is blind through touch, reassures them of his presence and communicates with them in a way that is meaningful to them. Jesus spits on the ground, creates some mud and wipes it on the man's eyes (John 9.6). Such an alternative reading of the narrative as that described above once again provides insights into the story that would not otherwise be found. This reading reveals insights into Jesus' praxes that become the locus of soteriological transformation. This man is in a minority in a crowd, unsure of what is going on around him, feeling insecure in the midst of people who do not understand him and have no desire to try to do so. His exclusion is not just religious and social, but embodied too. Jesus transforms the man's experience by engaging with him, reassuring him, touching him, striving to understand and engage with the man on his terms, treating him as an equal, a person of value and worth, bringing the person from the margins into full participation in the event.

One further note on the praxis of Jesus that has emerged out of disabled person's readings of these texts pertains to a question that Jesus often asks of the person in front of him: 'What do you want me to do for you?' (e.g. Mark 10.51). This question empowers the person who is ill, disabled, or thought to be demon-possessed, by ensuring the decision about what will happen to them is theirs. The removal of any kind of condition in these narratives invariably is not, therefore, imposed, but chosen. By implication, the removal of a disability, illness, or release from demon-possession is potentially only one outcome of the encounter with Jesus. There is a possibility of a multiplicity of potential new transformed existences and any particular form of salvation is not imposed on to anyone. While some disabled people feel angry with other people who are disabled and choose to have their

---

[21]J. M. Hull, *In the Beginning There was Darkness* (London: SCM Press, 2001), pp. 49–50 and J. M. Hull, '"Sight to the Inly Blind"? Attitudes to Blindness in the Hymnbooks', *Theology* CV(827), (2002), pp. 333–41.

disability taken away where that is possible, one of the key characteristics of
the disability movement has been the emphasis placed on giving people with
disabilities choice and the space to exercise autonomy over their own lives.[22]
The mantra of the disability rights movement from the 1980s onwards was
'Nothing about us without us'.[23] Jesus does not impose a state of embodied
normalization or cure onto those whom he encounters in these stories, but
instead empowers those whom he meets to choose their preferred state of
salvation, perhaps recognizing that salvation is not one universal state of
existence, but many possible alternative realities.

Summary: Salvation as healing

In all of the healing narratives, Jesus interacts physically with people who are
considered to be ritually impure and subsequently socially and religiously
outcast. To have touched the woman with the haemorrhage, for example,
would have led to Jesus himself becoming ritually impure. He touches a
woman deemed to be untouchable but, in so doing, her actions and his
touch transforms the impurity and subsequent exclusion into a new saved
state. Jesus' healing praxes subvert social and religious conventions and
expectations in a way that leads to a transformed existence in the present
for those whom he encounters. Such acts are transformative not only for the
persons involved, but potentially for the wider society too. In transgressing
social and religious boundaries that have been established to keep human
beings separate from one another, those who observe these acts of healing,
then and now, are likewise challenged to deconstruct practices of oppression
and marginalization. The person who was seen as 'other' and 'different', as in
some way 'less than human', is treated in another way by Jesus, through acts
that lead to the embodied well-being of each person who is encountered. The
person is enabled to participate fully in society, and this is achieved through
Jesus treating the person in front of him humanely, with care and respect for
their wishes and for their particular embodied needs. Drawing on traditions
such as that of Thomas a Kempis' *imitatio Christi*,[24] such praxes become
examples for Christian soteriological praxis today.

　　Perhaps the removal of a disability in the ancient world did constitute the
desirable state of well-being that persons with disabilities longed to have.
In a more contemporary context, however, for a hearing person to be well
means to be in a state of being able to hear, while for a Deaf person, to
be in a state of wellness may involve remaining in their Deaf condition.[25]
Contemporary responses to the question, 'What do you want me to do for

---

[22]See further discussion on this in Chapter 7.
[23]McCloughry and Morris, *Making a World of Difference*, p. 14.
[24]T. À Kempis, *The Imitation of Christ* (London: Fount, 1996).
[25]Morris, *Theology without Words*, p. 138.

you?' may well be different to those of the ancient world, but this question serves as a reminder that human persons are empowered to construct states of salvation and not to have them imposed upon them. In the contemporary world, there will be many different responses to Jesus' question. Wellness, health, the saved state of the body and the person in society cannot be universally determined categories because this is usually defined according to notions such as that of able-bodied normativity, which as we already have seen, creates ideals that serve to dehumanize some people over others.

However, salvation as a state of wellness, contextually understood, provides an important contribution to thinking about salvation in which the well-being of the human body in relation to the mind and spirit, together with the potential to engage with other human persons in community and society matters. The body matters and its well-being matters at every level of encounter, so that to engage in the praxis of salvation, means to attend to the well-being of human persons in the way that Jesus models. Conscious of the dangers of normalization that these narratives may encourage, the emphasis on salvation as healing is not on the cure of persons, but on the transformative praxis of Jesus that leads to a state of embodied well-being. Let us now bring this approach to salvation into conversation with the focus of this book: Christian soteriological praxis in a multi-faith world.

Salvation as healing: Critical conversations

Constructing new communities

It has been argued that healing as salvation is not simply concerned with a restoration of human bodies to a socially or politically constructed concept of normativity but, more importantly, it exercises a concern at a deeper level with overcoming marginalization and isolation. This 'tyranny of the normal' must be resisted in any attempt to reconstruct communities and societies in which those who exist in isolation or at the margins find ways of sharing public and communal spaces fully with everyone else. Christianity has been the dominant faith community of Europe for centuries and has become dominant also in the Americas, Australasia and parts of Africa and Asia too. It is a global movement, or more precisely a group of related movements that represent almost one third of the entire population of the planet. While Christianity's significance and influence has declined somewhat in Western societies, the way that Christianity has shaped Western cultures, philosophies and ways of living remains significant. In Chapter 3, when Bush invoked the language of the Crusades to justify his 'war on terror' the role of Christian language and thinking in Western contexts could not be more obvious. While contexts such as the United Kingdom, for example, are and, to varying degrees, always have been multi-faith contexts, the presence of people of other faiths has increased in number and visibility since the Second World War. One key challenge that has emerged has been related to how people of different faith communities and traditions, perhaps with conflicting views, share the same local, and increasingly global, spaces peacefully and graciously?

Miroslav Volf warns of the dangers of the language of 'inclusion'. His principal concern is that when communities and societies talk about 'inclusion', what is often meant is ways of developing mechanisms and systems whereby those at the margins or in isolation can 'fit' into the already existent way of doing things without the majority, or those exercising the greatest amount of power and control having to change at all.[26] Too many initiatives of Western governments to foster cohesive societies and nations of people of diverse ethnic and religious traditions have understood 'inclusion' in the way that Volf argues is so problematic. An inclusive society is thus envisaged as one in which people of different faith and spiritual pathways are encouraged, sometimes even forced to conform to the way that the majority population operates.

As already indicated, common norms for people who are different to be able to share the same space are essential, but become oppressive if the only voice that is heard in the construction of those norms are those of the powerful. If the notion of healing is to provide an alternative form of Christian soteriological praxis in a multi-faith world, the kind of communities that are created will need be formed as the result of attention being paid to all voices, but especially those who are often in minorities, or at the margins or isolated. If the saved state is one in which such isolation and marginalization of minority faith communities is to be transformed in contexts such as the United Kingdom, perhaps the praxis of Jesus might inform practice in this area. It calls us to ask the question that Jesus asked of many of those who came to him for healing, 'What do you want me to do for you?' New diverse multi-faith communities will surely only become positive and life-affirming spaces if the voices of all who make up those communities are involved in the constructive process and there is an openness to the possibility of multiple ways of living graciously together. Perhaps this principle applies to the global community too. As Western nations informed by Christian traditions and legacies engage with people in many different parts of the world, as we saw in Chapter 3, this is often shaped by an imposition of Western capitalist and democratic systems and structures. The assumed rightness of Western normativity is merely imposed onto groups who may not want it. Salvation as healing helps to challenge such practices and construct a praxis of creating new societies in which the voices of all are heard and contribute to creating an alternative state of salvation.

---

[26]M. Volf, *Exclusion & Embrace: A Theological Exploration of Identity, Otherness, and Reconciliation* (Nashville: Abingdon Press, 1996), p. 78.

The praxis of Jesus: Well-being and care for the body

In Chapter 2, it was argued that the dominant Christian understanding of salvation has involved the Christian seeking to escape from their bodies, as though their bodies were prisons preventing them from entering into communion with God. In Chapter 3, it was argued that salvation has been used to justify many kinds of atrocities to human bodies, such as sacrificing one's own or another's body through the shedding of blood to satisfy God's honour. The Holocaust, the murder of six million Jews, a hatred of a religious people that was, in part justified and made possible by a history of Christian anti-Semitism further exposes a tradition in which embodied human life has often been seen as of little value. While Christian traditions have, on the one hand, advocated a view that all human life is sacred,[27] on the other hand, the body and the life it contains has been understood as disposable, a prison and barrier to life in all its fullness. The healing narratives, it is proposed, offer an alternative understanding of the body and of the value of human life. They suggest that practices that lead to the realization of the embodied well-being of human persons in this world, including people of other faiths, are forms of Christian soteriological praxis.

To speak of healing is to speak of a concern for the well-being of the human in this world and the desire for the body to be in a state of wholeness. This is perhaps best understood, however, not simply as the normalization of bodies, the problems of which have already been discussed, but in the praxis of Jesus and his care for human embodied well-being. It has been proposed that in Jesus' praxis, read from disability perspectives, there is a particular care shown for the needs of the person who has come to him for healing. Not only does Jesus often empower the individual to tell him what they would like him to do, he also appears to show a particular awareness of the specific needs of the person in front of him and responds to them on their terms. He meets a person as an equal, as a friend, gives them autonomy and powers to make decisions about their own lives, he communicates and engages with them in a way they are likely to understand. The healing narratives are less of an imposition of a form of normativity onto anyone, but rather a radical subversion of practices of exclusion, marginalization and isolation.

The formation of new communities discussed above, in the first instance suggests that soteriological praxis is orientated towards the well-being of human persons in this world through finding means through which the full participation of everyone can be realized. Through relationships of equality between human persons, embodied well-being is fostered. However, that

[27]This has been particularly the case in Roman Catholic arguments surrounding ethical questions such as abortion or euthanasia.

the body is well is not unrelated to the place of bodies in relation to others in communities and it is no coincidence that the social marginalization of people of other faiths in Western contexts, for example is expressed in, among other things, poverty and the subsequent impact this usually has on the well-being of the body. The same can be said of the marginalization and isolation of non-Western nations by powerful, rich, Western countries, politically and economically and the impact this has on, for example, life expectancy. It was noted above that the social marginalization and isolation of many ill, demon-possessed and disabled people led to economic deprivation, a state that would only have worsened the well-being and state of the body too. The restoration to community had economic and social ramifications and therefore impacted on the well-being of the body too. If conformation to a particular state of embodiedness was not imposed, but rather chosen by those in the healing narratives, there is a sense in which the healing narratives represent Jesus' care for the body, not as something from which to be escaped, but as something that is of value and worth, the well-being of which is of paramount importance. Soteriological praxis in this model, therefore, is not orientated towards enabling people to escape from their bodies or to shed blood and harm bodies for sake of satisfying God's honour. Rather the state of salvation itself is a state of human, embodied well-being, and Christian soteriological praxis should be oriented towards realizing that in multi-faith contexts.

The healed wounds of Jesus: Remembering the past, transforming the future

In working towards such a possible earthly future, this soteriological understanding is perhaps usefully interpreted in light of Nancy Eiesland's understanding of the resurrected Christ as the disabled God.[28] The Christ of the resurrection, who bears the wounds of the cross in his hands, side and feet represents for Eiesland a God who embodies the paradox of woundedness and wholeness. Christ's resurrected divine body signifies for Eiesland a resistance to the sin of oppression for, while the wounds remain, they do so as a part of the body of the resurrected Christ who has subverted and overcome the sins that led to his death on the cross. These wounds that remain in the body of Christ suggest, for Eiesland, that woundedness and wholeness are compatible with each other.[29] Salvation as healing, therefore, may involve a person's body being transformed, but that transformation for Jesus did not mean conformation to able-bodied normativity. This is potentially significant in two key ways.

---

[28]N. L. Eiesland, *The Disabled God: Toward a Liberatory Theology of Disability* (Nashville: Abingdon Press, 1994), pp. 89–105.
[29]Ibid., p. 100.

First, Christ's wounded resurrected body is not transformed into a conforming able-bodied body and therefore it can be argued that embodied well-being is not the same as able-bodied normativity. Second, the wounded resurrected Christ stands as a sign that the sin of the cross is overcome, suffering is transformed and the powers of oppression are subverted and resisted. But the wounds of the cross remain, the body that has become as it is by being a part of this world remains in a wounded state. The wounds serve as a reminder, in the praxis of Jesus, that the sins that have caused suffering and pain in the past are not wiped away by working towards an alternative possible future. The wounds remain, or perhaps more accurately, the wounds may heal, but the scars will remain.[30] The wounds or scars of the resurrected Christ serve as a reminder that the injustices and sins of the past cannot be forgotten or ignored, but need to be continually acknowledged as at the foundation of the Christian motivation for creating a new and better future. The wounds and scars of people of other faiths at the hands of Christians throughout history cannot be taken away and history forgotten, the scars of sin are permanent, but the causes of the sins and even the wounds beneath the scars can perhaps be healed.

Subverting normalization: An alternative mission praxis

It has been argued that Christian approaches to people of other faiths have for centuries been dominated by agendas of normalization and conformation to Christians beliefs and practices. As a minority faith of the Roman empire in its early stages, Christianity was one spiritual pathway among many and there were many different expressions of Christian belief and practice within Christianity itself. Following Constantine's reunification of the Roman empire, he began to use Christianity to consolidate his power. Woodhead argues that what Christianity offered to Constantine was 'an exclusivist, universalist, monopolistic monotheism focused on a single, all-powerful God'[31] and, as Ariarajah argues, seeking religious unity served to secure him political unity too.[32] For Ariarajah it is the legacy of Constantine's association of Christianity with the empire that has shaped Christian approaches to people of other faiths. No longer was equivocity of theology and practice tolerated within Christianity, hence the initiation of

---

[30]This draws on the concept of the 'wounded healer' developed in H. J. M. Nouwen, *The Wounded Healer* (London: Darton, Longman & Todd, 2008).

[31]L. Woodhead, *An Introduction to Christianity* (Cambridge: Cambridge University Press, 2004), p. 9.

[32]S. W. Ariarajah, 'Power, Politics and Plurality: The Struggles of the World Council of Churches to Deal with Religious Plurality', in *The Myth of Religious Superiority* (ed. P. F. Knitter; New York, NY: Orbis Books, 2005), p. 178.

Church Councils to provide authoritative definitions on matters theological and practical. However, Christianity also could not tolerate any other rival religious or spiritual pathway. Christianity served Constantine's unification agenda well, forcing the empire's peoples to conform to one single religious authority: Christianity, and their imperial leader, Constantine.[33]

This has shaped Christian approaches to mission ever since, so that the normalization of people of other faiths has been understood to be necessary for the survival of Christianity. Ariarajah argues that 'when Islam sprang up and began to expand, the church responded much the same way an empire would to the rise of a rival power. The instinctive response was to see Islam as an illegitimate rival religious tradition'.[34] If Woodhead and Ariarajah are right about the origins of Christianity's agenda of insisting on its own superiority and that all other religious and spiritual pathways are illegitimate, and the evidence is substantial in favour of their cases as we saw in Chapter 3, then responding to the normalization discourses that have found their way into Christian soteriologies needs to begin with an acknowledgement of these origins. The normalization of people with disabilities is arguably rooted in the fear of difference or in fear that people with disabilities represent human vulnerability, contingency and even mortality. The normalization agenda of Christian churches towards people of other faiths is, however, rooted in a historical tradition of imperialism. Christianity secured its position by becoming the religion of a state that dominated other less powerful nations and tolerated no rivals. It was imperative that in order to maintain its position, Christianity also insisted that human beings could either submit to the authority of the dominant and powerful discourses of the state or else face marginalization, isolation or even obliteration. Soteriologies were developed to reinforce this 'presumption of superiority' and to justify imperialistic practices of normalization of people of other faiths and spiritual pathways. The mission practices of the Crusades and colonialism, together with centuries of anti-Semitic practice and various forms of neo-colonialism can all be understood as practices of normalization informed by a sense of Christian and subsequently Western superiority.

Soteriological discourses have reinforced this approach to difference. Dominant soteriological discourses have argued that it is necessary to conform to Christian normativity, or else face the consequences, an eternity of damnation. If this imperial agenda of unification and conformation to a single rule of law has so shaped Christianity and its theologies and practices of salvation, then in acknowledging the origins of this agenda provides a basis for deconstructing the practices of normalization of people of other faiths. Experience suggests that it is possible for human beings to live together differently without a threat to political and social unity, and many societies have lived with religious difference without always resorting to the

---

[33]Ibid.
[34]Ibid.

imposition of one pathway over another. If the political need for religious conformity and superiority over people of other faiths is no longer needed to secure the position of an emperor, and this has anyway been shown to be destructive and inconsistent with a Gospel of liberation, then alternative theologies of salvation need to be developed. No longer need mission and evangelistic practices be driven by conformation to Christian forms of normativity out of a fear of other religions perceived as rival powers. Rather, in following the example of Jesus, mission can be motivated by praxes that seek the embodied well-being of all human beings relationally, economically and bodily, including and especially towards people of other faiths.

Conclusion

Salvation as healing draws on an ancient soteriological tradition rooted in the New Testament that have historically been interpreted to reinforce agendas of normalization in particular towards people with disabilities. The healing narratives attend to 'making well' three conditions: illness, disability and demon-possession. The notion of healing in these narratives, however, it has been argued, is less concerned with imposing a form of embodied normativity and more concerned with realizing various expressions of embodied well-being. This praxis of salvation is modelled by Jesus attention to the specific needs of those whom society has ostracized and left isolated and Jesus subversion of established social and religious conventions. Salvation as healing, however, pays attention to the transformation of the lives of those who experience imposed marginalization and isolation from full participation in society and a care for the well-being of the body itself. If salvation can be understood to involve the creation of communities in which people of all kinds of difference have a place, and the well-being of bodies are cared for, this provides an important corrective and alternative to soteriological discourses and practices of the past that have led to the Christian 'presumption of superiority' and acts of violence, war and genocide towards people of other faiths.

7

'God of the Oppressed': Salvation as liberation

Introduction

In this final chapter, the notion of salvation as liberation is brought into the conversation. Liberation is a soteriological theme that can be discovered in ancient Hebrew texts in which God saved Israel from slavery. However, during the second half of the twentieth century, the notion of liberation was developed or, perhaps given its ancient roots rediscovered, in theologies emerging out of contexts and perspectives whose voices have historically been marginalized or silenced altogether. This concept of salvation as liberation provides the third framework for thinking about salvation as praxis that, it is argued, when brought into conversation with how Christian communities, institutions and individuals think about and act towards people of other faiths, might lead to a transformed 'saved' state for this world that seeks discontinuity with many of the travesties of the past. This chapter will thus first, explore the early developments of liberation theology, focusing in particular on the ways in which liberation as a soteriological theme emerged. Second, what might be termed the 'characteristics' of salvation as liberation will be outlined. Finally, this approach to salvation will be brought into critical conversation with questions regarding Christian beliefs and practices towards people of other faiths. In particular, the notion of 'God's preferential option for the poor' in their struggles for liberation will be the focus of this section.

Twentieth century liberation theologies:
Early developments

The concept of liberation as a way of speaking about the possible transformation of societies, in particular in the second half of the twentieth century, is not unique to theology. As Rivera-Pagan notes, it was a term coined by many different groups in the middle of the twentieth century who were variously struggling against patriarchy, racism, the war in Vietnam, homophobia and in student protests against repressive governments.[1] He explains, 'many of these agents of social protest adopted the title of "liberation movement" as the public card of presentation'.[2] It is no surprise, therefore, that by the end of the 1960s, this term had found its way into theological discourses that were likewise concerned with social and ecclesial change among those historically pushed to the margins of the churches and society. Gustavo Gutierrez explains that 'the name and reality of "liberation theology" came into existence'[3] at a conference in Chimbote, Peru, in a lecture he gave titled 'Toward a Theology of Liberation'.[4] This took place just before the famous conference at Medellin in July 1968. Rivera-Pagan, however, suggests that it was the 'final documents and the general tone prevailing in the [Medellin] conference'[5] that paved the way for liberation theology to be taken seriously in the church and academy, especially in Latin America. The conference at Medellin and its discourses on the poor of Latin America and the need for their 'liberation', affirmed later at Puebla, is described by Rowland as 'epoch-making' with its 'explicit commitment to take a "preferential option for the poor"'.[6] In 1971, Gutierrez's 'landmark'[7] book, *A Theology of Liberation,* was published outlining his particular critique of the sins of poverty and injustice in Latin America, the processes by which transformation might take place, and what the alternative reality might be like. Subsequently, many more books followed from a variety of Latin American contexts dedicated to themes of poverty, theology and liberation, building on the foundations of Medellin and Gutierrez. These theologies of liberation that emerged out of Latin America during the 1970s

---

[1] L. N. Rivera-Pagan, 'God the Liberator: Theology, History and Politics', in *In Our Own Voices: Latino/a Renditions of Theology* (ed. B. Valentin; Maryknoll, NY: Orbis Books, 2010), pp. 1–20 (2).

[2] Ibid., p. 2.

[3] G. Gutierrez, *A Theology of Liberation: History, Politics and Salvation* (London: SCM Press, rev. edn, 1988), p. xviii.

[4] Ibid.

[5] Rivera-Pagan, 'God the Liberator', p. 4.

[6] C. Rowland, 'Introduction: the theology of liberation', in *The Cambridge Companion to Liberation Theology* (ed. C. Rowland; Cambridge: Cambridge University Press, 2nd edn, 2007), pp. 1–16 (5).

[7] Rivera-Pagan, 'God the Liberator', p. 4.

and 1980s in particular must surely be understood as one of the most important and influential theological global movements of the twentieth century.

Latin America was not the only context, however, in which the concept of liberation as a theological theme could be found. Just as the Roman Catholic bishops and theologians of Latin America had been inspired to think about liberation theologically by the struggles in their own contexts against repressive political rulers and large-scale economic poverty, so in North America, inspired by the civil rights movement, liberation became a theological principle informing a new kind of 'black theology'. Rivera-Pagan rightly argues that the notion of struggle, resistance and transformation dates back much earlier among African Americans than during the period of the civil rights movements and can be found in the early songs of 'defiance' sung by slaves more than a century earlier.[8] Two years after Medellin and one year prior to the publication of Gutierrez landmark text, James Cone published *A Black Theology of Liberation*. As we have already seen, Cone proposed that 'Christianity is essentially a religion of liberation'.[9] By this, he argued, Christian theology has a role in 'analyzing the meaning of that liberation for the oppressed so they can know that their struggle for political, social, and economic justice is consistent with the Gospel of Jesus Christ'.[10] As Gutierrez's text was a landmark in the development of theologies of liberation in Latin America, so James Cone initiated new ways of thinking about theology and race with a particular focus on salvation as liberation. Both Gutierrez's and Cone's theologies proposed that the condition from which salvation was needed, the process by which it could be achieved and the desired state of salvation, each related to concrete earthly realities.

Rivera-Pagan further notes a third strand in the development or rediscovery of the concept of liberation as a soteriological motif, that is, those developed by particular feminist theologians. Most notably, he identifies the works of Letty Russell, Elisabeth Schussler-Fiorenza and Phyllis Trible, citing Schussler-Fiorenza's, *In Memory of Her,* as perhaps the most influential text, though by no means the earliest. Other key voices in feminist theology and liberation can also be found in the works of Rosemary Radford Ruether and Mary Grey whose contributions to thinking about both redemption and liberation have been foundational to much subsequent feminist soteriological discourse including and beyond feminist perspectives.[11] While Gutierrez was influenced by social and political movements in his own context alongside

---

[8]Ibid., p. 9.

[9]J. Cone, *A Black Theology of Liberation: Twentieth Anniversary Edition* (New York, NY: Orbis Books, 1990), p. v.

[10]Ibid.

[11]See for example, R. R. Ruether, *Women and Redemption: A Theological History* (Minneapolis: Fortress Press, 2nd edn, 2012) and M. Grey, *Redeeming the Dream: Feminism, Redemption and the Christian Tradition* (London: SPCK, 1989).

Marxist philosophy, and Cone was influenced by the civil rights movement, so also feminist theology was inspired by the wider feminist movement, much of which can also be dated back to a much earlier period than the second half of twentieth century, not least those women who campaigned for voting rights a century earlier (though Ruether looks at women's voices in theology in much earlier periods too[12]).

Early feminist perspectives on liberation, as with Latin American liberation theology and black theology faced in two principle directions: first towards society with a view to transforming poverty, racism, and patriarchy and secondly, to the church, to deconstruct theologies and practices that lead to oppression with a view to then search the tradition for alternatives or, if necessary, construct new theologies and practices. But they do this by drawing on different underlying principles. Thus, Gutierrez argued, along with many others in Latin America, that liberation theology is appropriately and necessarily 'connected' with tradition.[13] Ruether, however, argued that only theological ideas and biblical texts that liberate women are legitimately useful while those that perpetuated the oppression of women should be abandoned.[14] Daly, on the other hand, proposed that the tradition should be essentially ignored altogether because it was irredeemably patriarchal.[15] Theologies of liberation thus developed in three distinct ways, almost simultaneously in the second half of the twentieth century, addressing the oppressive experiences of poverty, the legacy of slavery and continuing racism, and patriarchy. What kinds of understandings of salvation as liberation did these perspectives begin to construct?

Characteristics of liberation theologies

The state from which salvation is necessary

Theologies of liberation begin with the realities of human experience, identifying as evil – as sin – poverty, slavery, racism, patriarchy, homophobia and other similar oppressive practices. These practices are understood to be sinful because they lead to injustices and inequalities through social, political and economic marginalization and exclusion, with human persons often experiencing violence and various kinds of abuse against them at the hands of others. In order to name and identify these experiences of evil,

---

[12]See, for example, R. R. Ruether, *Introducing Redemption in Christian Feminism* (Sheffield: Sheffield Academic Press, 1998), pp. 29–42.
[13]Gutierrez, *A Theology of Liberation*, p. xliv.
[14]R. R. Ruether, *Sexism and God-Talk: Toward a Feminist Theology* (Boston: Beacon Press, 1983), pp. 18–19.
[15]See M. Daly, *Beyond God the Father: Towards a Philosophy of Women's Liberation* (London: The Women's Press, 1973).

many theologies of liberation have turned to intellectual disciplines outside
of theology to locate tools that can help to critique oppressive theological
beliefs and practices and, where appropriate, to construct alternatives.
Gutierrez's own theology is thus informed and shaped by economic and
philosophical discourses that include those of Marx, Kant, Hegel, Freud,
Marcuse and others and he uses them for a particular purpose: to understand
and critique the context in which he is located, why poverty exists, how
theology and the church contributes to perpetuating lives of poverty and
how theology and the church might contribute to the transformation of
contexts of poverty.[16] Similarly, queer theologies often draw on, for example,
queer theory,[17] disability perspectives on the disability rights movement and
disability studies,[18] feminist perspectives on various feminist theories and
philosophies,[19] non-Western perspectives on postcolonial theories[20] and so
forth. Increasingly, theologies of liberation have used multiple perspectives
to help analyse complex and multiple layers of oppression.

Poverty, therefore, is described by Gutierrez as 'an evil'[21] and the need
for liberation from this evil can be understood to be in three parts. First,
'liberation from social situations of oppression and marginalization that
force many . . . to live in conditions contrary to God's will for their life'.
Second, he argues that liberation is needed for 'personal transformation
by which we live with profound inner freedom in the face of every kind
of servitude'. The third aspect is the need for liberation from sin which
he defines as 'the breaking of friendship with God and with other human
beings'.[22] It is noteworthy that for Gutierrez, therefore, not only is a life
of poverty not God's will for humanity, hence why it is evil, but that inner
freedom just as much as outer freedom is affected by the evils of poverty.
Further, he suggests that poverty leads to a breakdown of relationships
between human beings and God, and this is a condition that God also
does not desire for humanity. Therefore, it can be assumed that the only
way to restore those relationships is through bringing an end to poverty.
Consequently, in Gutierrez's own words, 'liberation theology is thus
intended as a theology of salvation'.[23]

---

[16]Gutierrez, A Theology of Liberation, pp. 16–22.
[17]For example, L. Isherwood, Liberating Christ: Exploring the Christologies of Contemporary
Liberation Movements (Cleveland: The Pilgrim Press, 1999), pp. 89–109.
[18]N. L. Eiesland, The Disabled God: Toward a Liberatory Theology of Disability (Nashville:
Abingdon Press, 1994).
[19]See H. Bacon, What's Right with the Trinity? Conversations in Feminist Theology (Aldershot:
Ashgate, 2009), especially her use of and engagement with Feminist Philosopher, Luce
Irigaray.
[20]See for example, R. S. Sugirtharajah, Exploring Postcolonial Biblical Criticism: History,
Method, Practice (Chichester: Wiley-Blackwell, 2012), pp. 7–30.
[21]Gutierrez, A Theology of Liberation, p. xxv.
[22]Ibid., p. xxxviii.
[23]Ibid., p. xxxix.

Salvation as liberation is thus rooted in a biblical and historic understanding of God's purposes for humanity and identifies those contexts where those purposes are not fulfilled, and then seeks to transform unjust structures and institutions that lead to the violence of poverty. That has involved not only critiques of social but ecclesiological structures and institutions as well as theological ideas that have justified poverty. If, therefore, the condition from which salvation – liberation – is needed is the condition of poverty, the evil that needs to be overcome is not some interior original sin, but the sin-filled theories, theologies, institutions and practices inside and outside of the churches that justify and perpetuate poverty.

'Sin' and salvation for Gutierrez is not, therefore, only about personal spirituality but 'is regarded as a social, historical fact, the absence of fellowship and love in relationships among persons, the breach of friendship with God and with other persons, and therefore, an interior, personal fracture'. To 'be saved', therefore, is not to be forgiven personally in the hope of a place in a future possible world, but is concerned with the recovery of 'fellowship and love' with God and one another.[24] He argues that 'salvation is not something otherworldly, in regard to which the present life is merely a test' but rather, sin is historical and this-worldly, and thus seeking 'communion of human beings with God and among themselves – orients, transforms and guides history to its fulfilment'.[25] Thus, the fulfilment of salvation history in Christ and the hope of a better world in the future, does not for Gutierrez, devalue this world. Rather, the transformation of this world leads to the possibilities of the world to come. Gutierrez seeks to deconstruct, therefore, 'old dualities':[26] the future and the present, God and other humans, this world and the world to come are each related to one another and they are dependent on one another to understand what salvation is about, as well as to realize salvation and bring it to completion.

Cone, like Gutierrez, is concerned to articulate a theology of salvation that seeks to address present oppressive realities with a view towards transformation and the realization of a new and improved existence, and his theology is also concerned with social oppression as well as ecclesial and theological oppression: 'American theology is racist',[27] he argues, and 'American white theology . . . . has been basically a theology of the white oppressor giving religious sanction to the genocide of Amerindians and the enslavement of Africans'.[28] Racism, slavery and the genocide of indigenous Americans are named, by Cone, as the evils and sins from which liberation into an alternative saved state is desired. He also makes clear why non-theological disciplines, discourses and insights are necessary to achieve

---

[24]Ibid., pp. 102–03.
[25]Ibid., p. 86.
[26]Ibid.
[27]Cone, *A Black Theology of Liberation*, p. 13.
[28]Ibid., p. 4.

that desired state: because theology itself has been part of the systems of oppression that he seeks to transform.[29] Once again, the condition of marginalized, oppressed peoples is named and identified as evil, sin that affects human lives here in the present, and the only salvation that really matters for those who live under such sin is liberation – salvation – in the present too.

For Rosemary Radford Ruether, as with Gutierrez and Cone, the sin and evil that her soteriological discourses seek to address is the structural and institutional sins that lead to the oppression of women; patriarchy. As was argued in Chapter 2, Ruether reconstructs the notion of original sin from a feminist perspective arguing instead that the sin of patriarchy is inherited by being passed on from one generation to another. As we have seen, original sin, she proposes, provides patriarchal theology with a means by which it can refuse to take responsibility for patriarchy by blaming ancestors for the presence of sin and suggesting that, as a result, we can do nothing about the sinful condition in which humans find themselves. Instead, if sin is understood as inherited and learned, rather than inherited and 'genetic' the possibility of the transformation of such sin becomes much more possible. Patriarchy, like poverty, racism and slavery, is understood as a form of evil and sin from which liberation, salvation, is desired. As with Cone and Gutierrez, that liberated and transformed state is, for Ruether, necessarily desired in the present.

The notion of sin is, therefore, redefined in liberationist perspectives in such a way as to re-orientate thinking away from a description of the human condition as 'sinful' irrespective of how they act, to an understanding of sin as something that is experienced concretely by the oppressed at the hands of the oppressors. Sin is properly understood, therefore, as acts of violence and oppression that cause certain individuals, communities and nations, to suffer needlessly, to live lives of exclusion or marginalization from social, political, economic and ecclesial systems where a dominant oppressive group occupy the centre and wield all the power; people are, therefore, 'sinned against'. Whether it be the sins of poverty, racism, slavery or patriarchy, a liberationist understanding of salvation is concerned with salvific acts that seek to transform such realities. If sin is defined in this way, then this has the potential to subvert the dominant understanding of salvation that has led to many similar craven acts justified by Christianity towards people of other faiths. The religious other is no longer perceived as in a state of 'original sin' from which they must be saved by conversion to Christianity so that they may enter a future post-mortem state. Rather, if sin is the violence and oppression that human beings live with and experience on a daily basis, soteriological praxes ought to be orientated towards the transformation of such sins and evils. This new form of Christian praxis might thus not seek

---

[29]Ibid.

to convert religious others, but to seek to transform injustice and oppression where it is experienced. It may involve an examination of Christianity's own theologies that have been used to justify such acts and to deconstruct them, and to work towards a transformation of this world. This will, in many instances involve de-throning Western and Christian beliefs and practices that oppress people of other faiths and necessitate establishing alternative, liberative possibilities.

Realizing salvation

Earlier, it was noted that the 1968 conference at Medellin made an 'explicit commitment to take a "preferential option for the poor"'.[30] This notion of a 'preferential option' is a concept that underpins Latin American liberation theology from Gustavo Gutierrez's first publication in 1971 through to that of Jon Sobrino in 2007[31] and beyond. Gutierrez defines 'preference' as a concept that 'denies all exclusiveness and seeks rather to call attention to those who are the first'.[32] For Gutierrez, that is not to deny the 'universality of God's love'[33] but that God has a 'predilection for those on the lowest rung of the ladder of history'.[34] God stands on the side of the poor, therefore, and engages with them in their struggles against the evils and violence of poverty. Thus, if God is with, and on the side of the poor, while the divine universal love is not diminished, God stands against those who create and sustain contexts of poverty: God engages in soteriological praxis with and alongside the poor. This preferential option for the poor, however, is not, for Gutierrez, simply concerned with God's relation to humanity. It also speaks of an attitude of mind that should inform the praxis of the church. Drawing on the writings of John Paul II, Gutierrez argues, 'In the final analysis, an option for the poor is an option for the God whom Jesus proclaims to us'.[35] To be a person of faith in the God of Christianity, the God of the poor, the church should engage, with God, in committed action with the poor to transform and end poverty. Soteriological praxis, therefore, can be understood as human-divine acts of co-operation in tasks that realize salvation. But who are 'the poor' for whom God, and subsequently those who believe in God, might exercise a 'preferential option'?

Poverty, in the work of Gutierrez, is not simply about an economic poverty, but about an 'all-inclusive' understanding of poverty as a context in which oppressed peoples experience 'institutionalized violence'

[30]Rowland, 'Introduction', p. 5.
[31]Gutierrez, A Theology of Liberation, and J. Sobrino, No Salvation Outside the Poor: Prophetic-Utopian Essays (New York: Orbis Books, 2008).
[32]G. Gutierrez, A Theology of Liberation, p. xxv.
[33]Ibid., p. xxvi.
[34]Ibid.
[35]Ibid., p. xxvii.

domination, exploitation, racism and marginalization.[36] It is often the case that people in such circumstances are also economically poor. However, Gutierrez has a broad definition of poverty and therefore a broad understanding of who God, and therefore the Church, should operate a preferential option towards. 'The poor' thus refers to any individual or group who experiences something akin to the various forms of oppression discussed above. However, the term 'a preferential option for the poor' is not universal in all theologies of liberation, although similar principles can often be found in them. James Cone argues, for example, that Jesus, is on the side of the 'poor and weak' and against the 'rich and strong'[37] and thus involved in their struggle for transformed lives in this world. He asserts that 'preaching the gospel is nothing but proclaiming to blacks that they do not have to submit to a ghetto-existence . . . . We are now redeemed, set free'.[38] Further, he argues that the person of Jesus reveals this divine collaboration with humanity in overcoming oppression. He claims that Jesus is 'for the oppressed, the poor and unwanted of society, and against oppressors'.[39] Jesus reveals a God who, in turn 'threatens the structures of evil'[40] and transforms society. Likewise, for Gutierrez, it is Christ who liberates for 'In Christ the all-comprehensiveness of the liberating process reaches its fullest sense'.[41] If the saved state from which salvation is desired is the sin of oppression, then the process by which salvation is realized is, once again, a form of soteriological praxis that involves God and human beings collaborating in the task of achieving the end goal of liberation.

The notion of 'preferential' option for the poor, of God and of the Church, is often referred to in Latin American liberation theologies also as 'solidarity' with the poor. Boff & Boff argue that in Liberation Theology, 'we need to have direct knowledge of the reality of oppression/ liberation through objective engagement in solidarity with the poor'.[42] Gutierrez echoes this notion: 'A spirituality of liberation will center on a conversion to the neighbor, the oppressed person, the exploited social class, the despised ethnic group, the dominated country'.[43] God's principle act of solidarity with the poor might thus be understood as the incarnation, the moment when God, in Christ discovers and experiences what oppression at the hands of others is like. Thus, if the churches too are to be in solidarity with the poor, they should strive to be actively involved

[36]Ibid., p. xxi.
[37]Cone, A Black Theology of Liberation, p. 120.
[38]Ibid., p. 131.
[39]Ibid., p. 6.
[40]Ibid., p. 121.
[41]Gutierrez, A Theology of Liberation, p. 104.
[42]L. Boff & C, Boff, Introducing Liberation Theology (Tunbridge Wells: Burns & Oates, 1988), p. 23.
[43]Gutierrez, A Theology of Liberation, p. 118.

in seeking to understand the lives of oppressed and marginalized persons. Thus salvation as liberation is realized through the identification of sin in contexts of oppression and transformed through the struggle and defiance of evil by those who are oppressed, in the company of God and the church, the latter of which is called to exercise with God a preferential option for the oppressed and engage in acts of solidarity that transform the sins that affect them.

Jon Sobrino, in a departure from the notion of solidarity and notions of a preferential option for the poor, argues that soteriological praxes can already be found among those who are oppressed. In a publication on salvation in 2007, he reworked the traditional Roman Catholic mantra *nulla salus extra ecclesiam* (no salvation outside the church) as *extra pauperes nulla salus* (no salvation outside of the poor). By this he argues that he does not mean that the poor automatically receive salvation but that among the poor can always be discovered 'something' of the nature of salvation. By looking to the lives of the poor, he suggests 'can come salvation for a gravely ill civilization'.[44] Sobrino is conscious of the critique of which many liberation theologians have been accused, that in such statements, there is a tendency to idealize the poor and ignore all that is bad in poor communities in which people struggle 'against one another to survive' or in contexts like El Salvador where there are a 'dozen daily murders' mostly among the poor.[45] But Sobrino argues that, too often the lives of the poor are portrayed in entirely negative terms without paying attention to the 'important elements of humanity in the world of the poor: joy, creativity, patience, art and culture, hope, solidarity'.[46] It is the possibility of such things in the face of and in spite of the horrors that the poor are forced to endure at the hands of others on a daily basis in which Sobrino glimpses something of what salvation is about. It is about the possibility of the good flourishing subversively in a context of economic and political oppression, among lives that are often lived in desperation at the hands of the rich of the world. It is in observing and following such defiance of evil through which, for Sobrino, salvation can come not just for the poor, but for all. Thus the possibilities of a liberated future existence on earth are not realized only by the educated and powerful converting to the world of the poor, oppressed and marginalized and standing with them and collaborating with God to bring about salvation. In addition, soteriological praxis, the means of bringing about the state of salvation is already underway in the lives of those who search and long for an alternative existence by making that future possibility a present reality despite the sins that strive to suppress them.

---

[44]Sobrino, *No Salvation*, p. 49.
[45]Ibid., p. 50.
[46]Ibid., p. 52.

The saved state: Salvation as liberation

As was argued in Chapter 2, liberation theologies often make reference to biblical texts and ancient practices to reinterpret salvation as liberation. Uses of narratives such as the liberation of Israel from slavery in Egypt, or the practices of slaves being freed through payment of some form of ransom, were given as examples. Salvation, for Gutierrez, is tied up with history right from the beginning: 'The creation of the world initiates history, the human struggle, and the salvific adventure of Yahweh'.[47] But, he explains, the 'Exodus experience is paradigmatic'[48] that is, not only as a tool for interpreting the Bible itself, but in its capacity to continue to speak to and transform the lives of the oppressed today. As with Gutierrez, the soteriological understanding of liberation in Cone is presented not as a new theological idea, but as the recovery of an ancient perspective. Thus salvation as liberation constitutes salvation into a new concrete reality: freedom from oppression in this world, the kinds of oppression that Israel experienced in ancient Egypt. A state in which a person, institution or state no longer exercises abusive control or oppressive domination over others, worked out in a more just, equal and fair environment for all. Thus, the saved state is a concrete reality in which poverty, injustice, patriarchy, slavery and racism are overcome and subsequently no longer exist.

Since these early formative theologies of liberation from the likes of Gutierrez and Cone, there has been a proliferation and diversification of approaches to liberation that have both developed early thinking on the notion of liberation but also addressed criticism to liberation theologies too. In subsequent editions of both Gutierrez and Cone's classic texts, they each acknowledge the limitations of their original publication.[49] Neither paid attention to, for example, the particular nature of the oppression of women among the poor of Latin America (Gutierrez) or among African Americans (Cone). There was a tendency to homogenize large numbers of people who could be identified by a single category with the supposition that their experience of oppression was all the same and therefore what constituted liberation was also the same. The development of key womanist voices such as those of Delores Williams, Katie Cannon and Jacquelyn Grant has been important in making the distinctive experiences and voices of black women heard with regard to the multiple oppressions they experience not only at the hands of Euro-Americans, but of African American men too.

---

[47]Gutierrez, *A Theology of Liberation*, p. 87.
[48]Ibid., p. 90.
[49]See J. Cone, *A Black Theology of Liberation*, pp. xv–xviii and Gutierrez, *A Theology of Liberation*, pp. xxi–xxv.

This led womanist theologians such as Jacquelyn Grant to argue that it is possible to be oppressed in multiple ways at the same time.[50] Similar perspectives have emerged in response to the largely male-dominated liberation theologies of Latin America.[51] Thus the state from which different groups and individuals sought salvation or liberation can no longer be defined simply as states of poverty, enslavement or patriarchy, but as realities that are often much more complex. Thus, if a woman in Latin America seeks transformation of her situation, it is likely that she will be fighting poverty and patriarchy at the same, struggling against men and women inside and outside of her own context as she strives to realize a space in which she can live in freedom. A person can be oppressed for multiple reasons at the same time, and thus, homogenizing terms such as 'the poor' or 'feminist' or 'black' to speak of theologies are terms that do not adequately represent the complexity of oppression. Consequently it is now possible to find liberation concepts in queer theologies, disability theologies, mujerista theologies, African theologies, African Women's theologies and so forth each defining the condition that demands a new soteriological response differently.

If contexts and experiences of oppression are multiple and complex as has been proposed, then the desired state of liberation will subsequently also not be universal and singular. While in Cone's early work, for example, the saved state might be one in which slavery is ended and racism is overcome and ceases to exist, that only represents a partial liberation for those black women who continue to live under repressive and multiple patriarchal systems operated by men from many different racial backgrounds. Further, however, Cone's vision for a liberated state along with those of the Euro-American white feminist vision does not constitute a state of liberation for black women who experience oppressive attitudes and practices from white men and women as well as black men. Thus just as the condition from which liberation is desired is often complex and includes many different realities globally, so the state of liberation necessitates individuals, groups and communities to work out what liberation will mean in their context. A new and transformed improved reality for one group of people may fail to represent a liberated state for another or indeed constitute the very reality from which another group wishes to escape. This creation of a space for multiple saved states has, it is argued shortly, important ramifications for Christian engagements with people of other faiths so that soteriological praxis does not lead to the imposition of a single Western, Christian paradigm of an improved transformed reality onto all cultures and peoples living in oppression.

---

[50]J. Grant, 'Black Theology and the Black Woman', in *Black Theology: A Documentary History Volume One: 1966–1979* (eds J. H. Cone and G. S. Wilmore; Belknap Press) (Maryknoll, NY: Orbis Books, 1993), pp. 323–38 (334).
[51]For example, E. Tamez, *Through Her Eyes: Women's Theology in Latin America* (Eugene, OR: Wipf & Stock, 2006).

Summary: Toward an understanding of salvation as liberation

Salvation as liberation can be described with reference to the three aspects of salvation that are found in many other Christian soteriologies: the state from which salvation is needed, the process by which salvation is realized and a proposal about the end state of salvation. All three aspects of liberatory soteriologies are concerned with a transformed existence in this world and actively seek to make that possible. Indeed, historic dominant understandings of salvation are critiqued for justifying a maintained state of oppression in the hope of a better post-mortem possibility and discouraging human beings from taking responsibility for identifying and transforming the systemic, institutional and repressive sins of this world. This approach to salvation begins, therefore, with social, political, economic analyses to understand such sins, and how they are framed and practiced: sin is named. The principle of the 'preferential option for the poor', developed at Medellin led to a widespread principle informing many Latin American theologies of liberation that God is on the side of (in solidarity with) the poor in the struggle for transformation and so, therefore, the churches should be also. Similar such principles can be found in many other theologies of liberation that locate the responsibility for transforming sin in a process of human and divine cooperation. Humans are not merely passive recipients of divine grace who simply accept it to be saved, but active participants in realizing salvation rooted in a principle that God cares about the sins of racism, discrimination, poverty, patriarchy and many others and is concerned to transform such sins in this world. Because the states that result from sin that need transformation are so many and complex, so, we can conclude, liberation itself is not a single universal vision of a proposed utopia. Rather, the state of liberation, transformation in this world, is multiple, complex and worked out contextually. Let us, therefore, begin to bring some of these principles of salvation as liberation into conversation with Christian engagements with people of other faiths.

Liberation and Christian praxis in a multi-faith world: Critical conversations

To speak of salvation as liberation is thus to discuss not the scope or possibility of salvation because the saved liberated state is intended not for a few but for everyone irrespective of faith or no faith. This liberated condition is especially orientated towards those who are politically oppressed or marginalized, socially excluded and economically poor. In what remains of this chapter, this approach to salvation will be brought to the ongoing conversation regarding Christian engagement with people of other faiths in the twenty-first century. This will include discussion of three main areas. First, if sin is not original but 'inherited' as Ruether proposes, how might that transform Christian engagements with people of other faiths, especially in contexts where Christian communities and nations have historically been the cause of oppression, and where soteriological motifs continue to be invoked to justify oppressive attitudes and practice towards people of other faith traditions? Second, Latin American liberation theologians have argued that God exercises a 'preferential option for the poor' and calls the churches to engage in solidarity with those who are poor, marginalized, oppressed and excluded. If that is so what kind of soteriological praxis might be shaped by this proposition with regard to people of other faiths, in particular in Western, predominantly Christian nations where faith and spiritual minorities are often viewed with suspicion and are socially and economically marginalized? Third, we will explore what kind of saved state of salvation might be hoped for as a result of this alternative salvation as praxis?

Thinking about inherited sin in a multi-faith world

In Chapter 2, and above, it was argued that the doctrine of original sin encourages human beings to be passive observers in the face of injustice and oppression, blaming our ancestors for the presence of sin in the world and suggesting that because it is so much a part of the human condition, there is nothing that can be done to change sin. Further, it was argued that to speak of a generic concept of sin rather than to address specific sins of injustice and oppression means that the person suffering as a result of racism, poverty, patriarchy or some other form of discrimination is perceived to be just as guilty of sin as the perpetrators of such acts. Sin, instead, it was argued, should be understood as something that humans inherit, learn and practice, and that specific acts of injustice and oppression should be identified as sin and challenged and transformed. This serves as a reminder that sin is not only about the 'sinner' but those also who are 'sinned against'.

Such sins are performed by human beings and affect people's lives in this world, but because that is the case, it is not unreasonable to propose that they can be changed in this world too. In Chapter 3, it was argued that Christianity has a long history of practices towards people of other faiths that have viewed them as inferior, in need of conversion or normalization so that they conform to Christian beliefs and practices. The legacy of this can be found in contemporary Western Christian churches and nations that have inherited these views and who continue to practice them to varying degrees in some contexts today. While it is by no means only Christian churches, and nations that claim to be Christian, that have acted in this way, nevertheless, Christianity has been used to justify many different kinds of atrocities towards people of other faiths. Understood as expressions of systemic sin, it is argued that liberation, a new and alternative improved reality, is one in which such forms of systemic and institutional sin are transformed. This will mean, in some instances, the transformation of Christian theology itself.

Acts of sin, however, do not belong to the Church and Christianity alone. As we saw above, those who live under systems of oppression and desire liberation can also be perpetrators of oppressive acts towards others. Simplistic analyses of oppression will, therefore, not suffice with regard to any context or experience. Many Christian persons have also experienced oppression at the hands of others, right from Christianity's inception through to the present time. It is also appropriate that acts of violence and the murder of human beings at the hands of those who identify with other faith traditions, such as of those in the twin towers in New York in 9/11 should be named as sinful from a Christian perspective because they involved acts that led to pain, suffering and death for many. However, when Western governments, such as the United States' Bush administration interpret such events as acts of pure evil and then seek to divide the world into the good, capitalist West and the evil, Islamic East, such interpretations of events are naïve and dangerous. Let us consider, therefore, in more concrete terms, the kinds of sin that 'salvation as liberation' may offer a response towards.

Reflecting on the events of 9/11, Forrester argues that contemporary Christian theology is now confronted with the 'urgent life and death question of how to understand, discipline, channel and criticize the powerful ideological forces of religion which in fact dominate the global political scene'.[52] El Fadl notes that 'Following 9/11, there has been a virtual avalanche of publications expressing unrestrained animosity to Islam as a religion and Muslims as a people'.[53] The global context influences local contexts. Reflecting on British public opinion polls since 9/11, Field explains that 'Within a week of the atrocities in America, 90% [in one poll] were pointing the finger of blame for the crisis at Islamic fundamentalist terrorism and 40% at Islam itself'.[54] Writing in 2007, he goes on to argue that 'Taking a cross-section of attitudinal measures, somewhere between one in five and one in four Britons now exhibits a strong dislike of, and prejudice against, Islam and Muslims'.[55] Gamal Mostafa argues that,

A review of literature indicates that the image of Islam and Muslims in the West is negative due to many factors such as: age-old prejudices

---

[52]D. Forrester, 'Theological and Secular Discourse in an Age of Terror', in *Pathways to the Public Square: Practical Theology in an Age of Pluralism* (eds E. Graham and A. Rowlands; Munster: Lit Verlag, 2005), pp. 31–40 (33).

[53]K. A. El Fadl, 'The Orphans of Modernity and the Clash of Civilisations', in *Islam and Global Dialogue: Religious Pluralism and the Pursuit of Peace* (ed. R. Boase; Farnham: Ashgate, 2005), p. 179.

[54]C. Field, 'Islamophobia in Contemporary Britain: The Evidence of the Opinion Polls, 1988–2006', *Islam and Christian Muslim Relations* 18(4), (2007), pp. 447–77 (453).

[55]Ibid., p. 465.

against Islam; tendentious discourse in the mass media and writings in
journals and on the internet; [a sense of the] under-developed condition of
the Muslims; the terrorist acts and violence attributed to some Muslims;
and finally the attitude of the Western media and its superficial coverage,
which relies on individual cases and generally presents the worst as the
normal state of affairs.[56]

Given the inherited sins of the past that continue to work themselves out
in political rhetoric and media portrayals of people of other faiths, such
as Muslims in the example above, alternative ways of thinking about and
acting towards people of other faiths are necessary if the despicable events
of the past are not to be repeated and the suspicions and mistrust of people
of other faiths in the present are not to be sustained indefinitely. Again, that
is not to say that a Christian heritage that shapes contemporary Western
beliefs and practices towards people of other faiths is the only player in
religious conflict and wars justified by religion. It is not, but the churches
must at least be willing to acknowledge their contributions to the way the
world is, to recognize the 'age-old prejudices' that have been inherited from
a Christian anti-Islamic past, and seek to transform it. If, therefore, this is
the kind of condition that demands an alternative soteriological praxis, the
role of Christian theology and practices in marginalizing and oppressing
people of other faiths and viewing them with suspicion, then do liberationist
perspectives on soteriology might provide an alternative way forward?

Realizing salvation: Solidarity with the oppressed

It is here proposed that, in articulating a liberatory understanding of
salvation, soteriological praxis might be understood in three stages: first,
having named and identified the kinds of systemic and institutional sins that
lead to oppression, it is important to begin by making a commitment to
seeking to transform it; second, to recognize that aspects of the desired saved
state may already be present among those who experience oppression which
will be discussed below; third, in expressing that commitment to exercise a
'preferential option for the poor', it is argued that Christian persons have a
responsibility to struggle with those who live under oppression, irrespective
of their faith commitments, to transform it. So let us consider each of these
three stages in a liberatory soteriological praxis in multi-faith contexts.

First, the kinds of conditions from which salvation is desired have been
discussed above: a legacy of oppressive Christian beliefs, attitudes and
practices towards people of other faiths that have often had disastrous,

---

[56]G. M. M. Mostafa, 'Correcting the Image of Islam and Muslims in the West: Challenges
and Opportunities for Islamic Universities and Organizations', *Muslim Minority Affairs* 27(3),
(2007), pp. 371–86 (372).

and even fatal, consequences for them. If oppression can be articulated as the lived experiences of attitudes and practices that marginalize and dehumanize human persons because they are not economically productive, a particular gender or race, or subscribe to particular religious beliefs systems, then Christianity has engaged in its fair share of oppression towards people of other faiths. Further that oppression is reinforced by discourses of normalization that suggest that if a person wishes to be free, liberated, saved, that person must become like the white Western able-bodied male who believes in and subscribes to particular Christian faith traditions. Given this history, and its ongoing legacy, a liberatory form of soteriological praxis challenges Christian communities, individuals and institutions, to engage in different ways of relating to people of other faiths. Soteriological praxis begins with a commitment therefore, to working with people of other faiths to seek to create new and improved ways of living together that do not forget the horrors of the past, but rather seek to transform them.

Second, if as Sobrino argues that all too often, the lives of those who are oppressed are understood to be lives entirely understood negatively, he proposes instead, that the state of salvation, what it means to be saved can be seen in the acts of resistence and defiance enacted by the poor against those who oppress and marginalize them. Such acts of resistance are not, however, for Sobrino, acts of violence towards others, but rather, as we have seen, expressions of 'joy, creativity, patience, art and culture, hope, solidarity'. Thus any liberatory soteriological praxis must not assume that the lives of those who are oppressed, including people of faith who are oppressed do not exhibit qualities of a realized soteriology already. Any quest to engage with people of other faiths living under oppression should begin by recognizing and affirming such extant practices of salvation where they are to be found. Such a way of thinking about salvation provides an important and potentially radical reorientation in Christian soteriological thinking in relation to people of other faiths by acknowledging that a Christian understanding of salvation might already be found among people of other faiths realized in the present. Sobrino goes beyond Medellin to suggest that there is no salvation outside the poor and so it might be argued that one of the places where Christians might glimpse what salvation is about, is not exclusively in their own communities or doctrines, but in the lives of people of other faiths, despite the lives they are often forced to live at the margins. This is not a new form of Rahnerian anonymous Christianity whereby it is suggested that people of other faiths are really Christian, they simply do not know it. Rather, it is to argue that this particularly Christian understanding of the praxis of salvation is not only found within the walls of Christianity itself and that what is meant by salvation as a form of liberative praxis is not unique to Christianity. Thus the soteriological question for Christian theology may be not, how might people of other faiths participate in Christian salvation, but rather, what can Christians learn about their own approach to salvation by engaging peacefully and respectfully with people from other faith contexts who live under oppressive systems and yet seek to resist them?

Third, if God operates a preferential option for the poor, and the church is called likewise to stand in solidarity with those who are oppressed, then perhaps this provides the most radical contribution of liberation theology to shaping Christian belief and praxis towards people of other faiths. Perhaps Sobrino's soteriology can take us in an entirely different direction. The term 'the poor' in its original usage was a term that described those who were actually economically poor, conscious of the implications that usually had for the lives of the poor. Drawing on Medellin and Puebla, Gutierrez describes poverty as 'institutionalized violence'[57] that destroys lives, acknowledging that poverty results from systems and institutions leads to poverty, an injustice towards some at the hands of others. As the influence of liberation theologies from Latin America spread, the notion of the poor is one that has become used to refer to any group that experiences economic deprivation and marginalization, political oppression, social exclusion at the hands of others, though usually economic poverty accompanies such experiences. Thus, where people of any faith tradition, including but not only within Christianity, live such lives it might be said that they are among 'the poor'. If God exercises a preferential option for the poor, as the Medellin conference argued and which has become a principle underpinning much liberation theology, we are left with the curious proposition that where people of other faiths experience institutionalized violence, then people of other faiths can be understood to be the ones alongside whom God stands in solidarity in their struggle for transformation. That may mean, when Christian persons have historically engaged in acts of violence towards people of other faiths, in this understanding of salvation, God is on the side of the victims of such violence. Consequently, a Christian soteriology of liberation suggests that God's praxis of salvation is actually active among people of other faiths in such instances, as God collaborates with them over against acts of violence that Christians have historically perpetrated.

The saved state: Salvation as liberation in a multi-faith world

As other liberation theologians, Jon Sobrino defines salvation in a particular way so as to locate salvation not in some other possible worldly reality but as a transformation of this world. He understands salvation to be concerned with what he terms 'constructing the kingdom' a process in which human persons and God work co-operatively to realize the kind of vision of an alternative way of living now that Sobrino suggests is articulated in the

---

[57]Gutierrez, *A Theology of Liberation*, p. xxi.

Gospels. This human-divine cooperation in realizing the goals of liberation is a soteriological praxis. Specifically for Sobrino, the sin from which humans need salvation is the sin of poverty and deprivation at the hands of other human persons that leads to 'disenchantment' of the poor in a world of abundance.[58] To know salvation, then is to see it in the poor who defy and resist such sin . . . who live differently, positively, even in the face of such sin, but above all to transform such sin. In summary, he defines the state of salvation, in contract to the conditions from which salvation is necessary thus:

> salvation is *life* (satisfaction of basic needs), over against poverty, infirmity and death; salvation is *dignity*, (respect for persons and their rights), over against disregard and disdain; salvation is *freedom,* over against oppression; salvation is *fraternity*, among human beings who are brought together as *family*, . . . salvation is *pure air*, which the spirit can breathe in order to move toward that which humanizes (honesty, compassion, solidarity, some form of openness to transcendence), over against that which dehumanizes (selfishness, cruelty, individualism, arrogance, crude positivism).[59]

Sobrino provides one account of the saved state in relation to the poor of Latin America, but the question of the nature of this saved reality cannot, as was argued above, be universally defined and applied.

Writing in the 1990s, Nancy Eiesland's landmark book, *The Disabled God*, brought liberation theology into conversation with disability studies, exploring liberation as a theme for talking about a transformed reality for people with disabilities. Drawing on the work of the discourses developed within the disability movement in the West, and in particular in North America, she defined liberation in terms of the disabled person's capacities to seize power and exercise autonomy over their own lives, a possibility not experienced by many disabled people historically.[60] Eiesland thus develops a notion of the liberated state that speaks directly to people with disabilities, in particular people who live with physical and sensory disabilities, though she does not make that distinction explicitly.

In a critique of Eiesland, Hans Reinders suggests that Eiesland does not sufficiently analyse or deconstruct the ways that in disability studies, the desired 'utopia' (saved state) for people with disabilities that she articulates is based problematically on an 'anthropology of liberal citizenship'.[61] He explains, that the 'key to this anthropology is the notion of purposive

---

[58]Sobrino, *No Salvation*, p. 50.
[59]Ibid., p. 57.
[60]See Eiesland, *The Disabled God*, pp. 49–67.
[61]H. S. Reinders, *Receiving the Gift of Friendship: Profound Disability, Theological Anthropology, and Ethics* (Grand Rapids, MI/Cambridge, UK: Eerdmans, 2008), p. 165.

agency aiming at self-representation'.[62] To be liberated is, therefore, to be in a state of having autonomy over one's life, economic independence, the ability to exercise choice and so forth, and he describes these qualities as essentially Western liberal values and ideals. Reflecting on the lives of people with profound intellectual disabilities, Reinders argues 'The consequence is that human beings incapable of self-representation have no place in this strategy'.[63] Paradoxically, Eiesland's disability theology that seeks to set out a liberative agenda that emerges out of the experience of people with disabilities has the potential to produce new forms of oppression and marginalization for those who cannot attain to such ideals. The necessity for contextually developed articulations of a possible liberated state, as with all approaches to salvation as praxis, is essential if liberation theology is to avoid proposing that the best possible future for human beings is one in which all humans can exercise freedom defined according to the kind of lifestyle that a western liberal democracy can offer.

Reinders is not alone in making such critiques of liberation theologies. Ivan Petrella is also critical of 'North American liberation theologies' that, he argues, have failed to see that liberation constituted as 'a program of "naming" or voice giving will benefit only the well-to-do middle class'.[64] He further critiques western philosophical and theological ideas that are often asserted as normative and universal. He explains the view that has emerged: 'If the Enlightenment is the release from immaturity, then Europe is the first mature region of the world. Today the United States would carry that mantle with Europe – the rest of us must watch, learn and emulate, until caught up.' Thus, Petrella explains, Europe and America become 'models for the rest of the world' and capitalism becomes the 'end goal for societies not fully developed'.[65] This theological concept of liberation rooted, in an 'anthropology of liberal citizenship' or shaped by an Enlightenment philosophy that idealizes Euro-American political and economic values and systems, can paradoxically lead to the construction of a new form of oppression. Such notions, exemplified most clearly in Fukuyama's notion of the 'end of history' themselves become oppressive if they provide the paradigm that informs any understanding for Christianity's engagement with people of other faiths. Learning from the past, new soteriologies must avoid justifying neo-colonial agendas that ultimately view the Western liberal lifestyle as normative and therefore necessarily the desired state of all human beings everywhere. To construct and use theologies that understand liberation in this way, evokes the same kinds of soteriologies used to justify colonialism. That is, that Western nations looked to themselves and saw

---

[62]Ibid.

[63]Ibid., p. 168.

[64]I. Petrella, *The Future of Liberation Theology: An Argument and Manifesto* (London: SCM Press, 2006), p. 147.

[65]Ibid., p. 148.

that they were already 'saved' and then determined that all nations and religions of the world must surely want to share in their good fortune, so that they had a responsibility to Westernize and Christianize the world. New soteriological constructions must stand apart from those of the past that have justified the Crusades, colonialism and Christian sensibilities about its own superiority over other faiths.

The saved state of liberation must, therefore, be worked out contextually, so that Christian soteriological praxis can be understood as standing in solidarity with those at the margins to realize that liberation, even when that may mean standing with the person of another faith over against systems of oppression located in institutions and nations that are explicitly Christian or continue to express the legacy of Christianity. However, liberation itself continues to be complex. Writing on questions of how to develop a British society that is welcoming and inclusive of people who migrate to the United Kingdom, Trevor Phillips, argues,

> that while the equality of women and the protection of children can never be modified in any way by cultural tradition, where fundamental protections are not undermined, we have to be ready to accept that minorities of which we are not a part ourselves have the right to be different.[66]

Phillips provides an important reminder that as communities and individuals might strive for a liberated state, and that the state of liberation itself must be determined contextually, there are dangers with a description of liberation that allows any definition of the proposed utopia for a multi-faith world. Not only can one group seeking liberation be agents of oppression as was argued earlier, and not only can one definition of a liberated state lead to the marginalization of others as with Eiesland, but desired liberated states can also come into conflict with one another. Recent examples in the United Kingdom include a state-funded registrar refusing to perform civil partnership ceremonies for gay couples because of her particular Christian beliefs.[67] Both she, and the gay couple involved, argued that by one group being allowed to exercise their rights, the other would experience a form of oppression. In such instances, who's 'utopia' will win out? If human beings are going to share the same spaces as they surely must, some norms for sharing that space must be developed.

---

[66]T. Phillips, 'Not a River of Blood, but a Tide of Hope: Managed Immigration, Active Integration', *Equality and Human Rights Commission*, www.equalityhumanrights.com/key-projects/race-in-britain/modern-multiculturism/not-a-river-of-blood-but-a-tide-of-hope/, accessed on 1 February 2013.
[67]British Broadcasting Corporation, 'Christians take "beliefs" fight to the European Court of Human rights', www.bbc.co.uk/news/uk-19472438, last accessed on 1 February 2013.

Criteria have been proposed to try to help determine such things. Take, for example, Nussbaum's quest to discover and articulate a set of criteria that gives a 'minimum account of social justice' that leads to a 'life with dignity' measured against 'ten capabilities'.[68] Without explicitly saying so, she seeks to find ways of articulating a desired saved state for human beings. Any attempt to transform for the better the way societies, cultures, institutions and governments think about human, and indeed, non-human life deserves consideration while also being open to people asking, can this truly make lives better? But like many of the accounts that aim to define and determine a saved state, Nussbaum's ten capabilities, while liberating of some people, may also be oppressive to others.

Nussbaum presents her ten capabilities as having universal significance. While she recognizes that the 'minimum thresholds' of her capabilities need to be established in context, even individually, it is essential to be suspicious of anything that claims to be universally applicable. When she addresses herself to people with disabilities, and in particular, people with severe intellectual disabilities, the problem of her universalizing comes to the fore. Drawing on an example of someone with a severe intellectual disability, someone who will never have the opportunity to experience some of Nussbaum's capabilities, such as 'senses, imagination and thought', 'practical reason' or 'control over one's environment',[69] she concludes that the life of such a person must be considered to be 'extremely unfortunate'.[70] In such a view, Nussbaum exposes her ten capabilities as not being a basic account of social justice with universal significance, but a Western, liberal able-bodied account of social justice. Her ten capabilities that constitute a life with dignity for all human beings are essentially based on yet another 'anthropology of liberal citizenship'.

The liberated state, a state free from suffering and pain, and a state free from political social and economic oppression, is not easily definable. It must be worked out contextually and seek to avoid constructions that create new forms of oppression and marginalization. Nevertheless, seeking a state of freedom, and seeking to work out what that really means in practice does, it is argued here, involve the churches and members of Christian communities standing in solidarity with all groups who identify as in some way oppressed and marginalized. What must necessarily be avoided is an imposition of a discourse of liberation that reflects a particular contextual understanding of a desired utopia. We already know from the past that this leads not to liberation, but renewed oppression. But neither can striving for liberation simply involve everyone marking out

[68]M. Nussbaum, *Frontiers of Justice: Disability, Nationality, Species Membership* (Cambridge, MA/London: Belknap Press/Harvard University Press, 2006), pp. 76–77.
[69]Ibid.
[70]Ibid., p. 192.

their space irrespective of the impact it has on others, or when liberation involves marginalizing others. Liberation necessarily involves continuous negotiation as people with conflicting desires and demands seek to inhabit the same spaces. Soteriological praxis in a multi-faith world thus involves throwing off the 'presumption of superiority' of Christians of the past, and working and participating in the struggle to discern what a liberated state looks like for all. This creates a new space of ambiguity which may feel uncomfortable in a tradition that has historically claimed to have all of the answers, but the goal of liberation as a soteriological discourse necessitates that.

Conclusion

Salvation as Liberation provides a particular understanding of soteriological praxis in which human persons and God co-operate to transform human suffering and oppression with a view to establishing contexts of human liberation. This is an anthropocentric approach to salvation focused on establishing the hoped for, utopian values of the 'kingdom of God' on earth. As with the other two approaches to salvation as praxis expounded in this book, however, the notion of the liberated state is not universal and singular. This has been recognized within theologies of liberation themselves where it has been acknowledged that those who seek liberation might also be the perpetrators of oppression and that others might desire liberation from multiple oppressed states. The state of oppression, however defined, can be understood as being caused by sin. Any discourse of liberation regarding people of other faiths should not impose any particular understanding of liberation on any experience, but allow liberation to be worked out contextually. However, it has been necessary to qualify this notion so as to aim to avoid affirming anything that an individual or community suggests is a state of liberation, even when that state leads to the oppression of others. Working towards liberation will involve constant negotiation that seeks an end to suffering and conflict for all human persons without one voice dominating those of others.

It has been argued also that what may constitute a state of liberation may be found outside of the Christian community. That is not to say that where such liberation is found, there is a form of anonymous Christianity in operation, but a recognition that what Christian theology might call liberation is not limited to Christian contexts. Where individuals and communities strive for liberation from any form of oppression, it is argued, God is on their side, even when that may mean people of other faiths seeking liberation from oppression at the hands of Christian and Western peoples and nations. It is proposed that if God is always on the side of the marginalized and oppressed, the challenge to Christian praxis is for Christian people to recognize that God is not always be on their side irrespective of how they act, simply because they subscribe to a particular set 'Christian' norms and beliefs. Thus salvation as liberation encourages Christian people and institutions to engage in self-examination of their practices to consider the extent to which they are consistent with the Gospel of liberation and, where they are not, to transform their practices so as to engage in co-operation with God in the struggle for the liberation of all people.

Conclusion

Christian soteriological discourses and practices have been central in shaping the way people of other faiths and spiritualities are viewed from within the Christian tradition. Often, these soteriologies have involved practices towards people of other faiths that have sought to insist on conformation to Christian normativity or even to suppress and, at times, annihilate people of other forms of religious and spiritual expression. The legacy of these traditions has shaped a Christian 'presumption of superiority' that no longer is sustainable in a post-Holocaust context and in an increasingly globalized world where multiple spiritual expressions can be found in one community. If human beings are to find ways of living together graciously, then alternative salvations are needed.

This was recognized when early contemporary theologies of religions began to emerge in the works of Karl Rahner and John Hick who acknowledge that traditional soteriologies made no sense if the Christian God was really a God of love, and that belonging to a particular religious or spiritual pathway was largely dependent on where a person was born. God could surely not condemn millions of human beings to complete oblivion through no particular fault of their own. Ruether's deconstruction of historic Christian understandings of messiahship, together with other post-Holocaust theologians like Moltmann, led to a thorough questioning of traditions and practices that directly or indirectly made such a horrific event possible in an historically Christian context. New ways of thinking and new theologies were needed and many rose to the challenge. The contention of this book, however, has been that an over-emphasis on post-mortem future eschatological understandings of salvation has the consequence of focusing attention away from addressing the questions that confront a multi-faith world today and, in particular, what an alternative role for Christian communities might entail that contrasts with the horrors of the past. Instead, it is argued that sin should be understood as concrete and real acts that affect human lives negatively in this world. Christian soteriologies that speak about an alternative reality in this world, while ancient and established parts of Christian soteriological thinking, have largely remained unexplored in conversation with Christian practices towards people of other faiths. Finally, it has been argued that it is important to speak about the notion of soteriological praxes, that is, both a way of speaking about alternative possible ways of living together graciously in this world as well as the mechanisms or processes by which such realities might be established.

Three notions of soteriological praxis have been developed here that draw on the traditions of deification, healing and liberation. All three, it is argued point towards a transformation of the person and, indeed, of societies in this world with a particular attention paid to those who are isolated, marginalized or oppressed. In many Western contexts, that is often people of other faiths, while much of the world's wealth and power remains, for now at least, in predominantly Western Christian or 'post-Christian' nations. However, in developing these three approaches to salvation, it is also argued that the process for achieving alternative lived possibilities is also a part of Christian responsibility and constitutes soteriological praxis. So that, if the end of humanity is to become like God and God exists as three persons in a relationship of communion and otherness, then seeking to realize that existence, without imposition of Christian paradigms for relationships provides an alternative form of salvation as praxis. If to be in a state of healing is to be restored from contexts of social and religious isolation and marginalization, then the process for realizing that possibility might be discovered in the healing narratives and praxes of Jesus; praxes in which the embodied well-being of the person and the human body were of paramount importance. And finally, if salvation is to be in a state of liberation, however defined and practiced, the notion of a 'preferential option for the poor' extended in the work of Jon Sobrino suggests that soteriological praxis will involve members of Christian communities recognizing that they cannot always be assured that God is on their side, especially when they are the perpetrators of oppression. If God is always on the side of the poor and marginalized, then often God will have been and remains alongside the person of another faith willing the transformation of their lives into renewed and alternative social political and economic realities.

Salvation as praxis is also a deeply practical theology, concerned with analyzing the historic practices of Christian communities towards people of other faiths while drawing on the notion that salvation as an earthly possibility can contribute to the formation of new Christian praxes. This understanding of salvation recognizes that salvation is a process that may, indeed, never be fully realized on earth but is, nevertheless, a possibility that can and should be worked towards in the present. This can shape Christian engagement with people of other faiths, it has been argued, away from relationships of domination, oppression, normalization and a sense of superiority over others, towards new ways of engaging and living with one another. These soteriologies of praxis are not proposed as universal paradigms for a new world order but as three related contributions to shaping alternative Christian praxes. They constitute distinctively Christian theological contributions to thinking about how people of different faiths and spiritual traditions might live together better, more 'graciously'. Some of the limitations of these contributions have already been outlined and discussed above and no doubt there are many more. This contribution does however challenge Christian theologians, church leaders, and all who form Christian communities to acknowledge within the traditions they share an alternative soteriological understanding. This will need refinement perhaps even deconstruction and new construction as it engages in the tests in practice. Nevertheless, despite the many limitations that may be uncovered, if this work can begin to draw on these ancient traditions to make a case that people of other faiths need not be transformed into a Christian or else be seen as of little value and worth, but rather that a better, more free, more whole future for all human lives in communion with one another in all our uniqueness and differences can help to foster a better future for all, then something of value has been achieved.

BIBLIOGRAPHY

Abbott-Smith, G., *Manual Greek Lexicon of the New Testament* (Edinburgh: T&T Clark, 1994).

Ahmed, A. S., 'Islam and the West: Clash or Dialogue of Civilisations?', in *Islam and Global Dialogue: Religious Pluralism and the Pursuit of Peace* (ed. R. Boase; Farnham: Ashgate, 2005), pp. 103–18.

Anselm, *Why God Became Man and The Virgin Conception and Original Sin* (Albany, NY: Magi Books, 1969).

Ariarajah, S. W., 'Power, Politics and Plurality: The Struggles of the World Council of Churches to Deal with Religious Plurality', in *The Myth of Religious Superiority* (ed. P. F. Knitter; New York, NY: Orbis Books, 2005), pp. 176–93.

Athanasius, *De Incarnatione* (trans. and ed. R. Thomson; Oxford: Oxford University Press, 1971).

Bacon, H., *What's Right with the Trinity? Conversations in Feminist Theology* (Aldershot: Ashgate, 2009).

Balasuriya, T., *Planetary Theology* (London: SCM Press, 1984).

Ballard, P. and J. Pritchard, *Practical Theology in Action: Christian thinking in the Service of Church and Society* (London: SPCK, 1996).

Bartholomew (Ecumenical Patriarch), 'The Necessity and Goals of Interreligious Dialogue – A Speech Given By His All Holiness Ecumenical Patriarch Bartholomew to the Plenary of the Parliamentary Assembly of the Council of Europe – Strasbourg, France' www.patriarchate.org/documents/speech-of-his-all-holiness-ecumenical-patriarch-bartholomew-to-the-plenary-of-the-parliamentary-assembly-of-the-council-of-europe-strasbourg-france, last accessed on 1 February 2013.

—*Encountering the Mystery: Understanding Orthodox Christianity Today* (New York, NY: Doubleday, 2008).

Bartos, E., *Deification in Eastern Orthodox Theology* (Eugene, OR: Wipf & Stock, 2006).

Baum, G., 'Introduction', in *Faith and Fratricide: The Theological Roots of Anti-Semitism* (Eugene, OR: Wipf & Stock, 1997).

Benedict XVI., *Deus Caritas Est* (Vatican City: Libreria Editrice Vaticana, 2005).

Bennett, Z., *Incorrigible Plurality: Teaching Pastoral Theology in an Ecumenical Context* [Contact Pastoral Monograph 14] (Edinburgh: Contact Pastoral Trust, 2004).

Bernhardt, R., 'The *Real* and the Trinitarian God', in *The Myth of Religious Superiority: A Multifaith Exploration* (ed. P. F. Knitter; Maryknoll, NY: Orbis Books, 2005), pp. 194–207.

Bevans, S. B., *Models of Contextual Theology* (New York, NY: Orbis Books, rev. edn, 2002).

Black, K., *A Healing Homiletic: Preaching and Disability* (Nashville: Abingdon Press, 1996).

Boff, C., *Theology and Praxis: Epistemological Foundations* (New York, NY: Orbis, 1987).

Boff, L., *Trinity and Society* (Eugene, OR: Wipf & Stock, 2005).

—*Fundamentalism, Terrorism and the Future of Humanity* (London: SPCK, 2006).

Boff, L. and C. Boff, *Introducing Liberation Theology* (Tunbridge Wells: Burns & Oates, 1988).

British Broadcasting Corporation, 'Christians take "beliefs" fight to the European Court of Human rights', www.bbc.co.uk/news/uk-19472438, last accessed on 1 February 2013.

Brock, R. N. and R. A. Parker, *Saving Paradise: How Christianity Traded Love of This World for Crucifixion and Empire* (Boston: Beacon Press, 2008).

Brown, R. M., 'Preface', in *The Power of the Poor in History* (London: SCM Press, 1983), pp. vi–xvi.

Brummer, V., *What are we Doing when we Pray? On Prayer and the Nature of Faith* (Aldershot: Ashgate, 2008).

Campbell, A., 'The Nature of Practical Theology', in *The Blackwell Reader in Pastoral and Practical Theology* (eds J. Woodward and S. Pattison; Oxford: Blackwell, 2000), pp. 77–88.

Carlton, C., *The Life: The Orthodox Doctrine of Salvation* (Salisbury, MA: Regina Orthodox Press, 2000).

Cheetham, D., 'Inclusivisms: Honouring Faithfulness and Openness', in *Christian Approaches to Other Faiths* (eds A. Race and P. M. Hedges; London: SCM Press, 2008), pp. 63–84.

Church of England, *The Book of Common Prayer* (Cambridge: Cambridge University Press, rev. edn, 1968).

—*Common Worship: Services and Prayers of the Church of England* (London: Church House Publishing, 2000).

Cone, J. H., *A Black Theology of Liberation: Twentieth Anniversary Edition* (New York, NY: Orbis Books, 1990).

D'Costa, G., *The Meeting of Religions and the Trinity* (Edinburgh: T&T Clark, 2000).

—*Christianity and World Religions: Disputed Questions in the Theology of Religions* (Oxford: Wiley-Blackwell, 2009).

Daly, M., *Beyond God the Father: Toward a Philosophy of Women's Liberation* (Boston: Beacon Press, 1985).

Davidson, I. J., 'Introduction: God of Salvation', in *God of Salvation: Soteriology in Theological Perspective* (eds I. J. Davidson and M. A. Rae; Farnham: Ashgate, 2011), pp. 1–14.

De Gruchy, J. W., 'Public Theology as Christian Witness: Exploring the Genre', *International Journal of Public Theology* 1(1) (2007), pp. 26–41.

De Lubac, H., *Christian Resistence to Anti-Semitism: Memories from 1940–1944* (San Francisco: Ignatius Press, 1990).

Eiesland, N. L., *The Disabled God: Toward a Liberatory Theology of Disability* (Nashville: Abingdon Press, 1994).

El Fadl, K. A., 'The Orphans of Modernity and the Clash of Civilisations', in *Islam and Global Dialogue: Religious Pluralism and the Pursuit of Peace* (ed. R. Boase; Farnham: Ashgate, 2005), pp. 179–88.

Elshtain, J. B., *Just War Against Terror: The Burden of American Power in a Violent World* (New York, NY: Basic Books, 2004).

Engelke, M., *A Problem of Presence: Beyond Scripture in an African church* (Los Angeles, CA: University of California Press, 2007).

Fiddes, P., *Participating in God: A Pastoral Doctrine of the Trinity* (London: Darton, Longman & Todd, 2000).

Field, C., 'Islamophobia in Contemporary Britain: The Evidence of the Opinion Polls, 1988–2006', *Islam and Christian Muslim Relations* 18(4) (2007), pp. 447–77.

Finlan, S. and V. Kharlamov, (eds), *Theosis: Deification in Christian Theology* (Eugene, OR: Wipf & Stock, 2006).

Forrester, D., *Apocalypse Now? Reflections on Faith in a Time of Terror* (Aldershot: Ashgate, 2005).

—'Theological and Secular Discourse in an Age of Terror', in *Pathways to the Public Square: Practical Theology in an Age of Pluralism* (eds E. Graham and A. Rowlands; Munster: Lit Verlag, 2005), pp. 31–40.

Friedman, T., *The Lexus and the Olive Tree: Understanding Globalization* (London: HarperCollins, 2000).

Fukuyama, F., 'The End of History?', *The National Interest* 16 (Summer) (1989), pp. 3–18.

—*The End of History and the Last Man* (London: Hamish Hamilton 1993).

Furlong, M., *Women Pray: Voices Through the Ages from Many Faiths, Cultures, and Traditions* (Woodstock, VT: SkyLight Paths, 2001).

Geivett, R. D. and W. G. Phillips, 'A Particularist View: An Evidentialist Approach', in *Four Views on Salvation in a Pluralistic World* (eds S. N. Gundry, D. L. Okholm and T. R. Phillips; Grand Rapids, MI: Zondervan, 1996), pp. 213–45.

Giddens, A., *The Consequences of Modernity* (Cambridge: Polity Press, 1990).

Gifford, P., *African Christianity: Its Public Role* (London: Hurst & Company, 1998).

Graham, E., *Making the Difference: Gender, Personhood and Theology* (London: Mowbray, 1995).

—*Transforming Practice: Pastoral Theology in an Age of Uncertainty* (Eugene: Wipf and Stock, 2002).

—*Words Made Flesh: Writings in Pastoral and Practical Theology* (London: SCM Press, 2009).

Graham, E., H. Walton and F. Ward, *Theological Reflection: Methods* (London: SCM Press, 2005).

Grant, J., 'Black Theology and the Black Woman', in *Black Theology: A Documentary History Volume One: 1966–1979* (eds J. H. Cone and G. S. Wilmore; Maryknoll, NY: Orbis Books, 1993), pp. 323–38 (334).

Green, L., *Let's Do Theology: A Pastoral Cycle Resource Book* (London: Continuum, 1990).

Greggs, T., *Barth, Origen and Universal Salvation: Restoring Particularity* (Oxford: Oxford University Press, 2009).

—'Legitimizing and Necessitating Inter-Faith Dialogue: The Dynamics of Inter-Faith for Individual Faith Communities', *International Journal of Public Theology* 4(2) (2010), pp. 194–211.

Grey, M., *Redeeming the Dream: Feminism, Redemption and the Christian Tradition* (London: SPCK, 1989).

Gunton, C. E., *The Promise of Trinitarian Theology* (London: T&T Clark, 2nd edn, 1997).

Gutierrez, G., *The Power of the Poor in History* (London: SCM Press, 1983).

—*A Theology of Liberation: History, Politics and Salvation* (London: SCM Press, rev. edn, 1988).

Hardt, M. and A. Negri, *Empire* (Cambridge, MA: Harvard University Press, 2001).

Hedges, P., 'Particularities: Tradition Specific Post-Modern Perspectives', in *Christian Approaches to Other Faiths* (eds A. Race and P. M. Hedges; London: SCM Press, 2008), pp. 112–35.

Heim, S. M., *Salvations: Truth and Difference in Religion* (New York, NY: Orbis Books, 1995).

Hick, J., 'A Pluralist View', in *Four Views on Salvation in a Pluralistic World* (eds S. N. Gundry, D. L. Okholm and T. R. Phillips; Grand Rapids, MI: Zondervan, 1996), pp. 29–59.

—*The Metaphor of God Incarnate* (London: SCM Press, 2nd edn, 2005).

Hick, J. and P. Knitter (eds), *The Myth of Christian Uniqueness: Toward a Pluralistic Theology of Religions* (Eugene, OR: Wipf & Stock, 2005).

Hull, J. M., *In the Beginning there was Darkness* (London: SCM Press, 2001).

— '"Sight to the Inly Blind"? Attitudes to Blindness in the Hymnbooks', *Theology* CV(827) (2002), pp. 333–41.

Hunt, V., 'The Place of Deaf People in the Church', in *The Place of Deaf People in the Church* (eds International Ecumenical Working Group; Northampton: Visible Communications, 1996), pp. 20–33.

Isasi-Diaz, A. M., 'Mujerista Theology', in *Feminism & Theology* (eds J. M. Soskice and D. Lipton; Oxford: Oxford University Press, 2003), pp. 91–96.

Isherwood, L. *Liberating Christ: Exploring the Christologies of Contemporary Liberation Movements* (Cleveland: The Pilgrim Press, 1999).

—'Will you Slim for Him or Bake Cakes for the Queen of Heaven?', in *Controversies in Body Theology* (eds M. Althaus-Reid and L. Isherwood; London: SCM Press, 2008), pp. 174–206.

Jantzen, G., *Becoming Divine: Towards a Feminist Philosophy of Religion* (Manchester: Manchester University Press, 1998).

John Paul II, 'General Audience, Wednesday, 9 September 1998', www.vatican.va/ holy_father/john_paul_ii/audiences/1998/documents/hf_jp-iI_aud_09091998_ En.html, last accessed on 1 February 2013.

— 'Address of His Holiness Pope John Paul II to the Representatives of the World Religions', www.vatican.va/holy_father/john_paul_ii/speeches/2002/january/ documents/hf_jp-iI_spe_20020124_discorso-assisI_en.html, last accessed on 1 February 2013.

— *Redemptoris Mater: On the Blessed Virgin Mary in the Life of the Pilgrim Church*, www.vatican.va/holy_father/john_paul_ii/encyclicals/documents/hf_jp-iI_ enc_25031987_redemptoris-mater_En.html, last accessed on 1 February 2013.

Kärkkäinen, V. M., *One with God: Salvation as Deification and Justification* (Collegeville: Liturgical Press, 2004).

Kempis, Thomas à., *The Imitation of Christ* (London: Fount, 1996).

Kilby, K., *The SPCK Introduction to Karl Rahner* (London: SPCK, 2007).

Klop, K. J., 'Equal Respect and the Holy Spirit: The Liberal Demand for Moral Neutrality in the Political Sphere and Christian Respect for Creation', in *Public Theology for the 21st Century* (eds W. F. Storrar and A. R. Morton; London: T&T Clark, 2004), pp. 95–106.

Knitter, P., *No Other Name? A Critical Survey of Christian Attitudes Toward the World Religions* (New York, NY: Orbis Books, 1985).

—'Is the Pluralist Model a Western Imposition: A Response in Five Voices', in *The Myth of Religious Superiority: A Multifaith Exploration* (ed. P. F. Knitter; Maryknoll, NY: Orbis Books, 2005).

Lacugna, C. M., *God for Us: The Trinity and Christian Life* (New York, NY: HarperCollins, 1991).

Lartey, E. Y., *In Living Colour: An Intercultural Approach to Pastoral Care and Counselling* (London: Cassell, 1997).

—'Practical Theology as Theological Form', in *The Blackwell Reader in Pastoral and Practical Theology* (eds J. Woodward and S. Pattison; Oxford: Blackwell, 2000), pp. 128–34.

—*Pastoral Theology in an Intercultural World* (Peterborough: Epworth, 2006).

Libânio, J. B., 'Praxis/Orthopraxis', in *The SCM Dictionary of Third World Theologies* (eds V. Fabella and R. S. Sugirtharajah; London: SCM Press, 2003).

McCloughry, R. and W. Morris, *Making a World of Difference: Christian Reflections on Disability* (London: SPCK, 2002).

McFague, S., *Models of God: Theology for an Ecological, Nuclear Age* (London: SCM Press, 1987).

McGrath, A. E., 'A Particularist View: A Post-Enlightenment Approach', in *Four Views on Salvation in a Pluralistic World* (eds S. N. Gundry, D. L. Okholm and T. R. Phillips; Grand Rapids, MI: Zondervan, 1996), pp. 151–80.

Miguez-Bonino, J., 'Marxist Critical Tools: Are they Helpful in Breaking the Stranglehold of Idealist Hermeneutics?', in *Voices from the Margin: Interpreting the Bible in the Third World* (ed. R. S. Sugirtharajah; London: SPCK, 1995), pp. 58–68.

Mitchem, S. Y., *Introducing Womanist Theology* (Maryknoll, NY: Orbis Books, 2004).

Moltmann, J., *The Trinity and the Kingdom of God: The Doctrine of God* (London: SCM Press, 1981).

—*The Crucified God: The Cross of Christ as the Foundation and Criticism of Christian Theology* (Minneapolis: Fortress Press, 1993).

—*A Broad Place: An Autobiography* (Minneapolis: Fortress Press, 2009).

Morris, W., *Theology without Words: Theology in the Deaf Community* (Aldershot: Ashgate, 2008).

—'Transforming Tyrannies: Disability and Christian Theologies of Salvation', in *Transforming Exclusion: Engaging Faith Perspectives* (eds H. Bacon, W. Morris and S. Knowles; London: T&T Clark, 2011), pp. 121–40.

Mostafa, G. M. M., 'Correcting the Image of Islam and Muslims in the West: Challenges and Opportunities for Islamic Universities and Organizations', *Muslim Minority Affairs* 27(3) (2007), pp. 371–86.

Nouwen, H. J. M., *The Wounded Healer* (London: Darton, Longman & Todd, 2008).

Nussbaum, M., *Frontiers of Justice: Disability, Nationality, Species Membership* (Cambridge, MA/London: Belknap Press/Harvard University Press, 2006).

O'Collins, G., *Jesus Our Redeemer: A Christian Approach to Salvation* (Oxford: Oxford University Press, 2007).

—*Salvation for All: God's Other Peoples* (Oxford: Oxford University Press, 2008).

Olson, R. E., 'Deification in Contemporary Theology', *Theology Today* 64(2) (2007), pp. 186–200.

Osmer, R. R., *Practical Theology: An Introduction* (Grand Rapids, MI/Cambridge: Eerdmans, 2008).

Parry, R. and C. Partridge (eds), *Universal Salvation? The Current Debate* (Carlisle: Paternoster, 2003).

Pattison, S., 'Some Straw for the Bricks: A Basic Introduction to Theological Reflection', in *The Blackwell Reader in Pastoral and Practical Theology* (eds J. Woodward and S. Pattison; Oxford: Blackwell, 2000), pp. 135–45.

—*A Critique of Pastoral Care* (London: SCM Press, 2000).

—*The Challenge of Practical Theology: Selected Essays* (London: JKP, 2007).

Pattison, S. and J. Woodward, 'Introduction to Pastoral and Practical Theology', in *The Blackwell Reader in Pastoral and Practical Theology* (eds J. Woodward and S. Pattison; Oxford: Blackwell, 2000a), pp. 1–19.

Pears, A., *Doing Contextual Theology* (London: Routledge, 2010).

Petrella, I., *The Future of Liberation Theology: An Argument and Manifesto* (London: SCM Press, 2006).

Phillips, T., 'Multiculturalism's Legacy is "Have a Nice Day" Racism', *The Guardian*, 20 April 2008, www.guardian.co.uk/society/2004/may/28/equality. raceintheuk, last accessed on 1 February 2013.

—'Not a River of Blood, but a Tide of Hope: Managed Immigration, Active Integration', *Equality and Human Rights Commission*, www. equalityhumanrights.com/key-projects/race-in-britain/modern-multiculturism/ not-a-river-of-blood-but-a-tide-of-hope/, accessed on 1 February 2013.

Pinnock, C. H., 'An Inclusivist View', in *Four Views on Salvation in a Pluralistic World* (eds S. N. Gundry, D. L. Okholm and T. R. Phillips; Grand Rapids, MI: Zondervan, 1996), pp. 95–123.

Placher, W. C., *Unapologetic Theology: A Christian Voice in a Pluralistic Conversation* (Louisville: Westminster/John Knox Press, 1989).

Quero, M. H. C., 'This Body Trans/Forming Me: Indecencies in Transgender/ Intersex Bodies, Body Fascism and the Doctrine of the Incarnation', in *Controversies in Body Theology* (eds M. Althaus-Reid and L. Isherwood; London: SCM Press, 2008), pp. 80–128.

Race, A., *Christians and Religious Pluralism: Patterns in the Christian Theology of Religions* (London: SCM Press, 1983).

Race, A. and P. M. Hedges (eds), *Christian Approaches to Other Faiths* (London: SCM Press, 2008).

Rahner, K., *Theological Investigations: Volume Six* (London: DLT, 1969).

Ratzinger, J., *Introduction to Christianity* (San Francisco: Ignatius Press, 2004).

Reader, J., *Reconstructing Practical Theology: The Impact of Globalization* (Aldershot: Ashgate, 2008).

Reddie, A. G., *Is God Colour-Blind? Insights from Black Theology for Christian Ministry* (London: SPCK, 2009).

Reinders, H. S., *Receiving the Gift of Friendship: Profound Disability, Theological Anthropology, and Ethics* (Grand Rapids, MI/Cambridge, UK: Eerdmans, 2008).

Reynolds, T., *Vulnerable Communion: A Theology of Disability and Hospitality* (Grand Rapids, MI: Brazos Press, 2008).

Rivera-Pagan, L. N., 'God the Liberator: Theology, History and Politics', in *In Our Own Voices: Latino/a Renditions of Theology* (ed. B. Valentin; Maryknoll, NY: Orbis Books, 2010), pp. 1–20.

Robinson, F., 'Islam and the West: Clash of Civilisations?', in *Islam and Global Dialogue: Religious Pluralism and the Pursuit of Peace* (ed. R. Boase; Farnham: Ashgate, 2005), pp. 77–89.

Rowland, C., 'Introduction: the theology of liberation', in *The Cambridge Companion to Liberation Theology* (ed. C. Rowland; Cambridge: Cambridge University Press, 2nd edn, 2007), pp. 1–16.

Ruether, R. R., *Sexism and God-Talk: Toward a Feminist Theology* (Boston: Beacon Press, 1983).

—*Faith and Fratricide: The Theological Roots of Anti-Semitism* (Eugene, OR: Wipf & Stock, 1997).

—*Introducing Redemption in Christian Feminism* (Sheffield: Sheffield Academic Press, 1998).

—'Feminism and Jewish-Christian Dialogue: Particularism and Universalism in the Search for Religious Truth', in *The Myth of Christian Uniqueness: Toward a Pluralistic Theology of Religions* (eds J. Hick and P. Knitter; Eugene, OR: Wipf & Stock, 2005), pp. 137–48.

—*Women and Redemption: A Theological History* (Minneapolis: Fortress Press, 2nd edn, 2012).

Russell, N., *The Doctrine of Deification in the Greek Patristic Tradition* (Oxford: Oxford University Press, 2004).

Sacks, J., *The Dignity of Difference: How to Avoid the Clash of Civilizations* (London: Continuum, rev. edn, 2003).

—*The Home We Build Together: Recreating Society* (London: Continuum, 2007).

Schmidt-Leukel, P., 'Pluralisms', in *Christian Approaches to Other Faiths* (eds A. Race and P. M. Hedges; London: SCM Press, 2008), pp. 85–110.

Schwöbel, C., 'Particularity, Universality, and the Religions', in *Christian Uniqueness Reconsidered: The Myth of a Pluralistic Theology of Religions* (ed. G. D'Costa; New York, NY: Orbis Books, 1990), pp. 30–46.

Second Vatican Council, *Unitatis Redintegratio*, www.vatican.va/archive/hist_councils/iI_vatican_council/documents/vat-iI_decree_19641121_unitatis-redintegratio_En.html, last accessed on 1 February 2013.

—*Lumen Gentium*, www.vatican.va/archive/hist_councils/iI_vatican_council/documents/vat-iI_const_19641121_lumen-gentium_En.html, last accessed on 1 February 2013.

—*Nostra Aetate*, www.vatican.va/archive/hist_councils/iI_vatican_council/documents/vat-iI_decl_19651028_nostra-aetate_En.html, last accessed on 1 February 2013.

Sobrino, J., *No Salvation Outside the Poor: Prophetic-Utopian Essays* (New York, NY: Orbis Books, 2008).

Sölle, D., *Thinking About God: An Introduction to Theology* (London: SCM Press, 1990).

Storrar, W. '2007: A Kairos Moment for Public Theology', *International Journal of Public Theology* 1(1) (2007), pp. 5–25.

Strange, D., *The Possibility of Salvation Among the Unevangelized: An Analysis of Inclusivism in Recent Evangelical Theology* (Eugene, OR: Wipf & Stock, 2002).

Suchocki, M. H., 'In Search of Justice: Religious Pluralism from a Feminist
   Perspective', in *The Myth of Christian Uniqueness: Toward a Pluralistic
   Theology of Religions* (eds J. Hick and P. Knitter; Eugene, OR: Wipf & Stock,
   2005), pp. 149–61.
Sudworth, R. J., 'Toward a Theology of Mission Amongst Muslims in Post July 7th
   Britain', *Practical Theology* 2(2) (2009), pp. 161–204.
Sugirtharajah, R. S., *The Bible and the Third World: Precolonial, Colonial and
   Postcolonial Encounters* (Cambridge: Cambridge University Press, 2001).
—*Exploring Postcolonial Biblical Criticism: History, Method, Practice* (Chichester:
   Wiley-Blackwell, 2012).
Sullivan, F. A., *Salvation Outside the Church? Tracing the History of the Catholic
   Response* (London: Geoffrey Chapman, 1996).
Swinton, J., *Raging with Compassion: Pastoral Responses to the Problem of Evil*
   (Grand Rapids, MI/Cambridge, UK: Eerdmans, 2007).
—'From Health to *Shalom*: Why the Religion and Health Debate Needs Jesus',
   in *Health to All Their Flesh: Jewish & Christian Perspectives on Spirituality,
   Theology & Health* (eds J. Levin and K. G. Meador; West Conshohocken, PA:
   Templeton Press, 2012), pp. 219–41.
Swinton, J. and H. Mowat, *Practical Theology and Qualitative Research* (London:
   SCM Press, 2006).
Talbot, T., 'Towards a Better Understanding of Universalism', in *Universal
   Salvation? The Current Debate* (eds R. Parry and C. Partridge; Carlisle:
   Paternoster, 2003), pp. 3–14.
Tamez, E., *Through Her Eyes: Women's Theology in Latin America* (Eugene, OR:
   Wipf & Stock, 2006).
Tinker, G. E., *American Indian Liberation: A Theology of Sovereignty* (Maryknoll,
   NY: Orbis Books, 2008).
Toensing, H. J., '"Living among the Tombs": Societym Mental Illness, and Self-
   Destruction in Mark 5:1–20', in *This Abled Body: Rethinking Disabilities in
   Biblical Studies* (eds H. Avalos, S. J. Melcher and J. Schipper; Atlanta: Society of
   Biblical Literature, 2007), pp. 131–43.
Torry, M. and S. Thorley (eds), *Together & Different: Christians Engaging with
   People of Other Faiths* (London: Canterbury Press, 2008).
Townes, E., 'Walking on the Rim Bones of Nothingness: Scholarship and Activism',
   Journal of the American Academy of Religion 77(1) (2009), pp. 1–15.
United State Catholic Conference, *Catechism of the Catholic Church* (Vatican City:
   Libreria Editrice Vaticana, 2nd edn, 1997).
Veling, T., *Practical Theology: 'On Earth as It Is in Heaven'* (Maryknoll, NY: Orbis
   Books, 2005).
Vogt, K., 'Becoming Male', in *Feminism & Theology* (eds J. M. Soskice and
   D. Lipton; Oxford: Oxford University Press, 2003), pp. 49–61.
Volf, M., *Exclusion & Embrace: A Theological Exploration of Identity, Otherness,
   and Reconciliation* (Nashville: Abingdon Press, 1996)
—*After Our Likeness: The Church as the Image of the Trinity* (Grand Rapids, MI:
   Eerdmans, 1998).
Ward, K., *What the Bible Really Teaches: A Challenge for Fundamentalists*
   (London: SPCK, 2004).
Ware, K., *The Orthodox Way* (New York, NY: St Vladimir's Seminary Press, rev.
   edn, 1995).

—*How are we Saved? The Understanding of Salvation in the Orthodox Tradition* (Minneapolis: Light and Life Publishing, 1996).

—*The Inner Kingdom* (New York, NY: SVS Press, 2000).

Ware, T., *The Orthodox Church* (London: Penguin Books, rev. edn, 1997).

Williams, D. S., *Sisters in the Wilderness: The Challenge of Womanist God-Talk* (Maryknoll, NY: Orbis Books, 2004).

Williams, R., 'A theology of health for today', in *Wounds that Heal: Theology, Imagination and Health* (ed. J. Baxter; London: SPCK, 2007), pp. 3–14.

Woodhead, L., *An Introduction to Christianity* (Cambridge: Cambridge University Press, 2004).

World Council of Churches, *Religious plurality and Christian self-understanding* (Geneva: World Council of Churches, 2006).

—*Constitution*, www.oikoumene.org/en/resources/documents/assembly/porto-alegre-2006/1-statements-documents-adopted/institutional-issues/constitution-and-rules-as-adopted.html?print=1_print%20african%20churches%20 address%20p, last accessed on 1 February 2013.

Yong, A., *Beyond the Impasse: Toward a Pneumatological Theology of Religions* (Carlisle: Paternoster, 2003).

—*Theology and Down Syndrome: Reimagining Disability in Late Modernity* (Waco: Baylor University Press, 2007).

—*Hospitality & The Other: Pentecost, Christian Practices, and the Neighbour* (New York, NY: Orbis Books, 2008).

Young, F., *Welcoming Difference* (Friends Day Lecture, 2002). (Birmingham: Queens Foundation, 2002).

Zizioulas, J. D., *Being as Communion* (London: Darton, Longman and Todd, 1985).

—*Communion & Otherness* (London: T&T Clark, 2006).

INDEX